פרקי אבות
דברי חכמים

Pirké Avot
Wisdom of the Jewish Sages

פרקי אבות
דברי חכמים

Pirké Avot
Wisdom of the Jewish Sages

•••

by

Rabbi Chaim Stern

Foreword by
Rabbi David H. Lincoln

KTAV PUBLISHING HOUSE
BROOKLYN, NY

Library of Congress Cataloging-in-Publication Data

Mishnah. Avot.
    [Pirke Avot : divre hakhamim = Pirké Avot : wisdom of the Jewish sages /
[edited] by Chaim Stern ; foreword by David H. Lincoln.
        p.   cm.
    Text of Avot in Hebrew and English translation; notes in English.
    Includes bibliographical references.
    ISBN 0-88125-595-5
    1. Mishnah. Avot—Commentaries. 2. Stern, Chaim. II. Mishnah. Avot. English.
III. Title.
BM506.A2E5   1997
296.1'234707—dc21   97-2736
                                                                      CIP
                                                                      HE

Manufactured in the United States of America
Ktav Publishing House
527 Empire Blvd.
Brooklyn, NY 11225
www.ktav.com | orders@ktav.com
(718) 972-5449

Contents

Foreword

Pirké Avot—The Wisdom of the Sages—is one of the two or three most loved books of religious literature of the Jewish people. Since this people has been called "The People of the Book," such affection by this people is no small compliment. There are innumerable commentaries to this book, and we can profit from all of them. It is all the more remarkable that our present edition can offer us so many special insights, references, and information. Teacher, students, the general public, all will find this volume an invaluable tool for a deeper examination of this great text.

Pirké Avot 5:15 tells us that "four kinds of people sit before the sages." These people are then compared to certain articles that will be found in every kitchen. One of these is a sponge. Rabbi Chaim Stern, author of our present work, points out that the Mishna "makes no explicit judgment about the four types, leaving the judgment to us." It will be evident to the reader that of the four categories, the four "kinds of people," Rabbi Stern is to be compared to the "sponge that absorbs everything."

A man of high standing in the ranks of American Jewry, Rabbi Stern has given us the benefit of his remarkable absorptive capacity, for this is not just a translation and commentary, but also a profound exploration of the background and teachings of the rabbis of the Pharisaic tradition, the tradition that formed the basis for the Judaism of the two millennia that followed them.

We are fortunate to live in an age which thirsts for knowledge; in such an age, the availability of texts in English enable all to be "learned of the Eternal One."

Pirké Avot brings its message of morality and ethical living not only to the Jewish world, but also to a wider community. Grounded in Jewish history and morality, its message has universal appeal. The commentary on Avot by the distinguished Christian scholar R. Travers Herford, among others, is evidence enough of this truth.

Because these chapters (Avot is divided into six) abound in wise observations and practical rules for living a righteous and fulfilled life, they occupy a special place in the liturgy of the synagogue. Many prayerbooks contain "the Perek," and it has therefore long been recited—a chapter a week—by worshippers, as a form of prayer on Shabbat afternoons. Many of us study it in groups or in classrooms, for its popularity far exceeds other works of moral instruction in our tradition.

I feel that this work will gain wide acceptance in the religious community, for it combines scholarship and inspiration. Rabbis of all streams of Judaism can reflect on the happy fact that this Mishna is most unusual in one particular respect. Quite simply put, there are no real differences of opinion, no arguments in all the many sayings of Pirké Avot. In this work we are all one, a people united in the love of learning and truth, in the search for wisdom and guidance in the art of living.

The massive source material that Rabbi Stern has gathered and organized will prove of value not only to the wider public for which the book has been written, but also to rabbis and other scholars of every faith community.

May Rabbi Stern's work prove an instrument for the wide dissemination of knowledge of Torah, and of admiration for it.

Rabbi David H. Lincoln
Senior Rabbi
Park Avenue Synagogue
New York, New York

Preface

At the end of the third century CE, Rabbi Judah the Prince compiled the legal and moral traditions of the Jewish people into an authoritative code called the Mishnah. It became the legal-religious guidebook of Judaism, and ultimately served as the foundation of the Talmud. Not long after the main body of the Mishnah was completed, a tractate called Pirqé Avot was added to this code. It was not devoted to matters of law but to the pursuit and practice of wisdom and ethics. It quickly became the best-known and best-loved tractate of the Mishnah, and was eventually included in the prayerbook; to this day it is found in every Jewish prayerbook, and read and studied with devotion.

Commentaries to Pirqé Avot are abundant, but the present work is unusual.

Here is what it includes:

• A new inclusive-language translation of the text.

• Explanatory commentary from many sources and by the editor.

• Readings from Talmud and Midrash about the sages mentioned in the text.

• Readings from Talmud and Midrash amplifying the themes of the text.

• Reference notes.

The result is a many-sided picture of the thought-world of Rabbinic-Pharisaic Judaism as it was forming itself and creating the Judaism that flourished until modern times, and that remains fundamental to the understanding of Judaism to this day.

And more: it provides the reader (or teacher) with a rich set of primary readings on subjects that touch the life of every individual. And it is our hope that this work will enrich the spiritual life of the reader.

Rabbi Chaim Stern
Senior Rabbi
Temple Beth El
Chappaqua, New York

Glossary

Agadah—(אגדה), exposition, fantasy, tales. The non-legal portion of rabbinic literature, generally presented as exposition of text, frequently in narrative form. (see also Midrash).

Am ha-aretz—(עם הארץ), literally, "the people of the land." That is, peasant, the folk, the masses. More broadly, the term came to mean "ignorant," "unlettered."

BCE—Before the Common Era.

CE—Common Era.

Charity—see Tzedakah.

Derech Eretz—(דרך ארץ), Literally, the "way of the land." It has a wide range of applications, and usually means good manners, graciousness, civility, worldly wisdom.

Divine Presence—See Shechinah.

Divine Voice—(בת קול), Literally, "daughter of a voice." A term for the "echo" of the divine voice. After the end of prophecy, in the rabbinic view, God continued occasionally to "speak," but, as it were, less directly than through prophecy, and unpredictably. Hence, "echo."

Elijah (the Prophet)—the Rabbis picture (the spirit of) the prophet Elijah as entering into conversation with one of the sages and providing information from the other world. Elijah appears in human guise. This entered into later Jewish folklore.

Gehenna—גי חנום, Gei Hinnom, a valley southwest of Jerusalem, was the site of the Canaanite worship of the god Moloch, to whom children were sacrificed. It quite naturally came to connote Hell or Purgatory, where the wicked are punished for a time. Its opposite was גן עדן, Gan Eden, the Garden of Eden—Paradise; see "World–to–Come."

Halachah—"the way to go," that is, the authoritative law. From the verb הלך, halach, "to go." Thus, it is the way of going and doing.

Ignorant, unlettered—see Am ha-Aretz.

Midrash—(מדרש), a vast collection of ethical, legendary, linguistic, and legal comments on the biblical text, referred to as "Midrash" (uppercase); a single comment from the collection is referred to as a "midrash" (lowercase). See also Agadah.

Mishnah—(משנה), The law-code compiled at the end of the 2nd century CE by Rabbi Judah the Prince, to which Pirqé Avot was subsequently added.

Repentance—Teshuvah (תשובה) is the noun usually translated by "repentance" or "penitence." Literally, however, it means (re)turning [to God], and is often so translated here.

Sage—From חכם, חכמים, chacham, chachamim (pl.): wise, hence, "sage(s)."

"Saint"—from חסיד, chasid (loyal [to God]). A "saint" is one who goes beyond the letter of the law. In Avot, chasid tends to blend with צדיק, tzaddik, "righteous (one)."

Talmud—(תלמוד), The immense body of law and lore using the Mishnah as a starting-point and compiled some centuries later. There are two "Talmudim;" the Babylonian Talmud is the better-known of the two. The other is called the Jerusalem or Palestinian Talmud.

The Omnipresent—From (ha-)makom (המקום), literally, "The Place;" that is, the One who is present and in whom we have our being.

World-to Come—(עולם הבא), Paradise, the Garden of Eden, where, in rabbinic thought, the righteous are rewarded. See "Gehenna."

Yetzer, Yetzer hara—(יצר, יצר הרע), The Will-to-evil, Evil Impulse. It drives us in this world and can drive us "out of the world." In rabbinic thought, the Yetzer is a good servant but a dangerous master. See the extended comment at Avot 2:11.

A Note

Avot chapter 1 sets the stage for the whole of Pirké Avot. It begins by establishing the credentials of the Sages, whose words form the content of the entire work. So the authority of the Sages is traced right back to the revelation at Sinai: the Oral Torah comes from the same Source as the Written Torah. Thus the entire Mishnah, for which Avot is an introduction, is validated and confirmed.

The authorities cited in chapter 1 are in the main eminent figures of the first century BCE and the first century CE, the time when the Pharisees rose to influence and authority. It was an adventurous and creative period, and one of conflict and confusion. The era of Roman domination of Judea began in the middle of the first century BCE. During the century and a half following, Judaism entered upon a renaissance under the guidance of the Pharisaic Sages; Christianity was born; and the first great war against Rome (66–73 CE) ended in defeat and the destruction of the Temple. This is the background of chapter 1, though as we read the words of the Sages it rarely intrudes.

•••••••

Additional readings on the sages whose sayings are featured in this chapter begin on page 34.

Avot 1:1

מֹשֶׁה קִבֵּל תּוֹרָה מִסִּינַי וּמְסָרָהּ
לִיהוֹשֻׁעַ, וִיהוֹשֻׁעַ לִזְקֵנִים, וּזְקֵנִים
לִנְבִיאִים, וּנְבִיאִים מְסָרוּהָ לְאַנְשֵׁי
כְנֶסֶת הַגְּדוֹלָה.
הֵם אָמְרוּ שְׁלֹשָׁה דְבָרִים:
הֱווּ מְתוּנִים בַּדִּין,
וְהַעֲמִידוּ תַלְמִידִים הַרְבֵּה,
וַעֲשׂוּ סְיָג לַתּוֹרָה.

MOSES RECEIVED Torah from Sinai and handed it on to Joshua, and Joshua [handed it on] to the elders, and the elders to the prophets. And the prophets handed it on to the members of the great assembly. They said three things:

Be deliberate in judgment.
Raise up many disciples.
Make a fence for the Torah.

Moses received Torah—Not the whole Torah, but only as much as he was capable of taking in. Each generation receives Torah according to their varying capacities.
The members of the great assembly—They followed Ezra in the late 5th century BCE. Little is known of them. The Talmud (Berachot 33a) credits them with the composition of parts of the liturgy.
--- *A lesson in humility*: "God's self-revelation occurred at Mt. Sinai because it is the smallest of the mountains." (Talmud Megillah 29a)
--- *A lesson in universality*: "The Torah was revealed in the wilderness because it is a place belonging to no one, and therefore to everyone. The Torah belongs to anyone who wishes to possess it." (after Midrash, Mechilta to Exodus 19:2)
deliberate in judgment—This refers only to a case that calls for extended analysis. [see 5:8] (Midrash Shemuel). More generally, show good judgment in dealing with others, avoiding haste, impatience, stubborness, etc. (ARN)
a fence--It is better to have a vineyard surrounded by a fence. Do not, however, make the fence more important than what it surrounds: should the fence fall in, all would then be lost. (ARNB)
--- Do not make a rigid system in which freedom is lost, yet keep definite boundaries. The sages created an 'early warning' system to keep us from violating Mitzvot; e.g., since work on the Sabbath is prohibited, so is the handling of work-tools.

Revelation

1. *When Moses came down from Mount Sinai...Moses did not know that the skin of his face sent forth beams...* (Exodus 34:29). Where did Moses get those beams of glory? Rav Judah bar Nehemiah says: "When Moses was writing the Torah, a little was left over in his pen, and he passed it over his head." (Midrash Tanchuma to Exodus 34)

2. *Moses led the people out of the camp toward God, and they took their place at the foot of the mountain.* (Exodus 19:17).

 Rabbi Abdimi bar Chama bar Chassa said: This teaches that the Holy One lifted up the mountain over the people of Israel, held it like an inverted barrel, and said to them: "Accept the Torah and it will be well with you; otherwise this will be your burial place." (Talmud Shabbat 88a)

3. Rabbi Yochanan said: When the divine voice came forth at Mount Sinai, it divided itself into the 70 human languages, so that the whole world might understand it.

Rabbi Tanchuma said: All at Mount Sinai—old and young, women, children, and infants—heard the voice of God according to their ability to understand.

Moses, too, understood only according to his capacity, as it is said (Exodus 19:19), *Moses spoke, and God answered him with a voice.* With a voice that Moses could bear. (Midrash Exodus Rabbah 5:9)

4. God said to Israel: Because you have seen Me in many guises, do not suppose that there are many gods. It is always the same God—*I am the Eternal your God.* (Exodus 20:2).

Rabbi Levi said: The Holy One appeared to them like a mirror, in which many faces can be reflected: a thousand people look at it; it looks at all of them, So when the Holy One spoke to the people of Israel, all felt themselves personally addressed by God, and thus it says in the singular (ibid.), *I am the Eternal your God.*[1] (Midrash Pesikta de Rav Kahana 109b–110a)

5. *The Eternal spoke with you face to face at the mountain.* (Deuteronomy 5:4). Rabbi Yochanan said: A thousand people look at a statue, and each one thinks, 'The statue is looking at me.' So the Holy One looks at every Israelite and says, *I am the Eternal your God.*[2] Rabbi Levi said: You can learn the same lesson from everyday life. One voice can enter ten ears, but ten voices cannot enter one ear. Yet God hears the prayers of all creatures as if they were one prayer, as it is said (Psalm 65.2), *O God who hears prayer, to You shall all flesh come.* It does not say 'prayers,' but "prayer." (Pesikta Rabbati 100b)

6. *I am your Eternal God.* (Exodus 20:2) Because the Holy One appeared to Israel on the sea as a warrior doing battle, and at Sinai as a scribe teaching Torah, and in the days of Solomon as a young man, and in the time of Daniel as an elder filled with compassion, the Holy One was careful to say to them: Since you see Me in many different guises, do not suppose that there many gods. It is I: I am the One at the sea, I am the One at Sinai, I am the One everywhere: *I am your Eternal God.* (Midrash Tanchuma, Yitro; Mechilta, B'shalach, Shira, 4)

Avot 1:2

שִׁמְעוֹן הַצַּדִיק הָיָה מִשְּׁיָרֵי כְנֶסֶת

הַגְּדוֹלָה. הוּא הָיָה אוֹמֵר:

עַל שְׁלֹשָׁה דְבָרִים הָעוֹלָם עוֹמֵד:

עַל הַתּוֹרָה, וְעַל הָעֲבוֹדָה,

וְעַל גְּמִילוּת חֲסָדִים.

SIMEON THE RIGHTOUS[3] was one of the [last] members of the great assembly. He would say: The world is based on three things:
On the Torah,
On worship,
On deeds of lovingkindness.

On the Torah—The three fundamentals given here (there are other formulations elsewhere) are revelation (the received tradition of law and wisdom), spiritual inwardness (worship/the Temple Service), and love of neighbor. And they are interrelated. (CS)

--- Once when Rabbi Tarfon, Rabbi Yosé the Galilean, and Rabbi Akiba were together in Lydda, the question arose: Which is more important, study or practice? Tarfon argued, "practice." Akiba argued, "study." They concluded: "Study is more important, for it leads to practice." (Midrash Sifrei to Deuteronomy 41)

--- The world is a ball suspended in space and all that keeps it going is the breath of Torah from the mouths of students—like a balloon kept afloat by currents of air. (after Duran)

deeds of lovingkindness–Once, as Rabban Yochanan ben Zakkai was coming forth from Jerusalem, Rabbi Joshua, following him, beheld the Temple in ruins. "Woe is us," he lamented, "that the place where Israel found atonement for its sins is laid waste." "Do not grieve, my son," said Yochanan. "We have a means of atonement equally good—deeds of loving kindness, as it is said (Hosea 6:6), *It is steadfast love I desire, and not sacrifice.*" (ARN)

--- *Love your neighbor as yourself* (Leviticus 19.18). Rabbi Akiba says: This is the great principle of the Torah. Ben Azzai says: *This is the book of the generations of Adam...God made them in the divine image* (Genesis 5:1). This is an even greater principle, for then you cannot say, 'Since I despise myself, I can despise another as well; since I curse myself, let the other be accursed as well.' Rabbi Tanchuma said: [Ben Azzai is right, for] if you do thus, know that the one you are despising—God made in the divine image. (Jerusalem Talmud Nedarim 9:4; Genesis Rabbah 24) (see 3:14)

Loving kindness

Rabbi Simlai expounded: The Torah begins and ends with lovingkindness. It begins with a loving deed, as it is said (Genesis 3:21), *And the Eternal God made for Adam and his wife garments of skins, and clothed them.* And it ends with a loving deed, as it is said (Deuteronomy 34:6), *And God buried him [Moses] in the valley.* (Talmud Sotah 14a)

2. Rabbi Elazar said: Lovingkindness is greater than charity, as it is said (Hosea 10:12), *Sow for yourselves righteousness, reap the fruit of steafast love.* We may or may not eat of what we sow; what we reap we will surely eat.[4]

And Rabbi Elazar said: Charity is not fulfilled except through the lovingkindness involved in it, as it is said (ibid.), *Sow for yourselves righteousness, reap the fruit of steafast love.* (Talmud Sukkah 49b)

Avot 1:3

אַנְטִיגְנוֹס אִישׁ סוֹכוֹ קִבֵּל תּוֹרָה
מִשִּׁמְעוֹן הַצַּדִּיק. הוּא הָיָה אוֹמֵר:
אַל תִּהְיוּ כַּעֲבָדִים הַמְשַׁמְּשִׁין
אֶת־הָרַב עַל מְנָת לְקַבֵּל פְּרָס;
אֶלָּא הֱווּ כַּעֲבָדִים הַמְשַׁמְּשִׁין
אֶת־הָרַב שֶׁלֹּא עַל מְנָת לְקַבֵּל
פְּרָס. וִיהִי מוֹרָא שָׁמַיִם עֲלֵיכֶם.

ANTIGONUS OF Socho[5] received [Torah] from Simeon the righteous. He would say:

Do not be like servants who serve their master in the hope of reward—

be rather like servants who serve their master without thought of reward.

And let the fear[6] of Heaven be upon you.

Reward—It may be that we really cannot escape self-interest, but we can aim for selflessness. So doing, we get closer to the ideal.

Fear—We should not confuse "fear of Heaven" with being afraid. The "God-fearing" person is one who lives reverently and acts ethically.

Without thought of reward–Once it happened that the child of Dov Baer, the Great Maggid, became dangerously ill. They had little with which to feed him, and there came a point when he was too weak to cry. The Maggid's wife brought the child to him in wordless reproach. Until now, he had been silent, in silence accepting whatever might be. Now, finally, a low sigh forced its way past his lips. Immediately a voice came to him, saying, "You have lost your share in the world–to–come." And he replied, "All the better—now I can serve without hope of reward." (after Buber, *Tales of the Hasidim*, vol 1, p. 99)

[A literal reading of this story can mislead us. Its essential message is that a saint can serve so selflessly that questions of "reward" for service are stilled, and that the faith of the saint may be so complete that no hint of petition for one's own needs, and no whisper of complaint, will pass through his/her lips. Needless to say, perhaps: saints are not all alike.] (CS)

--- *Blessed is the one ... who greatly delights in God's commandments* (Psalm 112:1).— and not in the reward of the commandments. (Talmud)

Fear of Heaven—"Everything is in the hands of Heaven, except the fear of Heaven." (Talmud Berachot 33b) [see 3:15]

--- Out of love, one fulfills the 248 positive commandments; out of fear. one avoids transgressing the 365 negative commandments. (Maimonides)

Planting

Hadrian emperor of Rome was walking along a road near Tiberias when he noticed a very old man planting fig saplings not far off the side of the road.

He said: "Had you worked in the morning you would not have had to work in the evening."

"As God pleases," replied the man. "I did work in the morning; now I work in the evening."

"How old are you, man?"

"Near enough to one hundred years," replied the man.

"At your age you still go to all this trouble planting trees! Do you expect to live long enough to enjoy their fruits?"

"My lord," the man answered, "If I live I will eat. If not: my parents planted for me, I plant for my children."

"If you live to eat this fruit, come see me," the emperor said.

Three years later, the old man took some ripe figs and brought them to the palace. He presented them to Hadrian, saying: "I have lived to enjoy the fruits of my labors, and here are some of them."

In reply, Hadrian commanded that the basket in which he had received the figs be returned, filled with gold coins.

His servants were taken aback: "You honor this old Jew so richly?"

"His Creator honored him, so do I," was Hadrian's reply.

The wife of the old man's neighbor heard of this and said to her husband: "Worthless! The emperor likes figs and pays for them with gold!" He filled a bag with figs and brought them to Hadrian. "I have heard that the emperor loves figs and gives gold for them," said he.

"Make him stand in front of the palace," commanded the emperor, "and throw these figs at him."

They let him go toward evening. He came home and said to his wife: "I will honor you the way they honored me."

She responded: "Thank your lucky stars they were figs and not lemons."

Avot 1:4

יוֹסֵי בֶּן יוֹעֶזֶר, אִישׁ צְרֵדָה, וְיוֹסֵי
בֶּן יוֹחָנָן, אִישׁ יְרוּשָׁלַיִם, קִבְּלוּ מִמֶּנּוּ.
יוֹסֵי בֶּן יוֹעֶזֶר אוֹמֵר:
יְהִי בֵיתְךָ בֵּית וַעַד לַחֲכָמִים,
וֶהֱוֵי מִתְאַבֵּק בַּעֲפַר רַגְלֵיהֶם,
וֶהֱוֵי שׁוֹתֶה בְצָמָא אֶת־דִּבְרֵיהֶם.

YOSÉ BEN Yo'ezer of Zareida and Yosé ben Yochanan[7] of Jerusalem received [Torah] from them. Yosé ben Yo'ezer says:

Let your home be a meeting-place for the wise,

sit in the dust of their feet,

and with thirst drink in their words.

the wise—Pharisaic/Rabbinic Judaism places great emphasis on the respect due teachers of Torah, for they are the Torah's guardians and expositors. In a sense, they are Torah. One sage remarked (Talmud Makkot 22a), "How foolish people are, who rise in honor of the Torah-scroll, but not for a sage!" (CS)

with thirst—the words of the Torah are like water: drink them. More than that, take them in with the eagerness of someone who is dying of thirst and finds water. [The Talmud (Ta'anit 7a, etc.) compares the Torah to water.] (CS)

Hospitality

The way things go when one has a guest is that on the first day one serves fowl, the second day meat, the next day fish, then cheese, then beans...till they get to eat nothing but lettuce! (Midrash Pesikta 31; Socher Tov 23)

Avot 1:5

יוֹסֵי בֶּן יוֹחָנָן, אִישׁ יְרוּשָׁלַיִם, אוֹמֵר:
יְהִי בֵיתְךָ פָּתוּחַ לִרְוָחָה, וְיִהְיוּ עֲנִיִּים
בְּנֵי בֵיתֶךָ. וְאַל תַּרְבֶּה שִׂיחָה עִם
הָאִשָּׁה. (בְּאִשְׁתּוֹ אָמְרוּ, קַל וָחֹמֶר
בְּאֵשֶׁת חֲבֵרוֹ.) מִכָּאן אָמְרוּ חֲכָמִים:
כָּל־זְמַן שֶׁאָדָם מַרְבֶּה שִׂיחָה עִם
הָאִשָּׁה גּוֹרֵם רָעָה לְעַצְמוֹ, וּבוֹטֵל
מִדִּבְרֵי תוֹרָה, וְסוֹפוֹ וְיוֹרֵשׁ גֵּיהִנָּם.)

YOSÉ BEN Yochanan of Jerusalem says:
Let your house be opened wide,
and let the poor be members of your household.
And do not talk too much with women.
(Even to one's wife—how much more to another man's wife.[8] This led the sages to say: Who talks too much with a woman brings disaster upon himself, begins to neglect Torah, and ends up an heir to Gehenna.)

And do not talk too much with women–Though they made some efforts to improve the lot of women, the sages were on the whole children of their time and their attitude toward women is fairly represented (but not exhausted) by this passage. This should not distract us from the rest of the message, although we keep in mind the fact that in the main it was the male half of the population that recorded its story and made the rules. Thus we have read of the "members of the great assembly," but the usual translation of אנשי כנסת הגדולה is "*men* of the great assembly." (CS)

Let your house ... Let the poor–The obligations of hospitality and compassion for the poor are hallmarks of biblical teaching, and are carried forward by Rabbinic Judaism. (CS)

Let your house ... Let the poor—The two teachings may be linked, meaning: even if your own household is the poorer for it, let your house be opened wide to the poor. (Meam Loez, Avoth, p. 29, citing Midrash Shemuel)

--- Once when the Baal Shem Tov was sitting with his chasidim, a poor man entered. He had no special distinction, yet the Baal Shem called him to the head of the table and seated him at his side. His chasidim, astonished, asked later why he had so greatly honored this man: was he perhaps a hidden saint? The Baal Shem explained: "When I want a seat of honor in the world–to–come, and I am asked what I did to deserve it, what will I have to say? The only answer I will have is that once I too gave a poor man a seat of honor." (Chasidic)

The Poor

1. *And if your kin become poor and cannot maintain themselves with you, you must maintain them*. (Leviticus 25:35) Do not let them fall down. A poor person is like a

load resting on a wall: while it is still in place one person can hold it steady; once it falls to the ground, five people cannot lift it. (Midrash Sifra, Behar, 109b)

2. *Defend the poor and the orphan; do justice to the afflicted and the destitute.* It does not say "pity" but "do justice." Give a righteous judgment. Do not say we will give them what belongs to the rich because they are poor or orphaned. *The earth is God's and all its fullness* (Psalm 24:1), and if you take unjustly from the rich and give it to the poor, you rob Me, says the Holy One. You give what is Mine—all the earth is Mine—and I gave them the wealth that you are taking away from them. (Midrash on Psalms on 83:2)

3. *If you pour yourself out for the hungry* (Isaiah 58:10) Rabbi Levi said: If you have nothing else to give, give consoling words; say: "My heart goes out to you, that I have nothing to give you." (Midrash Leviticus Rabbah 34)

4. Rabbi Yannai, seeing a man give a zuz in public to a pauper, said: "It would have been better to have given him nothing than to have shamed him."[9] (Talmud Chagigah 5a; Midrash Ecclesiastes Rabbah 12)

4. For the sake of [the ways of] peace[10] one may not keep foreigners [non–Jews] from gleaning, the forgotten sheaf, and the corner of the field. [See, for example, Leviticus 19]

Our sages taught: The non-Jewish poor are to be sustained along with the Jewish poor, the non-Jewish sick are to be visited along with the Jewish sick, and the non-Jewish dead are to be buried along with the Jewish dead, for the sake of [the ways of] peace. (Talmud Gittin 61a)

6. Rabbi Pinchas ben Ya'ir was living in a southern city, and two poor men came there to make a living. They had two measures of barley and they left it in his care. Eventually they forgot about it and left town. Rabbi Pinchas ben Ya'ir did not forget. He planted them and for years harvested the barley and brought it to the granary after each harvest. Seven years later the two paupers returned and asked for their barley. Rabbi Pinchas ben Ya'ir recognized them and said: "Bring camels and donkeys and collect your fortune." (Midrash Deuteronomy Rabbah 3; Jerusalem Talmud Demai 1:3)

Three On Women

1. Rabbi Chelbo said: Take good care of your wife's honor, for blessing enters your house only because of her. (Talmud Baba Metsia 59a)

2. When the daughters of Zelophehad[11] heard that the land was being divided among men to the exclusion of women, they came and took counsel together. They said: "Heaven's compassion is not like that of men. Men care more about men than about women, but the compassion of Heaven extends to men and women equally, as it is

said (Psalm 145:9), *Eternal One, You are good to all; Your mercies are over all Your works.* (Midrash Sifre Numbers, Pinchas, 133)

3. The daughters of Zelophehad said to Moses (Numbers 22:4): *Give us a possession among our father's kin.* Rabbi Nathan said: The strength of the women was thus greater than that of the men, for the men had said (Numbers 14:4), *Let us choose a captain, and go back to Egypt.* (Midrash Sifre Numbers, Pinchas, 133)

Avot 1:6

יְהוֹשֻׁעַ בֶּן פְּרַחְיָה וְנִתַּי הָאַרְבֵּלִי
קִבְּלוּ מֵהֶם.

יְהוֹשֻׁעַ בֶּן פְּרַחְיָה אוֹמֵר:

עֲשֵׂה לְךָ רַב,

וּקְנֵה לְךָ חָבֵר,

וֶהֱוֵי דָן אֶת־כָּל־הָאָדָם לְכַף זְכוּת.

JOSHUA BEN Perachiah[12] and Nitai the Arbelite[13] received [Torah] from them.

Joshua ben Perachiah says:

Find yourself a teacher.

Get yourself a friend.

And give everyone the benefit of the doubt.

Find ... a teacher—Literally, "Make yourself a teacher." I think this says that there is no teaching without learning, and learning is as much a creative act as teaching. The student, as it were, makes the teacher. This teaching is repeated in 1:16. (CS)

Get ... a friend—Literally, "Buy yourself a friend." For a real friend is not easily acquired. The coinage paid is effort, interest, responsiveness, tolerance. We get what we are willing to pay for. (CS)

a teacher–to learn from; *a friend*—to study with. (ARN)

a teacher–Even if you are already a considerable scholar. Studying by yourself does not begin to compare with studying with another person. (Maimonides)

a friend—According to the Greek philosophers, a friend is someone outside yourself and yet in truth is you: though you inhabit separate bodies, your souls hold fast to each other. (Aknin)

--- "Either companionship or death." (Talmud Ta'anit 23a)

"buy" yourself a friend—with the coinage of an open and generous heart.

the benefit of the doubt—"One who mistrusts the virtuous will suffer affliction." (Talmud Shabbat 97a)

--- Once, when Rabbi Levi Yitzchak of Berditchev (1740-1809) was in the bath-house, his coat was stolen. He returned home and his wife noticed he was without his coat and asked him where it was. The rebbe replied that someone had taken the coat, doubtless mistaking it for his own. His wife then asked, "In that case, where is his coat?" Levi Yitzchak said, "He must have forgotten to leave it!" (Chasidic)

Friendship

1. One who greets a friend [with honor] is like one who greets the Shechinah. (Jerusalem Talmud Erubin 5.1)

2. Three things ingratiate us to others: An open hand, a prepared table, a light heart. (ARNB 31, S. Buber ed.)

3. Rabbi Joshua ben Levi said: Who sees a friend after 30 days should say: "Blessed is the One who has given us life, sustained us, and brought us to this day." Who

sees a friend after 12 months should say: "Blessed is the One who gives life to the dead."[14] (Talmud Berachot 58b)

4. Rabbi Jeremiah ben Elazar said: Be moderate in praising people in their presence; but in their absence give them all the praise they deserve. How do we know this in regard to moderate praise? It is said (to Noah, Genesis 7:1), *for I have seen that you are righteous before Me in this generation;* and all the praise they deserve? It is said (of Noah, Genesis 6:9), *a righteous man, perfect in his generation.* (Talmud Erubin 18b)

5. This one gains and the other doesn't lose. (Talmud Baba Kama 20a)

6. Rava said to Rabbah bar Mari: "The popular saying, 'Don't throw a stone into the well you drink from'—where do we find support for it?" "From this," he answered (Deuteronomy 23:8): *You must not abhor an Egyptian, in whose land you were a stranger.* (Talmud Baba Kama 92b; Midrash Numbers Rabbah 22)

7. *If you return evil for good, evil will not depart from your house.* (Proverbs 17:13). Rabbi Judah said in the name of Rav: "And beyond this: if you return evil for *evil,* evil will not depart from your house." (Midrash Genesis Rabbah 38)

8. Rabbi Chama ben Rabbi Chanina said: "You may give a friend a gift without letting your friend know it, as it is said (Exodus 34:29), *And Moses did not know that his face was shining because he had spoken with God.*"[15]

They said in the name of Rav: "You may give a friend a gift without letting your friend know it, as it is said (Exodus 31:13*), That you may know that I, the Eternal, make you holy.* (Talmud Shabbat 17a)

9. If you seek mercy for a friend—needing that very thing yourself—you will be answered first. (Talmud Baba Kama 92a)

10. Rabbi Samuel bar Nachman said in the name of Rabbi Jonathan: When Moses was writing the story of creation, he reached this sentence (Genesis 1:26): *And God said: Let us make a being in our image, in our likeness...* he said: "Ribbono shel olam, why do you give heretics a talking point? I don't understand!" He answered: "Son of Amram, write—and let those who choose go astray!"

The Holy One added: "Do not both great and humble descend from Adam, My creation? Therefore, when the exalted have occasion to consult with a lesser, let them not say, 'Why bother seeking the views of one beneath me?' Rather, let them learn from their Maker, the Creator of the heights and the depths. Though supreme over all, I consulted the ministering angels before the creation of humankind. (Midrash Genesis Rabbah 8)

Avot 1:7

נִתַּי הָאַרְבֵּלִי אוֹמֵר:

הַרְחֵק מִשָּׁכֵן רַע,

וְאַל תִּתְחַבֵּר לְרָשָׁע,

וְאַל תִּתְיָאֵשׁ מִן הַפּוּרְעָנוּת.

NITAI THE Arbelite says:
Keep your distance from a bad neighbor.
Do not associate with a villain.
And never despair [because of your fear]
of judgment.[16]

a bad neighbor—The warning against associating with villains seems simple common sense. Given our nature, the bad drives out the good more often than the good influences the bad. Creation is harder that destruction. It does not, however, suggest that we withdraw from the effort to help turn people toward the good. Teachers, social workers, police officers, community and youth workers, and others, are in the front lines, and they need the support of every citizen. In this context, the admonition never to despair takes on real force. (CS)
--- "Woe to the wicked, woe to their neighbors." (Talmud Sukkah 56b)
--- "Whoever has a synagogue in his locality and does not go in to pray, is called a bad neighbor; moreover he incurs exile for himself and his children." (Jerusalem Talmud Berachot 5:1)
the wicked—your own inclination to be wicked, the Yetzer that rules your body and lies in wait for your heart to stray. As soon as you decide to transgress, it bends your whole body to that purpose. (after ARNB)
never despair ... of judgment—When all is well with you, do not imagine yourself immune from trouble; when in the midst of trouble, do not despair of better times. (after ARNB)

Deceivers

A pious fool,[17] a crafty knave, a woman who hypocritically does charitable works, and the plagues of the Pharisees[18] ruin the world. (Mishnah Sotah 3:4.)

Avot 1:8

יְהוּדָה בֶּן טַבַּי וְשִׁמְעוֹן בֶּן שָׁטַח
קִבְּלוּ מֵהֶם.

יְהוּדָה בֶּן טַבַּי אוֹמֵר:

אַל תַּעַשׂ עַצְמְךָ כְּעוֹרְכֵי הַדַּיָּנִין,

וּכְשֶׁיִּהְיוּ בַּעֲלֵי הַדִּין עוֹמְדִים לְפָנֶיךָ,

יִהְיוּ בְעֵינֶיךָ כִּרְשָׁעִים,

וּכְשֶׁנִּפְטָרִים מִלְפָנֶיךָ,

יִהְיוּ בְעֵינֶיךָ כְּזַכָּאִין,

כְּשֶׁקִּבְּלוּ עֲלֵיהֶם אֶת־הַדִּין.

JUDAH BEN Tabai[19] and Simeon ben Shetach[20] received [Torah] from them.

Judah ben Tabai says:

Do not act like one who counsels the judges.

And when the litigants stand before you, look upon them as guilty.

And when they accept your decision and leave your presence, look upon them as innocent.

judges—So fundamental is the need for a community in which people can be confident that in a dispute they will receive fair treatment—justice—that the sages hold the establishments of courts of justice to be one of the seven Noachide laws: that is, one of a handful of natural moral laws so basic that they do not need divine sanction by revelation—they apply to all people everywhere. (CS)

who counsels the judges—When you are a judge, do not be an advocate—as though you were one of the lawyers or litigants. (CS)

equal treatment—Rabbi Meir would say: Why is it said (Deuteronomy 1:17), *You must hear the weak and the strong alike*? So that you do not keep one litigant standing while the other sits, you do not let one talk forever while saying to the other, "Cut your words short!" (ARN)

look upon them as innocent—Do not assume that the person who loses a lawsuit was lying. In complex business dealings both sides may believe different things about a single set of facts, and neither may be lying: their interpretations may honestly differ. (Bertinoro)

--- Once a dispute is over and settled, all should go forward with a clean slate. (CS)

Bribery

1. We have learned (Exodus 23:8): *...and take no bribe.* What does this teach: 'Do not acquit the guilty nor condemn the innocent?' It is already stated (Ibid., 23:6), *You shall not pervert justice...*What then? 'Take no bribe even to acquit the innocent and to condemn the guilty.'

If someone takes payment to sit as a judge, his judgment is invalid. How do we know this? Rav Judah said in the name of Rav: It is said (Deuteronomy 4:5), *See, I have taught you laws and rules of justice as my Eternal God has commanded me.* As I[21] receive no payment, neither must you.

We have learned: A judge who takes payment is condemned, but the judgment stands. But have we not learned: "If someone takes payment to sit as a judge, the judgment is invalid?" Here is meant payment for loss of time.

Karna would take an Istera[22] from both parties and would judge between them.

How could he have done this, when we have learned that a judge who takes payment is condemned?

This applies where the time lost is not fixed [and known]. With Karna the loss was clear, for he was employed in a wine warehouse[23] and was payed a Zuz.

When people with a case came before Rav Huna he would say: Get me someone to replace me watering my field and I'll sit as judge.

The full-time Head Judges in Jerusalem would be paid 99 Maneh[24] from the Temple treasury. If that was not enough to sustain them, they would be given more, even if they did not ask. (Talmud K'tubot 105a; Bechorot 89a)

2. *...for a bribe blinds the eyes of the wise...* (Deuteronomy 16:19). If you take a bribe, you will not depart this world before your heart is blind, even if you have been a great sage. *...and subverts the words of the righteous.* (Ibid.) If you take a bribe—even if you were a complete saint[25]—you will not depart this world without losing your mind. (Talmud K'tubot 105a)

3. Rav Papa said: You must not judge another whom you love or hate, for you cannot avoid partiality in either case. (Talmud K'tubot 105b)

4. *You shall hear the small and the great alike* (Deuteronomy 1:17). Resh Lakish said: Let a case about a penny be as important to you as a case about millions.[26] (Talmud Sanhedrin 8a)

5. *Hear the cases between your neighbors and judge them ...* (Deuteronomy 1:16). Rabbi Chanina said: This is a caution to the judge, not to listen to one side before the other person arrives, and a caution to litigants, not to begin speaking to the judge before their adversary is there. (Talmud Sanhedrin 8a)

6. How do we know that when two come for judgment, one dressed in rags and the other in a cloak worth 100 Maneh that they say to the latter: "Either dress like your opponent or clothe him like yourself?" Scripture says (Exodus 23:7), *Keep far from a false matter.* (Talmud Shevuot 31a)

Avot 1:9

שִׁמְעוֹן בֶּן שָׁטַח אוֹמֵר:
הֱוֵי מַרְבֶּה לַחֲקֹר אֶת־הָעֵדִים,
וֶהֱוֵי זָהִיר בִּדְבָרֶיךָ,
שֶׁמָּא מִתּוֹכָם יִלְמְדוּ לְשַׁקֵּר.

SIMEON BEN Shetach says:
Be painstaking in examining the witnesses.
And watch your words, lest, through them, they may learn to lie.

This teaching complements its predecessor, and spells out a few details. The tendency of the sages is to particularize general principles, to spell out their implications. (CS)

be painstaking—Say nothing that might show the witnesses what you expect them to say, or that might give an advantage to one of the litigants before you. (Duran)

watch your words—Through your very diligence you may inadvertently give the litigants a clue, so be aware of this and watch your words.

Avot 1:10

שְׁמַעְיָה וְאַבְטַלְיוֹן קִבְּלוּ מֵהֶם.
שְׁמַעְיָה אוֹמֵר:
אֱהֹב אֶת־הַמְּלָאכָה.
וּשְׂנָא אֶת־הָרַבָּנוּת.
וְאַל תִּתְוַדַּע לָרָשׁוּת.

SHEMAYAH[27] AND Avtalyon[28] received [Torah] from them. Shemayah says:
Love work.
Hate authority.[29]
Do not make yourself known to the government.[30]

Love work—Neglect of work leads to dishonesty.

Hate authority—Those who seek power and high office are least likely to be worthy of them. We speak of public or civil service, of public servants—a noble concept. Unfortunately, they all too often come to think of the public as their servants. Hence Lord Acton's dictum, so resonant: "Power tends to corrupt ...;" But note the word *tends*. It need not happen, and sometimes it does not happen. (CS)

--- Shun domination over others, and resist or avoid those who seek to dominate you. (CS)

--- Status destroys those who seek it. (Rashi)

--- Do not put a crown on your own head; let others do it, as it is said (Proverbs 27:22), *Let another praise you and not your own mouth, a stranger and not your own lips.* (ARN)

--- Rabbi Yosé says: Go down to go up, go up to go down. (ARN)

Do not make yourself known—Intimacy with rulers leads to excessive ambition. (Maimonides)

Avot 1:11

אַבְטַלְיוֹן אוֹמֵר:
חֲכָמִים, הִזָּהֲרוּ בְדִבְרֵיכֶם, שֶׁמָּא
תָחוּבוּ חוֹבַת גָּלוּת וְתִגְלוּ לִמְקוֹם
מַיִם הָרָעִים, וְיִשְׁתּוּ הַתַּלְמִידִים
הַבָּאִים אַחֲרֵיכֶם וְיָמוּתוּ, וְנִמְצָא שֵׁם
שָׁמַיִם מִתְחַלֵּל.

AVTALYON SAYS:
Sages, watch your words, lest you become liable to the penalty of exile and are carried off to a place of bad water, and lest the disciples who follow you [there] drink and die, and the name of Heaven be thereby profaned.

N.B.: The Pharisees were persecuted by the heads of state throughout most of the 1st century BCE; some were killed, some fled to other lands. All were compelled to face the challenge of Hellenism, assimilation, and general upheaval. The teachings of 1:10 and 1:11 probably reflect this. (CS)

watch your words—Teachers (sages) must not mislead: those who do and those who are misled are in "exile," a "place of bad water"—confusion, loss of faith, error, etc. Thus the teacher profanes Heaven's name, by failing to serve God properly. (CS)

--- Teachers (sages) must choose their disciples with care, for if they teach fools, their teaching will be distorted, and they, not their [hapless] disciples, will be held responsible. (Vitry)

--- Teachers are responsible for what they teach, so they must make sure that they avoid misinterpretation. Do not say, "I don't care about my audience; let them come up and inquire, if they don't understand." They may not do it; in fact, they may already be predisposed to a false interpretation and be happy to hear you appear to confirm it. (after Meiri)

Companionship

1. *The Eternal One said to Moses: Take Joshua unto yourself.* (Numbers 27:18). "Take" always means "acquire" [by purchase], for nothing worthwhile is acquired without paying a price. Thus they said: "One should acquire[31] a friend with whom to read, to learn, to eat and drink, to share secrets." (Midrah Sifre, Vayeilech; ARN 8)

2. *Who goes with the wise grows wise.* (Proverbs 13:20). As the fragrance of balsam will cling all day to anyone who has spent time in a shop that sells spices. *But the companion of fools suffers harm.* (ibid.) As the smell of a tannery will cling all day to anyone who has spent time there. (Midrash to Proverbs)

3. A chavurah and a family are both like a mound of stones: take one stone away and they all will tumble and scatter. (Midrash Genesis Rabbah 100)

Avot 1:12

הִלֵּל וְשַׁמַּאי קִבְּלוּ מֵהֶם.

הִלֵּל אוֹמֵר:

הֱוֵי מִתַּלְמִידָיו שֶׁל אַהֲרֹן,

אוֹהֵב שָׁלוֹם וְרוֹדֵף שָׁלוֹם,

אוֹהֵב אֶת־הַבְּרִיּוֹת וּמְקָרְבָן לַתּוֹרָה.

HILLEL[32] AND Shammai[33] received [Torah] from them. Hillel says:
Be a disciple of Aaron,
loving peace[34] and pursuing peace,
loving people[35] and drawing them near to the Torah.

This well-known saying of Hillel's is one connected thought. "Oheb Shalom" and "Rodeph Shalom" [love peace/pursue peace] have been adopted as names by many synagogues.

N.B.: The desire of the Pharisees to draw "all people" near to the Torah is a corollary of love, and means: bring them to a fuller knowledge of God. (CS)

Hillel—A certain heathen came to Shammai and said to him, "I will convert, provided that you teach me the entire Torah while I stand on one foot." Threatening to thrash him, Shammai drove him away. He went to Hillel with the same proposal. Hillel (accepted him and) said to him, "What is hateful to you, do not do to anyone else: that is the whole Torah; the rest is commentary—go and learn it." (Talmud Shabbat 31a)

Peace- So long as there is peace in Israel's midst, no people or nation can have dominion over them, even were they to worship idols. (Midrash Genesis Rabbah 38:6)

--- We find that in the case of the Generation of the Dispersion, the people [building the Tower of Babel] loved one another, and for that reason were spared by the Holy One. Despite the fact that they waged war against Heaven, they did not share the fate of the Generation of the Flood, but were merely scattered over the earth. On the other hand, the people of Sodom hated one another, and therefore lost both this world and the world–to–come. (ARN)

pursuing peace—What was Aaron's way of reconciling people who had quarrelled? To each he would go and say, "Your friend feels terrible over your quarrel, and wants only to accept the blame for this dispute." Thus, when the two met, they would embrace and make peace. He would do the same thing when there was a dispute between husband and wife. For this reason, when Aaron died, it says (Numbers 20:29), *All the house of Israel wept for him*. Everyone wept for him, because he was the great peacemaker. When Moses died, what does it say (Deuteronomy 34:8)? *The sons of Israel wept for Moses*. Only the men, to whom he had taught Torah, wept for him. (ARN 12, etc.)

Jesters

Rav Beroka of Bei Chozai often came to the market of Bei Lapat. There, from time to time, he would encounter Elijah the Prophet.

At one of their meetings, he said to Elijah: "Is there anyone in this market who has earned Paradise?"

Elijah's answer was: "No."

For a time, there was a silence between them. Then two men came along.

When he saw them, Elijah said: "These two will enter Paradise."

Rav Beroka went to them and said: "Who are you and what are your deeds?"

They answered: "We are jesters."

"And your deeds: what are they?"

"When people are dejected we make them laugh. When people quarrel we find a way to help them make peace." (Talmud Ta'anit 22a)

Avot 1:13

הוּא הָיָה אוֹמֵר:

HE WOULD say:[36]

נְגַד שְׁמָא, אֲבַד שְׁמֵהּ,

A name made great is a name lost.

וּדְלָא מוֹסִיף יָסוּף,

Who does not add, subtracts.

וּדְלָא יָלֵף קְטָלָא חַיָּב,

Who does not learn commits [spiritual] suicide.[37]

וּדְאִשְׁתַּמֵּשׁ בְּתָגָא חֲלָף.

Who uses the crown passes away.

Four teachings. The first and last address the inauthentic; one who seeks fame, one who acts insincerely, out of ulterior motives will not benefit. The second and third sayings call on us to keep growing in our ability to contribute to ourselves and others. (CS)

A name made great—"The camel went to look for horns, and had its ears cut off." (Talmud Sanhedrin 106a)

--- "Honor flees the one who pursues it, and pursues the one who flees it." (Talmud Erubin 13b)

Who does not learn—Scholars who have given up learning: have they not given up living? Who are they? Those who decide they have learned all there is to know, or who are weary of their labor, or tired of pondering what they consider cannot be understood (Rabbi Jonah ben Abraham) [compare Maimonides' comment at 1:6]

lost—Or, "destroyed." That is, one achieves distinction as a byproduct of devoted service, not for its own sake. (CS)

subtracts—It is not enough to memorize the past, nor to hand on the achievements of others; one must try to add something new of one's own. (CS)

the crown—That is, the crown of Torah. Torah learning must not be used as a means of self–aggrandizement, or to enrich oneself with material possessions. This may be understood to say that we must be unselfish in our use of any noble gift we may possess. (TH)

Avot 1:14

הוּא הָיָה אוֹמֵר:

HE WOULD say:

אִם אֵין אֲנִי לִי, מִי לִי?

If I am not for myself, who will be for me?

וּכְשֶׁאֲנִי לְעַצְמִי מָה אֲנִי?

And if I am [only] for myself, what am I?

וְאִם לֹא עַכְשָׁיו אֵימָתַי?

And if not now, when?

If I am not for myself—Self–reliance is viewed favorably, but balanced by a warning against selfishness; though self–love precedes love of neighbor, it should lead to it. (CS)

--- This can be translated literally to yield the meaning: "If I am not mine, who then is mine?" That is, if I do not belong to myself, who belongs to me? Since I do not own even myself, how can I imagine that I own anyone—or anything—else? On the other hand, how can I make a claim on another human being until I am in possession of myself?

--- Rabbi Mendel of Kotzk was told that a certain man was greater than another. He responded, "If I am I because I am I, and you are you because you are you, then I am truly I and you are truly you. But if I am I only because you are you, and if you are you only because I am I, then I am <u>not</u> I, and you are <u>not</u> you." (Buber, *Or ha–Ganuz*, p. 438)

who will be for me—or, who is for me?

And if not now—If I do not acquire good qualities when young, when will I? In old age? By that time behavior patterns have become firmly fixed, and it is difficult to give up habits already formed. (Maimonides)

--- If I do not work at perfecting myself today, I may not get the chance tomorrow. But even if I do, today's chance to serve God has been lost, never to return. (Rabbi Jonah ben Abraham)

Avot 1:15

שַׁמַּאי אוֹמֵר:

SHAMMAI SAYS:

עֲשֵׂה תוֹרָתְךָ קֶבַע.

Make your Torah a fixed routine.

אֱמֹר מְעַט וַעֲשֵׂה הַרְבֵּה.

Say little, do much.

וֶהֱוֵי מְקַבֵּל אֶת־כָּל־הָאָדָם

בְּסֵבֶר פָּנִים יָפוֹת.

Greet everyone with a cheerful counte-nance.[38]

a fixed routine—Set aside regular times for study. And see 2:13, which warns against "routine" prayer. The Hebrew makes for a more striking contrast between the two passages than the English. The intent may be to point out that both are sacred, yet different. The sages teach that Torah is God's word to us and therefore not to be modified to suit our convenience; prayer, our word to God, should ever be fresh and from the heart—not formal, lifeless, routine. (CS)

-- Raba said: At the final judgment we are asked: "Did you conduct your business honestly? Did you set aside times to study Torah? .... Did you wait hopefully for redemption?" Did you study Torah with all your powers? Did you understand that your acts have consequences? And with all that, if *reverence for the Eternal was your treasure* (Isaiah 33:6), then it is well with you—but only then. (Talmud Shabbat 31b)

--- We need to be consistent, neither easy on ourselves and hard on others, nor hard on ourselves and lenient with others (though the latter is preferable to the former). In a matter where we are easy on ourselves, let us be easy on others; and where we are hard on ourselves, let us be the same with others. (ARN)

Say little, do much—This is the way of the righteous. Abraham offered his visitors bread, then went and prepared them oxen and fine meal (Genesis 18). The wicked, on the other hand, say much and do not even do a little. Ephron the Hittite first offered Abraham the land as a free gift, and ended up selling it to him for 400 shekels of sil-ver (Genesis 23.15–16). (ARN)

with a cheerful countenance—One who showers you with gifts, but with a downcast face, has given you nothing; but one who greets you with nothing more than a cheerful countenance, has given you all the gifts in the world. (ARN)

L'shon Hara[39]

1. Rav Chisda said in the name of Mar Ukba: The Holy One says of one who speaks ill of another: "There isn't room in the world for the two of us," as it is said (Psalm 101:5), *Who slanders his neighbor in secret...I cannot endure.* Read this אתו, *ito*, instead of אותו, *oto*, [and it yields the meaning]: I cannot endure with him. (Talmud Sotah 42a)

2. Resh Lakish said: When is says (Leviticus 14:2), *This is the law concerning the leper* [m'tzora],[40] it should be understood as saying, *motsi shem ra*, giving someone a bad name.[41] (Talmud Arachin 15b)

3. *A warrior's sharp arrows, with glowing coals of the broom tree!* (Psalm 120:4). Why did the Psalmist liken malicious speech to an arrow, of all weapons? Other weapons strike only in their place, the arrow strikes from afar. Speak ill of someone in Rome and it kills in Syria. And the coals of the broom tree are unusual in that, unlike other coals, they burn within even after they are cool on the outside. When you engage in malicious speech, even though you later apologize, its victim continues to burn inwardly. (Midrash Genesis Rabbah 98; Jerusalem Talmud Peah 1:1)

4. The tongue is like an arrow. How? If you take up a sword to slay another, you may yet be persuaded to return the sword to its sheath. Once the arrow has been released, however, there is no calling it back. (Midrash Socher Tov 120)

5. And they said: *We came to the land...and indeed it is flowing with milk and honey...but its inhabitants are [too] powerful [for us].* (Numbers 13:27,28). That's the way of those who speak maliciously: they begin with praise and end with derogation. (Midrash Tanchuma A, Sh'lach)

6. Rav Amram said in the name of Rav: There is no day in which one escapes these three transgressions: illicit thoughts, distraction during prayer, malicious speech. Malicious speech? Can this really be what he meant? Rather, the 'dust' of malicious speech. (Talmud Baba Batra 164a)

7. It is forbidden when leaving a session of the court to say: "I was for acquittal but my colleagues were for conviction, and what could I do? They were in the majority." How do we know this? It is said (Proverbs 11:13), *Who goes about as a talebearer reveals secrets [but one who is trustworthy in spirit keeps a thing hidden.]* (Talmud Sanhedrin 29a)

Avot 1:16

רַבָּן גַּמְלִיאֵל אוֹמֵר:
עֲשֵׂה לְךָ רַב.
וְהִסְתַּלֵּק מִן הַסָּפֵק,
וְאַל תַּרְבֶּה לְעַשֵּׂר אוֹמָדוֹת.

RABBAN GAMALIEL[42] says:
Find yourself a teacher,[43]
keep clear of doubt,
and do not make it a habit to tithe by guesswork.

tithe by guesswork—The tithe went to the Levites, and was set at 10% of the harvest (Numbers 18:21). Before tithing, the farmer had to allocate an offering (called T'rumah) for the priests. The Torah does not specify the amount, but the rabbis (see Mishnah T'rumot 4:3) set parameters for this offering: 1/40 of the harvest was 'generous,' 1/50 was 'average,' 1/60 was 'grudging.' Although the tithe due the Levites was set, one could "tithe by guesswork," making sure to overestimate what was due. This practice is discouraged by our mishnah. (CS)

Find ... a teacher—This repeats a teaching of 1:6; see comment there.

clear of doubt—Rabban Gamaliel urges us toward clarity of thought and purpose. Do not take the easy way, saying: "It's sort of like this." (CS)

--- Do not make this a habit: if you overtithe it doesn't matter, but it may be you will undertithe, to your own harm, for then your own produce will be forbidden you. (after Vitry)

--- This is a figure of speech for the way we arrive at our opinions. It is better to think things through than to rest on vague conjectures. (Rabbi Jonah ben Abraham)

--- One should not render decisions by guesswork or conjecture but by careful examination, or by consulting others. (Meiri)

Avot 1:17

שִׁמְעוֹן בְּנוֹ אוֹמֵר:

כָּל־יָמַי גָּדַלְתִּי בֵּין הַחֲכָמִים,

וְלֹא מָצָאתִי לַגּוּף טוֹב אֶלָּא שְׁתִיקָה.

וְלֹא הַמִּדְרָשׁ הוּא הָעִקָּר, אֶלָּא הַמַּעֲשֶׂה,

וְכָל־הַמַּרְבֶּה דְבָרִים מֵבִיא חֵטְא.

SIMEON HIS son[44] says:
I have lived all my life among the sages,
and I have found nothing better for one's well-being[45] than silence.
Doing is the essential thing, not learning,[46]
and too much talk causes sin.

Doing—This could be translated more fully as "It's not what you know that matters, but what you do [with what you know]." As in the old saying, "Actions speak louder than words." What is notable about this is that it comes from the sages, who, as is well known, devoted themselves to teaching and learning. They never doubted that we learn in order to serve. (CS)

silence—Speech is becoming only in the mouth of those who practice what they preach. (Yebamot 63b)

--- If silence is becoming to the sage, how much more to the fool! (ARN)

--- But the fool identifies himself by his speech! (CS)

--- Notice that you have two ears but only one tongue. This suggests that you ought to speak less and listen more. (Duran)

--- silence in the face of insult is the best revenge. (Bertinoro) [One might then say, living "good"—not "well"—is the best revenge. (CS)]

--- Our rabbis have taught: Those who are persecuted and do not persecute in turn, those who listen to contemptuous insults and do not reply, those who act out of love and are glad of sufferings, concerning them Scripture says (Judges 5:31), *They that love God are like the sun going forth in his strength.* (Yoma 23a, etc.)

doing—Simeon does not set up doing without learning as the ideal; without learning, how can one know what to do? He means that the best learning is the learning that leads to doing. (Duran)

too much talk—Simeon is not referring to such things as slander, for such speech is obviously forbidden. But he teaches us to be sparing even in words of praise. (Vitry)

Silence

1. Bar Kappara taught: Silence being fitting for the wise, how much the more for fools! And so says Solomon (Proverbs 17:28), *Even a fool who keeps silent is deemed wise.* And one needn't add, "a sage who keeps silent." (Jerusalem Talmud Pesachim 9:9; Talmud Pesachim 99a)

2. *A time to be silent and a time to speak.* (Ecclesiastes 3:7). At times you are silent and are rewarded for your silence; at times you speak and are rewarded for your speech. (Talmud Z'vachim 115b)

3. The king of Persia became sick unto death and his physicians told him that the only remedy was milk from a lioness. One of them volunteered to go and fetch it, saying: "Give me ten goats and I'll get the milk." He went to the forest and found a lioness suckling her cubs. On the first day he stood at a great distance and sent a goat. The lioness devoured it. On the second day he came a little nearer and sent the second goat. By the tenth day he was playing with her and was able to milk her and go on his way.

Halfway back he dreamt that his limbs were engaged in argument. The legs claimed preeminence over the rest, for they had conveyed the entire body to the forest: "Without me there would have been no milk and no cure for the king." The hands pointed out that they had done the actual milking. The eyes said: "How do you imagine you could have found the way without my sight?" And the brain insisted that it was responsible for the idea in the first place. Then the tongue spoke up: "Where would you be without my power of speech?" All the limbs together rounded on the tongue: "Where do you get off making claims for yourself, you who are least of us all? Stay in your darkness, you boneless wretch!" And the tongue replied: "Before long you will all agree that I am your ruler."

The man woke up and kept his dream in mind. Upon his return to the palace he said to the king: "I have brought you the bitch's milk to drink." This angered the king, who gave orders to have the man hanged. As he was led to the gallows his limbs began to tremble and the tongue spoke up: "Didn't I tell you that you don't amount to anything? Will you acknowledge my dominion if I save you?" "Yes," they told him, and the tongue then said to the executioners: "Return me to the king!" They did this, and the man then asked the king: "Why did you tell them to hang me?" "Because you brought me the milk of a bitch," said the king. "If it cures you, what's the difference?" said the man. "Besides, a lioness is also called a bitch. Have the milk inspected and you will see." The milk turned out to have come from a lioness and the king drank it and recovered.

The body's other limbs then acknowledged the tongue's preeminence. And thus it is said (Proverbs 18:21), *Life and death depend on the tongue.* (Midrash Socher Tov 39; Yalkut Shimoni, Psalm 34)

4. Our sages said: Two rhetoricians stood before Hadrian and debated the question: Which is better, speech or silence? "My lord," said the one, "there is nothing better than speech. Without it there would be no songs in praise of brides, no business conducted anywhere, no ships dispatched to sea."

The king turned to the other and asked him: "What have you to say about silence?"

As the man began to speak, his colleague went over and clapped his hand over his mouth.

"Why did you do that?" asked the emperor.

"My lord," the man explained, "I defended my view with the appropriate means—I spoke about speech. Now let him argue his case the same way!" (Midrash Yalkut Shimoni, B'haalot'cha)

5. Rabbi Judah of Kefar Giboraya expounded: "The words (Psalm 65:2), *Unto You silence is praise* tell us that silence is the sovereign remedy." When Rav Dimi came he said: "In the West we say, Speech is worth a Sela,[47] silence two." (Talmud Megillah 18a)

6. Silence is tantamount to consent. (Talmud Yebamot 87b)

7. Silence can validate, silence cannot annul. (Tosefta Nedarim 7)

Avot 1:18

רבָּן שִׁמְעוֹן בֶּן גַּמְלִיאֵל אוֹמֵר:
עַל שְׁלֹשָׁה דְבָרִים הָעוֹלָם קַיָּם:
עַל הַדִּין,
וְעַל הָאֱמֶת
וְעַל הַשָּׁלוֹם.
שֶׁנֶּאֱמַר: אֱמֶת וּמִשְׁפַּט שָׁלוֹם שִׁפְטוּ
בְּשַׁעֲרֵיכֶם.

RABBAN SIMEON[48] ben Gamaliel says:
The world is sustained by three things:
by justice,
By truth,
and by peace,
as it is said (Zechariah 8:16), *Execute the judgment of truth and peace in your communities.*

The world is sustained—What saves this noble saying from mere abstraction? I think it is the combination of virtues that Simeon ben Gamaliel selects. We have seen societies destroy themselves: justice was their aim, and to achieve it they scorned truth and lied about their violent and unjust ways of realizing their utopian dreams. Justice and peace are not to be arrived at dishonestly—nor, for that matter, by means of injustice and violence. (CS)

--- This passage forms a fitting conclusion to Avot 1. Avot 1:2 speaks of the (three) things on which the world is based or founded, while 1:18 speaks of the (three) things by which the world sustains itself and carries on.

--- The world sustains itself by obedience to law, but that is not enough, for the judgment (of law) must be a judgment of truth. And even that is not enough: law and truth will not sustain the world unless there is also peace. (after Vitry)

--- Rabbi Simeon ben Gamaliel said: Never sneer at justice, for it is one of the three pillars of the world. The sages taught that the world is sustained by three things: justice, truth, and peace. Consider, then, that if you pervert justice, you shake the world, you make it unstable. It is written (Proverbs 21:3), *To do justice and righteousness is more acceptable to the Eternal than sacrifice.* For sacrifices could be brought only when the Temple existed, but justice and righteousness apply both then and since. Sacrifices atoned only for involuntary sins, but justice and righteousness atone both for voluntary and involuntary sins. Sacrifices were offered only by human beings, but justice and righteousness apply also to the world above. Sacrifices were offered only in this world, justice and righteousness are for this world and for the world-to-come. (Midrash Deuteronomy Rabbah, Shof'tim, 5:1,3)

Justice and Mercy

When the Eternal God made heaven and earth...(Genesis 2:4). A king had some fragile drinking glasses. He considered: If I put hot drinks in them, they will crack.

But if the drinks are too cold, they may shatter all the same. So he poured lukewarm liquid into them, and all was well.

This was the thought of the Holy One: If in creating the world I show nothing but mercy, sinners will abound. But if, on the other hand, I display nothing but strict justice, the world will not endure. Let me combine the two, and hope that the world will survive. (Midrash Genesis Rabbah 12)

Scoundrels and Saints

And God said: Let us make a being in our image, in our likeness...(Genesis 1:26). Rabbi Berechiah said: Before creating the first Adam, The Holy One saw that scoundrels as well as saints would be numbered among his descendants. God considered: If I create human beings, I create scoundrels as well; but if I do not create them, how will saints come into existence? So the Holy One ignored the scoundrels, took hold of mercy, and created humankind. (Midrash Genesis Rabbah 8)

The Righteous

1. One righteous human being is equal in God's sight to the whole world, as it is said (Proverbs 10:25), *The righteous is the foundation of the world.* (Midrash Tanchuma, B'shallach, 10)

2. *You stand this day, all of you, before the Eternal, your God...* (Deuteronomy 29:10). All of you are pledges for one another: if but one among you is righteous, all of you endure through that one's merit—you, and all the world, as it is said (Proverbs 10:25), *The righteous is the foundation of the world.* If one sins, the whole generation suffers, as happened with Achan.[49] If one does good, all the more do all reap the benefit. (Midrash Tanchuma B, Nitzavim, 25a)

3. *Now the brothers of Joseph, being ten, went down to Egypt* (Genesis 42:3). Why is a particular point made of the number ten? Because [being ten] they had the power to cancel the sentence of [of exile and affliction] and annul the decree.

In the same way, you can see how, in regard to Sodom, Abraham reduced his pleading from "for the sake of fifty" to "for the sake of ten." When ten righteous people could not be found, Abraham was silent. The generation of the Flood, too, could not be saved because they lacked ten righteous souls, for among them were only Noah and his sons and their wives, eight altogether. (Midrash Tanchuma B, Miketz, 98a)

4. By these two marks is Israel known: the effort to penetrate to the very essence of the Torah, and to love God with a perfect love, in good days and in bad. (Leviticus Rabbah, Vayikra, 3:7)

5. Rabbi Chiyah and Rabbi Jonathan were strolling in a cemetery and Rabbi Jonathan's ritual fringes were dragging on the ground. Rabbi Chiyah said to him: "Lift them up; you don't want them [the dead] to say, 'Tomorrow they join us, yet

today they mock us!'" He wondered: "Are they aware of anything? Doesn't it say (Ecclesiastes 9:8), *The dead know nothing?*" He replied: "If you learned[50] you did not repeat, if you repeated you did not go over it, and if you did go over it, they did not correctly explain it to you. For the living know that they must die—those are the righteous, who even when they have died are called 'living;' *The dead know nothing*—those are the wicked, who even while they are alive are called 'dead.' (Talmud Berachot 18a)

On Truth

1. Rabbi Chanina said: The seal of the Holy One is truth. (Shabbat 55a)

2. Rava said: Jerusalem was destroyed because of a dearth of truth-sayers, as it is said (Jeremiah 5:1), *Run through the streets of Jerusalem and take note; search her squares and see if you can find one who does justice and seeks truth, and I will pardon her.* (Talmud Shabbat 119b)

3. *You shall have a just ephah and a just hin.*[51] (Leviticus 19:36). Rabbi Yosé son of Rabbi Judah said: Why does Scripture speak of a just "hin," when it is included in the larger "ephah?" Read it as *hein*, [yes], meaning: let your Yes be just and your No just. (Talmud Baba Metsia 59a)

4. The letters of *EMeT*, Truth [אמת] stand on two legs, while the letters of *SHeKeR*, Falsehood [שקר] stand on one leg. The truthful endure, the falsifiers do not. The letters of Truth [אמת] are set apart from one another,[52] while the letters of Falsehood [שקר] are closer together.[53] Truth is hard to do; deceit stands right to hand. (Midrash Yalkut Shimoni, Genesis 3)

5. Such is the fate of liars: even when they tell the truth they are not believed. (Talmud Sanhedrin 89b)

6. Rabbi Zeira said: Never make a promise to a child that you don't keep, for thereby you teach that child to lie, as it is said (Jeremiah 9:4), *they have taught their tongue to speak lies.* (Sukkah 46b)

13. "Yes, Yes" is an oath; "No, No" is an oath. (Talmud Shevuot 36a)

14. It is improper to take an oath even on the truth. (Midrash Tanchuma, Vayikra)

15. It is told that a man entrusted Bar–Talmion with 100 denarii. Some time later he asked for their return. Bar–Talmion said: "I have returned what you entrusted to me." The man said: "Come and take an oath to that effect." What did Bar–Talmion do? He hollowed out a reed and put the dinarii into it and used it as a walking–stick. Arriving at the Synagogue he said to the man: "Hold on to this stick while I take the oath." He then said: "I have returned to this man what he entrusted to me." The [astonished] man took the stick and threw it to the ground. It broke open and the coins rolled out over the floor. Bar–Talmion said: "Take them, take them—they're yours!" (Midrash Leviticus Rabbah 6; Pesikta De Rab Kahana 22)

16. King Yannai said to his wife: Fear neither the Pharisees nor those who are not Pharisees, but the people who wear both colors. They seem like Pharisees, yet their deeds are like those of Zimri and they ask the reward of Pinchas.[54] (Sotah 22b)

17. This pig lies down and shows his hooves, as if to say: "See, I'm Kosher!" (Midrash Genesis Rabbah 65; Leviticus Rabbah 13)

Peace

1. Rabbi Simeon ben Chalafta said: The Holy One found no vessel better suited to hold blessing for Israel than peace, as it is said (Psalm 29:18), *Eternal One: give strength to Your people; Eternal One, bless Your people with peace.* (Talmud Uktzin 3)

2. Bar Kappara said: Great is peace, for even the upper worlds are in need of it, as it is said (Job 25:2), *Who makes peace on high.* We reason from minor to major: If the upper beings, in whom there is neither enmity nor hatred nor jealousy nor competition nor an evil eye, are in need of peace, how much the more do humans need it!

3. Great is peace, for even the Holy One told a lie for its sake, as it is said (Genesis 15:13), *Will I really have a child when I am so old?* [55] (Various sources)

4. Hezekiah said: Great is peace, for concerning all the [other] Mitzvot it is written: *If you find your enemy's ox that has strayed* (Exodus 23:4), *If you should see your foe's donkey* (ibid., 23:5), *If you should happen upon a bird's nest* (Deuteronomy 22:6)— that is, only if the Mitzvah comes your way are you called upon to do it; but what is said about peace? *Seek peace and pursue it.* (Psalm 34:15)—seek it where you are and pursue it elsewhere. (Midrash Leviticus Rabbah 9; J. Peah 1:1)

5. Why were not the words *[God saw] that it was good* said concerning the second day [of creation]? Rabbi Chanina said: That was the day when conflict was created, as it is said (Genesis 1:7), *Let there be a division between the waters.* Rabbi Tavyomi said: If *it was good* is not said of a division that was for the upbuilding and settlement of the world, all the more is this true of a division that is to its detriment! (Talmud Berachot 4a)

6. *God hangs the earth upon nothingness.* (Job 26:7). Rabbi Illai said: The world endures only through such as make nothing of themselves in the hour of conflict. (Talmud Chullin 89b)

7. ...*for if you wield your tool upon it [the altar] you profane it.* (Exodus 20:25).
The altar was made to add to human life,
the iron blade shortens human life.
It is not right to wield that which shortens
over that which lengthens. (Midrash Tanchuma, Yitro, 17, 126b)

Sages 1

The following section supplements Pirké Avot, by adding passages from elsewhere in the rabbinic literature that either quote or tell about the sages of Avot.

The Chain Remains Unbroken

1. When Rabbi Akiba died, Rabbi was born.
When Rabbi died, Rav Judah was born.
When Rav Judah died, Rava was born.
When Rava died, Rav Ashi was born.
—To teach you that no tzaddik departs the world until another tzaddik like him is created, as it is said (Ecclesiastes 1:5), *The sun rises and the sun goes down.*
Before the High Priest Eli's sun had set, the sun of Samuel of Ramah had risen, as it is said (I Samuel 3:3), *The lamp of God had not yet gone out, and Samuel was*[56]...
(Talmud Kiddushin 72b)

1:2

Simeon the Righteous

1. Simeon the Righteous said: Only once have I eaten of a Nazarite's guilt offering. A man from the south once came to me. He had a ruddy countenance, beautiful eyes, was handsome, and his hair hung in curly locks. I said to him: "Why do you want to cut off this beautiful hair?" He answered: "I was a shepherd and, going to fill the trough from the well, I saw my image in the water. My yetzer[57] took hold of me then and would have driven me out of the world. So I said to myself: 'Wicked one, what makes you so proud of what isn't yours, of what belongs to the dust, to the worm? I am going to consecrate you to Heaven and cut you off for Heaven's sake.'" I bowed my head and kissed him, and I said: "May there be many like you in Israel who do the will of Heaven."
Rabbi Muna said: Why did Simeon the Righteous ordinarily not eat the Nazirite's offering? Did he consider that the Nazarite sinned by abstaining from wine? No, it was because he thought that people often took the Nazirite vow in haste, and so ended by regretting it. [And why did he make an exception in this instance?] Because this young man took the vow calmly and with full reflection: mouth and mind were at one. (Midrash Numbers Rabbah, Naso, 10:7)

1:4

Yosé ben Yo'ezer of Zereida;
Yosé ben Yochanan of Jerusalem

1. With the death of Yosé ben Yo'ezer of Zereidah and José ben Yochanan of Jerusalem, there were no more "complete men,"[58] as it is said (Micah 7:1), *There is not a cluster to eat, not a ripe fig I could desire.* And no complete man rose up until Rabbi Akiva. (Jerusalem Talmud Sotah 29:10; SA 2.11:18.144)

1:6

Rabbi Joshua ben Perachiah

1. In the time of Rabbi Joshua ben Chananiah, Rome agreed to the rebuilding of the Temple. In the end, the plan was frustrated. A large crowd was gathered in the valley of Bet Rimmon when the royal writ was received. There was groaning and talk of rebellion. They [the Sages] said: "Someone wise is needed to calm the crowd down. Let it be Rabbi Joshua ben Perachiah, a Father in Torah."
Rabbi Joshua entered and spoke: "A lion caught its prey and was left with a bone in its throat. He said: "I will reward anyone who can extract it." A long–beaked Egyptian Heron came along. Putting its beak in the lion's mouth, he extracted the bone and claimed his reward. The lion replied: "Get yourself away from here, and content yourself with the boast that you went into the lion's mouth and lived to tell the tale. That's reward enough for you."
"If we can boast the same about this nation, let us be content." (Midrash Genesis Rabbah 64; Yalkut Shimoni, Tol'dot, 26)

1.8

Simeon Ben Shetach

1. When one of King Yannai's servants killed a man, Simeon ben Shetach said to the Sages: "Take jurisdiction over him and let us judge him." They sent word to King Yannai: "Your servant has killed a man." He handed the man over to them. They sent to him: "You too must come, for the Torah says (Exodus 21:29), *and it has been testified against to its owner... let the owner come and take responsibility for his ox.*" He came and they seated him near Simeon ben Shetach, who said to him: "Stand up and let testimony be given against you." He [Yannai] replied: "Not as you say but as your colleagues say." He turned to his right, he turned to his left: they hung their heads. Simeon ben Shetach said to them: "You cowards, let the One who sees thoughts come and punish you!" The angel Gabriel came and threw them to the ground till they were lifeless. The king was shaken. Simeon ben Shetach said to him: "Stand up and let testimony be given against you. You stand not before us but before the One whose word created the world, as it is said (Deuteronomy 19:17),

Then those who have a dispute shall stand before the Eternal. Yannai stood up. (Talmud Sanhedrin 19a)

2. Rabbi Simeon ben Shetach lived in extreme poverty.

His disciples purchased a donkey with the intention of presenting it to their teacher It would ease his labors and enable him to earn a little more.

They were admiring the donkey and examining it, when one of them found a pearl hidden in its bridle. overjoyed, they brought the donkey to their master. "Now," they cried, "you can live without care and spend all your time in the study of Torah."

When he asked them their meaning, they told him: "We bought this donkey from an Arab and have found a pearl hidden in its bridle. That pearl will make you rich."

Simeon ben Shetach took little time to say to them: "Did its owner know about the pearl?" His disciples answered: "He could not have known. Who knows when it was hidden, or by whom?"

Hearing their reply, Simeon ben Shetach commanded them: "Go and give the pearl back to the man. You bought a donkey from him, not a pearl."

When they returned the pearl, the vendor cried: "Blessed is the God of the Jews!" (Midrash Deuteronomy Rabbah 3; Jerusalem Talmud Baba Metsia 2:5)

1:12

Hillel the Elder

1. It was told of Hillel the Elder, that every day he would earn a half–dinar. One half went for access to the House of Study, and the other sustained him and his household. Once he did not earn anything, and the doorkeeper refused him admittance. He climbed the wall and sat by a skylight, in order to hear the words of the living God from Shemayah and Avtalyon. They say it was the eve of Shabbat, at the end of Tevet, and snow fell and covered him. At dawn Shemayah said to Avtalyon: "Brother, it's unusually dark in here today, as though it were cloudy." Looking up, they saw a man's shape through the skylight. There were three cubits of snow on him. They cleared it off him, washed and covered him, and put him by the fire. "It's worth profaning the Sabbath for this one." (Talmud Yoma 38b)

2. *The kind benefit themselves* (Proverbs 11:17). —Hillel the Elder, for example. Concluding a session he would walk along with his disciples. They asked him once: "Master, where are you going?" "To perform a Mitzvah." "What is the Mitzvah?" "To bathe in the bath–house." "That is a Mitzvah?" "Yes," he said. "They put ikons of kings in front of theaters and meeting-halls, and they appoint people to guard them and see to their 'care and feeding'—all the more so I, who am flesh and blood, and created in the image and likeness Of God." (Midrash Leviticus Rabbah 34)

3. Our sages taught: When the last prophets died—Haggai, Zechariah, and Malachi—the Holy Spirit departed from Israel. Nevertheless they had access to a Bat

36

Kol. They were gathered once in the upper story (attic) of Bet–Goria in Lydda and a Bat Kol from Heaven was granted them: "One here is as worthy as Moses our Teacher to have the Shechinah rest on him, only his generation does not merit that." The Sages all turned their eyes on Hillel the Elder. When he died they said of him: "A saint, a humble man, a disciple of Ezra." (Talmud Sanhedrin 11a)

4. Hillel the Elder would say: Do not be appear naked—where others are clothed; do not appear standing—where others are sitting; do not appear laughing—where others are crying, as it is said (Ecclesiastes 3:4), *a time to weep and a time to laugh.* (Tosefta Berachot 2)

Beit Hillel and Beit Shammai[59]

1. Rabbi Aba quoted Rabbi Samuel: The School of Shammai and the School of Hillel debated for three years. Each held that the Halachah was according to their view. Then a Bat Kol proclaimed: "The words of both sides are the words of the living God, but the Halachah follows the School of Hillel."

Since both of them expounded the words of the living God, why did the Halachah follow the views of the School of Hillel? Because they were gentle and conciliatory, and would teach their own view and that of the School of Shammai; moreover, in teaching they gave priority to the School of Shammai—demonstrating that the Holy One exalts those who humble themselves, and humbles those who exalt themselves. (Talmud Erubin 13b)

2. A man who is half–slave and half–free works one day alternately for his master and for himself. Such was the view of the School of Hillel.

The School of Shammai said: You have worked things out for his master, but not for him: he is not allowed to marry a female slave, for he is half-free; and he cannot marry a free woman, for he is half–slave: is he not to marry? But the world was created to be populated, as it is said (Isaiah 45:18), *I did not create it to be a waste, I made it to be inhabited.* Rather, for the common good they make his master set him free and write a contract for half his future wages to go to the master.

The School of Hillel reconsidered and came around to the view of the Shammaites. (Talmud Pesachim 88ab; Baba Batra 13a)

3. Despite the fact that the School of Shammai and the School of Hillel differed— these forbidding and those permitting—the men of the School of Shammai did not hesitate to marry the women of the School of Hillel, and vice versa. This teaches that they treated one another with love and friendship, fulfilling what is said (Zechariah 8:19), *Love truth and peace.* (Talmud Yebamot 14a)

1:16

Rabban Gamaliel

1. Rabban Gamaliel married and recited the Sh'ma on the first night. His disciples said to him: "Did you not teach us, Rabbi, that a bridegroom is exempt from the obligation of reciting the Sh'ma?" He said to them: "Yes, but personally I am unwilling to separate myself from the Kingdom of Heaven even for a single hour." When his wife died, he bathed on the first night. His disciples said to him: "Did you not teach us, Rabbi, that a mourner is forbidden to bathe?" He said to them: "I am different from others—I am infirm." (Talmud Berachot 16a)

2. Two people came and bore witness: "In the morning we saw the New Moon in the east; in the evening [we saw it] in the west." Rabbi Yochanan ben Nuri said: "They are false witnesses," but when they came to Yavneh, Rabban Gamaliel accepted them. Another time two people came and said: "We saw it in its time [on the thirtieth], but on that evening it was not visible." Rabban Gamaliel accepted them. Rabbi Dosa ben Hyrcanas said: "They are false witness—today they see the woman giving birth and tomorrow her belly is between her teeth [she is very pregnant]!!" Rabbi Joshua said to him: "I agree with you."
Rabban Gamaliel [then] summoned Rabbi Joshua. "I command you to come to me with staff and wallet on the day that by your reckoning is Yom Kippur!" He departed and Rabbi Akiba found him in distress. "Why are you distressed, Rabbi?" He replied: "Akiba, better I be bedridden twelve months than have such a decree fall on me." He answered: "I can show that whatever Rabban Gamaliel has done is valid, as it is said (Leviticus 23:4), *These are the Eternal one's appointed times, the holy meeting-days that you shall proclaim*—whether in their due time or not I have no other festivals than these [*that you proclaim*]." He then came to Rabbi Dosa ben Hyrcanas (for another opinion), who said: "If we reject the court of Rabban Gamaliel, we must reject every court in Israel since the days of Moses, as it is said (Exodus 24:9), *Moses, Aaron, Nadav and Avihu and seventy of Israel's elders went up*—why weren't the names of the elders spelled out? To teach that every three who stand over Israel as a court are the equivalent of the court of Moses."
So Rabbi Joshua took his staff and wallet in hand and went to Yavneh, to appear before Rabban Gamaliel on the day that was Yom Kippur by his reckoning. When Rabban Gamaliel saw him, he arose and kissed his head. He said: "Well met, my master and disciple! My master in wisdom, my disciple in obedience. Happy the generation where the great listen to the small!" (Talmud Rosh Hashanah 24b–25a)

3. We have learned: In the old days the arrangements for the funeral were worse for the family than the death itself.[60] It came to the point where they would leave the body and flee. Then Rabban Gamaliel decreed for himself an inexpensive funeral and they buried him in a flaxen garment. Thus it came about that everyone emulated

him. Rav Papa said: Nowadays people use even the cheapest of materials. (Talmud K'tubot 8b)

4. Rabban Gamaliel issued a proclamation: No disciple whose heart and hand are not one[61] may enter the House of Study. (Talmud Berachot 28a)

1:18

Rabbi Simeon ben Gamaliel

1. Rabbi Simeon ben Gamaliel would say: They had a wonderful custom in Jerusalem: If one were entrusted with preparing [catering] a feast and spoiled it, he would pay his client an additional sum for the humiliation he and his guest had suffered.[62]

They had another fine custom there: A banner would be displayed at the entrance as a signal; When it was there people would know they might enter. (Talmud Baba Batra 93b)

2. Rabbi Illai said in the name of Rabbi Elazar son of Rabbi Simeon: It is permitted to speak with deliberate inaccuracy for the sake of peace, as it is said (Genesis 50:16f.), *Your father commanded ... tell Joseph ... "Please forgive..."*[63]

Rabbi Simeon ben Gamaliel said: See how much ink has been spilled, how many quills broken, how many skins used, how many schoolchildren disciplined, to get them to learn in the Torah something that never happened: that's how great is the importance of peace. (Talmud Yebamot 65b)

3. We have learned: Rabban Simeon ben Gamaliel says: One must violate the Sabbath to save the life of a day–old infant. The Torah says: "Violate one Sabbath for him so that he may observe many Sabbaths." On the other hand, once he has died one may not violate the Sabbath even for David king of Israel. The dead are free of [responsibility for] the Mitzvot. That is what Rabbi Yochanan said: *Free among the dead* (Psalm 88:6)—The dead are free of [responsibility for] the Mitzvot. (Talmud Shabbat 151b)

1. Rabbi Eliezer, Rabbi Joshua, and Rabbi Zadok were gathered at the feast for Rabban Gamaliel's son, and Rabban Gamaliel was standing and serving them drinks. He gave the cup to Rabbi Eliezer, who did not accept it; he gave it to Rabbi Joshua, who took it.

Rabbi Eliezer wondered: "How can it be right that we sit while Rabban Gamaliel stands and serves us?" He replied: Abraham was the greatest of his generation, and greater certainly than Rabban Gamaliel, yet concerning him it says (Genesis 18:8), *And he was standing over them* [to serve them]. Do you argue that they (the men Abraham was serving) looked like angels? No—they looked to him like Arabs. Why then should not Rabban Gamaliel stand and serve us?"

Rabbi Zadok said to them: "How long will you prefer to speak in honor of human beings and not in honor of the Presence? The Holy One makes the wind blow and exalts princes and brings down the rain and makes the earth fruitful and prepares a table for each and every one of us—[If God can serve us,] why then should not Rabban Gamaliel stand and serve us?" (Talmud Kiddushin 32b)

2. We have learned, Rabban Gamaliel says: *God will give you pity and will pity you* (Deuteronomy 13:18)—Heaven shows compassion for all who show compassion for others. (Talmud Shabbat 151b)

In Sum

Between the three things that form the world's foundation and the three that keep the world going, what do the sages of chapter 1 have to say to us? Much that is recorded deals with the life of the sage and the sage–in–training, the disciple. The path of the sage is one of selfless devotion to God; the path of the one who would be wise is the same. In addition, more specific advice is offered the Sage who is both teacher and judge. Summing up the teaching, we may say: be diligent is preparing yourself for what you have to do, and be considerate to everyone. There is little or nothing that cannot be applied to each of us. A few passages may reflect more obviously the historical moment, but on the whole the teaching is timeless, and it is addressed to every reader, every seeker.

•••••••

Notes

[1]אֱלֹהֶיךָ, *Elohecha,* 'your God,' is in the singular.

[2]אֱלֹהֶיךָ, *Elohecha,* 'your God,' is in the singular.

[3]Ca. 3rd C. BCE, High Priest from 219–199.

[4]חֶסֶד, *chesed,* is 'loving kindness; צְדָקָה, *Tzedakah,* is both "righteousness' and 'charity.' This gives Rabbi Elazar his point: we only sow צְדָקָה, while we reap the fruit of חֶסֶד.

[5]Late 3rd C. BCE.

[6]Or, awe. God is to be served out of love, but also out of awe or reverence, expressed by us through ethical behavior.

[7]Ca. 200–160 BCE. They, and the 'pairs' that follow, served, respectively, as Nasi (President) and Av Bet Din (Chief Justice) of the Sanhedrin.

[8]חבר, *chaver*—companion, colleague, comrade, fellow.

[9]By giving in public where all could see his humiliation.

[10]To promote communal harmony מפני דרכי שלום, *mipnei darkei shalom,* 'for the sake of [the ways of] peace' is a phrase frequently invoked in rabbinic literature.

[11]Numbers 22.1–12.

[12]Late 2nd C. BCE.

[13]Late 2nd C. BCE.

[14] After 12 months mourners no longer say Kaddish for the dead, except on the anniversary of their death. So it's as though your friend had died and has now comback to life.

[15] That shining face was a gift from God.

[16]Or, "And do not imagine yourself immune from disaster."

[17]Or, a foolish saint.

[18]Who give advice which enables people to circumvent the law legally.

[19]1st C. BCE.

[20]1st C. BCE. He was the brother of Queen Salome Alexandra who, as the widow of King Alexander Yannai, reigned 76–67 BCE. Unlike her husband, who persecuted the Phaarisees, Salome Alexandra treated them favorably.

[21]Moses.

[22]A coin worth 2 shekels.

[23]Estimating which wine barrels should be sold first.

[24]9900 Zuz.

[25]צַדִּיק, *tzaddik,* a righteous person.

[26]To make his point, he treats 'great' and 'small' as referring to the case rather than to persons.

[27]1st C. BCE.

[28]1st C. BCE.

[29]Or, power, high office.

[30]See II Kings 4:8–13.

[31] קנה, *kanah,* 'acquire,' means, literally, 'buy.'

[32]End of 1st C. BCE–beginning of 1st C. CE.

[33]End of 1st C. BCE–beginning of 1st C. CE.

[34]שלום, the word usually translated as 'peace,' also conveys 'completeness' 'harmony', and 'well-being.'

[35]Literally, "the creatures," That is, the (human) creatures that God has created.

[36]This passage is in Aramaic.

[37] Or, deserves to die.

[38]And see 3:12.

[39]Malicious gossip, slander, speaking ill of another.

[40]A play on words turns מצרע, *m'tzora,* 'leper,' into מוציא שם רע, *motsi shem ra,* 'slanderer'.

[41]That is, this is a form of 'moral leprosy.'

[42]1st C. CE. Hillel's grandson and the first to hold the title 'Rabban', a variant on 'rabbi.'

[43]Or, mentor, guide

[44]1st C. CE. It is unclear whether Simeon was Gamaliel's son, or Hillel's. In the latter case, of course, this mishnah is out of order.

[45]Or, for the body

[46]And see 3:9, 3:17, 4:5, 5:14.

[47]A coin valued at two shekels.

[48]1st–2nd C. CE.

[49] Joshua 22:20.

[50]The verse (Ecclesiastes 9:8) you just quoted. Rabbi Chiyah holds that the verse is metaphorical, not to be understood literally.

[51] These are units of measure.

[52] They are at the beginning, middle, and end of the alphabet, respectively.

[53] The three letters are adjacent to one another in the alphabet.

[54] See Numbers 25.

[55] God is telling Abraham what Sarah said; in fact, she said: *when **my lord** is so old.*

[56]A pun on Eli\Elohim.

[57]יצר הרע, *yetzer hara,* The Will–to–evil, Evil Impulse. It drives us in this world and can drive us "out of the world."

[58]אשכול, *eshkol* (biblical 'grape-cluster,' mod. 'grapefruit') = אשכולות, *ashkolot,* slang for איש שהכל בו, *ish sheh-hakol bo,* 'one in whom there is everything.'

[59]The School [House] of Hillel and the School [House] of Shammai. These represented rival points of view on a wide range of issues.

[60]The expense was so great.

[61]Literally, whose inside is not the same as his outside.

[62]That is, in addition to the refund for the feast itself.
[63]And Jacob gave no such command.

Avot 2

A Note

Chapter 2 carries on the line of authorities from chapter 1, and in an interesting way. There are in fact two lines: the first line of leaders traces its ancestry to Hillel the Elder through Simeon ben Gamaliel (1.18), Rabbi (2:1) and their descendants; the second traces its spiritual ancestry to Hillel, beginning with his disciple Yochanan ben Zakkai and continuing with his disciples (2.8–16). By the end of chapter 2, as Neusner points out, the two lines of authority have effectively merged. Instead of rivalry for power we have cooperation for the sake of Heaven. The first part of chapter 2 looks back at the first two centuries CE, with its disasters and controversies. The second half bridges the time between 70–135, the time that follows one disastrous war, and continues to the end of an even more calamitous second war—the Bar Kochba uprising.

•••••••

Additional readings on the sages whose sayings are featured in this chapter begin on page 75.

Avot 2:1

רַבִּי אוֹמֵר: אֵיזוֹ הִיא דֶרֶךְ יְשָׁרָה
שֶׁיָּבוֹר לוֹ הָאָדָם? כָּל-שֶׁהִיא תִפְאֶרֶת
לְעֹשֶׂיהָ וְתִפְאֶרֶת לוֹ מִן הָאָדָם.
וֶהֱוֵי זָהִיר בְּמִצְוָה קַלָּה כְּבַחֲמוּרָה,
שֶׁאֵין אַתָּה יוֹדֵעַ מַתַּן שְׂכָרָן שֶׁל מִצְוֹת,
וֶהֱוֵי מְחַשֵּׁב הֶפְסֵד מִצְוָה כְּנֶגֶד
שְׂכָרָהּ, וּשְׂכַר עֲבֵרָה כְּנֶגֶד הֶפְסֵדָהּ.
וְהִסְתַּכֵּל בִּשְׁלֹשָׁה דְבָרִים וְאִי אַתָּה
בָא לִידֵי עֲבֵרָה: דַּע מַה לְמַעְלָה מִמְּךָ:
עַיִן רוֹאָה,
וְאֹזֶן שׁוֹמַעַת,
וְכָל-מַעֲשֶׂיךָ בַּסֵּפֶר נִכְתָּבִין.

RABBI[1] SAYS: What is the right path to choose?[2] Whatever is a thing of beauty for the one who follows it, and a thing of beauty in the eyes of others.[3]

Be as eager to do a minor Mitzvah as a major,[4] for you do not know the [relative] rewards of the Mitzvot. And balance what you may lose by [doing] a Mitzvah against your gain, and what you may gain from a transgression against your loss. And keep your eye on three things and you will not fall into the grip of sin: know what is above you—

an eye that sees,

an ear that hears,

and all your actions inscribed in the Book.

the right path—As it is in many other cultures, the image of a path or way is frequently encountered in Jewish thought. The entire system of law is called הלכה, *Halachah*, from the root הלך, *halach*, to walk or go; the life of the spirit is pictured as a journey: *Walk before Me with integrity*, says God to Abraham and all his descendants; The call to righteous action, as here, is put in terms of "the right path." And it should be noted that the text can, and perhaps should, be understood to speak not of "the right path" but of "a right path." For no single path can be right for all, even if they have a common destination. (CS)

---You may adopt a course of action that you think right, and that you would think right were others to do the same—yet others might not approve your course. And the other way around: others may honor you for what you do, yet you yourself might think it wrong. What to do? Take the path that brings you honor which you too think is honorable. (Duran)

major and minor Mitzvah—The primary meaning of "major" and "minor" is probably "difficult" and "easy" (to fulfill). Some have made the following distinction between the Mitzvot: There are two types of commandment—those that are between the individual and God, and those that are directed at other people. The former group includes "ritual," that is, such commandments as wearing a tallit, building a sukkah, and the like. The latter includes the "ethical," that is, good deeds, honesty, and the like. Where they conflict, the "ethical" have priority; within categories, however, one performs the commandments as they come along, and one should not ignore "minor" commandments while waiting for a more important one to fulfill. (see Meam Loez, Avoth, pp. 68f., citing Midrash Shemuel)

--- Lit., "light" and "heavy:" this is not a reference to the relative importance of the commandments, but to their relative difficulty of fulfillment, or their rarity. We should do the commandment at hand, whether "light" or "heavy." (Meam Loez, Avoth, pp. 70f.)

your actions inscribed—There are people in whose presence you would be ashamed to do something dishonorable or say something improper; keep in mind, then, that you are always in the presence of the Holy One, and conduct yourself accordingly. (after Rabbi Jonah ben Abraham)

--- God's attention to us is one of love. (Neusner)

Avot 2:2

רַבָּן גַּמְלִיאֵל, בְּנוֹ שֶׁל רַבִּי יְהוּדָה
הַנָּשִׂיא, אוֹמֵר:

יָפֶה תַלְמוּד תּוֹרָה עִם דֶּרֶךְ אֶרֶץ,
שֶׁיְּגִיעַת שְׁנֵיהֶם מְשַׁכַּחַת עָוֹן.

וְכָל־תּוֹרָה שֶׁאֵין עִמָּהּ מְלָאכָה סוֹפָהּ
בְּטֵלָה וְגוֹרֶרֶת עָוֹן.

וְכָל־הָעֲמֵלִים עִם הַצִּבּוּר יִהְיוּ עֲמֵלִים
עִמָּהֶם לְשֵׁם שָׁמַיִם. שֶׁזְּכוּת אֲבוֹתָם
מְסַיְּעָתָן, וְצִדְקָתָם עוֹמֶדֶת לָעַד.

וְאַתֶּם, מַעֲלֶה אֲנִי עֲלֵיכֶם שָׂכָר הַרְבֵּה
כְּאִלּוּ עֲשִׂיתֶם.

RABBAN GAMALIEL[5], son of Rabbi Judah the Prince, says:

The study of Torah along with a craft[6] is fitting, for this dual labor banishes iniquity from the mind. All Torah not accompanied by labor is doomed to fail and leads to iniquity.[7]

And let all who labor with the community[8] labor with them for the sake of Heaven. For then the merit of their ancestors upholds them and their righteousness endures forever. As for you, I deem you worthy of great reward, as though you yourselves had done [the labor].

a craft (derech eretz)—How you make a living. Since on the one hand you will learn from the Torah not to oppress nor rob, and on the other you are engaged in making a living, it will not even occur to you to steal, to rob, or to engage in violence. (after Vitry)

Torah and derech eretz—The learned are prone to think too highly of themselves, and this mishnah warns them not to be arrogant. Thus it says, "The study of Torah along with derech eretz is fitting"—that is, scholars must have derech eretz, good manners; they must practice humility, care for others, and get along with them. And derech eretz means, literally, "the way of earth." Scholars must add to their learning the ordinary way of earth, and not think themselves separate and superior. (See Meam Loez, Avoth, pp. 74f.)

dual labor—The Hebrew for "labor" is in the singular, teaching that the labor of Torah and the labor of a craft are a single labor, for you are expected to pursue your craft by the standards you have learned from the Torah. (see Vitry, above)

who labor with the community—"The Holy One makes good intentions bear fruit" (Talmud Kiddushin 40a). If, despite all your labors, you have not accomplished all that you set out to do, do not throw up your hands in despair: God takes note even of your labors that do not succeed, and reckons you as having accomplished your task. (Vitry)

Labor

1. We have learned (Deuteronomy 24:14f.): *You shall not oppress hired hands who are poor and needy...You must pay their wage on the day they earn it ...for they have set their heart on it.*
Why did they climb to the top of this ladder? Why did they perch on that fruit–tree, risking life and limb? Was it not for their wages?
Another interpretation: *for they have set their heart on it* —anyone who holds back payment of wages tears the hired hand's heart out, as it were. (Talmud Baba Metzia 112a)

2. *You must pay their wage on the day they earn it ...for they have set their heart on it. ...* (Deuteronomy 24:14f.)
It's like the story of a man who was walking along ahead of his donkey. He bought a sheaf and put it on his shoulder. The donkey now walked along behind the sheaf yearning to eat it. What did its master do? When he arrived home he put the donkey in its stall and put the sheaf high up, where the donkey could not reach it. They said to him: "Villain! The donkey goes on your errands and runs the whole way back wanting that food and you don't give it to him!"
So the hired hands work and toil all day yearning for their wages, and they are sent forth empty! (Midrash Exodus Rabbah 31; Tanchumah, Mishpatim)

3. *For they are My servants* (Leviticus 25:42)—My contract with them [says God] preceded all others. ...*whom I brought out of the land of Egypt.* (ibid.)—on condition that they not hire themselves for the hire of slaves.[9] (Midrash Sifra, Behar)

4. Our sages taught (Leviticus 25.43): *Because it goes well for them with you. With you*—in regard to food; *with you*—in regard to drink. You may not eat a fine loaf while they eat a coarse loaf; you may not drink vintage wine while they drink new wine; you may not sleep on feathers while they sleep on straw. That's why it is said: "Who acquires a Hebrew slave acquires a master." (Talmud Kiddushin 22a)

Avot 2:3[10]

הֱווּ זְהִירִין בָּרָשׁוּת, שָׁאֵין מְקָרְבִין
לוֹ לָאָדָם אֶלָּא לְצֹרֶךְ עַצְמָן.
נְרְאִין כְּאוֹהֲבִין בִּשְׁעַת הֲנָאָתָן,
וְאֵין עוֹמְדִין לוֹ לָאָדָם בִּשְׁעַת דָּחְקוֹ.

BE CAUTIOUS of the government, for they befriend you only when it suits them. They seem like friends when it is to their advantage, but when you need them they don't stand by you.

Be cautious—We have already encountered one statement of distrust of political power or high office. Further along we will come upon other reflections. They will not all agree. Perhaps they reflect particular personalities, perhaps different times and conditions. (CS)

They seem like friends—People say, "When the lion bares his teeth do not mistake it for a smile; it is only to eat you." Lions are the animal kingdom's equivalent of human monarchs. (Nachmias)

Turncoats

Following the defeat in the war led by Bar Kochba against Rome, during the time of the Roman persecution, two of Rabbi Joshua's disciples tried to avoid capture by disguising themselves as non-Jews.

A Roman officer came upon upon them and saw through their disguise.

He said to them: "If you are sons of Torah, you should be ready and willing to give up your lives for her without dissembling; if not, why should you be martyred for her sake? Give her up, once and for all!"

"We are sons of Torah", said they, "and we are willing to be slain for her sake; but it is not natural deliberately to give up one's life." (Midrash Genesis Rabbah 83.88)

Avot 2:4a[11]

הוּא הָיָה אוֹמֵר:
עֲשֵׂה רְצוֹנוֹ כִּרְצוֹנֶךָ,
כְּדֵי שֶׁיַּעֲשֶׂה רְצוֹנְךָ כִּרְצוֹנוֹ.
בַּטֵּל רְצוֹנְךָ מִפְּנֵי רְצוֹנוֹ,
כְּדֵי שֶׁיְּבַטֵּל רְצוֹן אֲחֵרִים מִפְּנֵי רְצוֹנֶךָ.

HE WOULD say:
Do God's will as [though it were] your will, so that God may do your will as [though it were] God's. Set aside your will in favor of God's, so that God may set aside the will of others in favor of yours.

Do God's will—It has been said that this falls short of the unconditional trust in God displayed by "Your will be done." There seems to be some bargaining for a quid pro quo in our passage. But this may be selling Rabban Gamaliel a bit short. Rabbi Jonah ben Abraham (below) clearly derives the "higher" meaning from our text. The Christian Gospel's words "Your will be done" come from the Kaddish, though there the context is a prayer for divine deliverance, not, as here, advice to the individual. (CS)

--- One's own will and the will of God should be the same; there should be no distinction between them—that is to say, one should have no other wish than to please God. Thus we are advised to rise above our own nature and use our wealth and possessions as God wishes, for all that we have is but on loan from the One who has given us everything. (Rabbi Jonah ben Abraham)

--- Lincoln, when told the Union would win "because God is on our side." replied, "I do not at all worry, whether God is on our side. I only worry whether we are on God's side."

Compassion

1. *This is my God whom I will glorify* (Exodus 15:2). Abba Saul said: *whom I will glorify*—by imitation: As God is gracious and compassionate so must you too be gracious and compassionate. (Talmud Shabbat 133b)

2. Let 'these' be filled with pity for 'those,' and the Holy One will be filled with pity for all. (Midrash Genesis Rabbah 33)

3. Rav Judah said in the name of Rav: One is forbidden to taste a thing before feeding one's animal, for first it is said (Deuteronomy 11:15), *I will put grass in your field for your cattle*, and only then does it say (ibid.), *and you shall eat and be satisfied*. (Talmud Gittin 62a)

4. Levi ordered a public fast, but no rain fell. He said: "Ruler of the World, You sit in the heights, and have no compassion on Your children." The rain began to fall. But Levi became lame. (Talmud Ta'anit 25a)

2:4b[12]

הִלֵּל אוֹמֵר:

אַל תִּפְרֹשׁ מִן הַצִּבּוּר.

וְאַל תַּאֲמֵן בְּעַצְמְךָ עַד יוֹם מוֹתָךְ.

וְאַל תָּדִין אֶת־חֲבֵרְךָ עַד שֶׁתַּגִּיעַ

לִמְקוֹמוֹ.

וְאַל תֹּאמַר דָּבָר שֶׁאִי אֶפְשָׁר לִשְׁמֹעַ,

שֶׁסּוֹפוֹ לְהִשָּׁמַע.

וְאַל תֹּאמַר: לִכְשֶׁאֶפָּנֶה אֶשְׁנֶה,

שֶׁמָּא לֹא תִפָּנֶה.

HILLEL SAYS:

Do not separate yourself from the community.

Do not be too sure of yourself until the day you die.

Do not judge your friends until you are in their place.

Say nothing that cannot be understood[13] [at once], supposing that in the end it will be understood.

And do not say, "When I have time I will study"—you may never have the time.

These sayings are so familiar that we ought to read them with special care. They are familiar, after all, because we all can see their profound wisdom. To take one example: Do you think you have achieved? And what is it that you have achieved? Self-understanding? Virtue? A correct point of view? "Do not be too sure of yourself...." That is to say, our achievements, like our life itself, are ours on loan; we have to keep on earning them. Hillel is saying: "What have you done for yourself [or others] lately?" (CS)

Do not separate—You have an obligation to take part in the life of the community, to share its joys and its sorrows, to help improve it. (CS)

--- One should entertain views not far different from those of the community, but if the people are corrupt, one should go even into the wilderness to escape their influence. (Aknin)

Do not too sure—Even when a virtue is second nature to you, do not be overconfident and say, "It can never leave me." There is always the possibility that it will. Therefore, never neglect an opportunity to do good, and thus to strengthen yourself in that habit. (Maimonides)

Do not judge—This goes along with the injunction not to be too sure of yourself. When people behave unjustly, it is easy to say, "Had I been in their position I would not have done that." You might have done just as badly, had you been there. (Rabbi Jonah ben Abraham)

... in their place—That is, do not judge others until you are their equal. (Raanach, cited in Meam Loez, Avoth, p. 82)

Living with Others

1. Rabbi Tanchum ben Chanilai said: One should never depart from established usage. Thus, when Moses ascended to Heaven he did not eat, and when the ministering angels came down to earth, they did (appear to) eat. (Talmud Baba Metzia 86b)

2. Abayei was always saying this: Always be clever in fear;[14] a soft answer turns away wrath; speak peaceably with your family, relatives, and everyone else—even a foreigner in the marketplace—and you are loved Above and held dear below and are acceptable to everyone. (Talmud Berachot 17a)

Avot 2:5

הוּא הָיָה אוֹמֵר:
אֵין בּוֹר יְרֵא חֵטְא,
וְלֹא עַם הָאָרֶץ חָסִיד,
וְלֹא הַבַּיְשָׁן לָמֵד,
וְלֹא הַקַּפְּדָן מְלַמֵּד,
וּבִמְקוֹם שֶׁאֵין אֲנָשִׁים, הִשְׁתַּדֵּל
לִהְיוֹת אִישׁ.

HE WOULD say:
A boor does not fear sin;
the ignorant are not pious;
the bashful do not learn;
the hot–tempered do not teach;
one too steeped in business does not grow wise;[15]
and where none are real persons,, endeavor [yourself] to be one.

does not fear sin—Would this have been better stated in reverse, that is, "One who does not fear sin is a boor"? (CS)

The bashful—Those willing to seem foolish in order to learn Torah will in the end be lifted up, but those afraid to ask questions will end up by showing themselves to be fools. (Vitry)

--- No one who wants to learn should think, "How can a fool like me ask questions of a brilliant sage? I neither know nor understand enough to ask." Feeling like this, how will you ever acquire wisdom? (Rabbi Jonah ben Abraham)

too steeped in business—That is, business alone will not make one wise: one who would be wise must engage in all kinds of social enterprises, in business, and in all other matters where instruction may be found, for a successful life demands a broad understanding. (Vitry)

Where none are real persons—Or, "individuals." A reference to character, integrity, courage, authenticity. Literally, "Where there are no men, strive to be a man." In other words, be a "mensch." (CS)

--- When no one is ready to assume responsibility, you are required to do it. (Vitry) On the other hand, do not interfere when someone is already doing the needed work. (Hertz)

--- When no one is available to help and correct you, try to do it yourself. Another interpretation: Where no one is wiser than you or better at what you do, do not (on that account) give up trying to improve yourself. Even if you are the best of your generation, think of the giants of the past. That will help you learn and improve. (after Rabbi Jonah ben Abraham)

Avot 2:6

אַף הוּא רָאָה גֻּלְגֹּלֶת אַחַת

שֶׁצֶּפָה עַל פְּנֵי הַמָּיִם. אָמַר לָהּ:

עַל דַּאֲטֵפְתְּ אַטִיפוּךְ,

וְסוֹף מְטִיפַיִךְ יְטוּפוּן.

ONCE, HE happened to see a skull floating on the water and said to it:[16]
Because you drowned others, others drowned you;
in the end, those who drowned you will themselves be drowned.

you drowned others—All who do evil and introduce violence and corruption victimize themselves, for they teach themselves an occupation that can only injure them and others. (Maimonides)

Others drowned you—The pharaohs of this world deserve punishment even when they carry out God's will, because their purposes are their own—not God's. God works through them, even if it be said that they know it not; and even though they care only to carry out their own maleficent ambitions. Suppose one thief steals from another—should that thief gain our approbation? And suppose one murderer takes another murderer's life—that act would surely remain foul and deserving of retribution. No good end can justify an evil act; no bad beginning in life can justify a bad continuation. This is not to suggest that we should ignore the "root causes" of crime and other evils, but it does mean that people should be given the honor of being held responsible for what they do. (see Talmud Shabbat 42a, and Meam Loez, Aboth, p. 86) (CS)

Avot 2:7

הוּא הָיָה אוֹמֵר:

מַרְבֶּה בָשָׂר, מַרְבֶּה רִמָּה;

מַרְבֶּה נְכָסִים, מַרְבֶּה דְאָגָה;

מַרְבֶּה נָשִׁים, מַרְבֶּה כְשָׁפִים;

מַרְבֶּה שְׁפָחוֹת, מַרְבֶּה זִמָּה;

מַרְבֶּה עֲבָדִים, מַרְבֶּה גָזֵל;

מַרְבֶּה תוֹרָה, מַרְבֶּה חַיִּים;

מַרְבֶּה יְשִׁיבָה, מַרְבֶּה חָכְמָה;

מַרְבֶּה עֵצָה, מַרְבֶּה תְבוּנָה;

מַרְבֶּה צְדָקָה, מַרְבֶּה שָׁלוֹם.

קָנָה שֵׁם טוֹב קָנָה לְעַצְמוֹ.

קָנָה לוֹ דִבְרֵי תוֹרָה

קָנָה לוֹ חַיֵּי הָעוֹלָם הַבָּא.

HE WOULD say:

Add flesh, add worms;

add possessions, add worries;

add wives, add witchcraft;

add slavegirls, add lust;

add slaves, add theft;

add Torah, add life;

add schooling,[17] add wisdom;

add counsel, add understanding;

add Tzedakah, add peace.

When[18] you have earned a good name you have earned it for yourself.

When you have earned knowledge[19] of Torah you have earned life eternal.

earned a good name—See, also, 2:1, 3:10, 4:13. There may be no intention here to compare unfavorably one who earns a good name with one who earns knowledge of Torah, but the passage is open to that interpretation; in that event, however, 4:13 would contradict this passage. (CS)

add possessions—"No one leaves this world having gained even half his desires." (Midrash Kohelet Rabbah 1.34)

add schooling—"Much have I learned from my masters, more from my colleagues, and from my disciples, most of all." (Talmud Ta'anit 7a)

add Tzedakah—In a cold room you may warm yourself by heating it or by donning a fur coat. In the former case, you warm whoever else is in the room with you; in the latter, only yourself. The person who chooses to provide only for himself is called in Yiddish a tzaddik in pelts—"A saint in furs." (Bunim, I, pp. 164f.)

Avot 2:8a[20]

רַבָּן יוֹחָנָן בֶּן זַכַּאי קִבֵּל מֵהִלֵּל
וְשַׁמַּאי. הוּא הָיָה אוֹמֵר:
אִם לָמַדְתָּ תּוֹרָה הַרְבֵּה, אַל תַּחֲזִיק
טוֹבָה לְעַצְמְךָ, כִּי לְכָךְ נוֹצָרְתָּ.

RABBAN YOCHANAN ben Zakkai[21] received [Torah] from Hillel and Shammai. He would say:
If you have learned much Torah, do not let it go to your head, since that is what you were created for.

If you have learned—However much Torah you have learned, you are still at the very beginning: how then can you take credit when you have done a thousandth of the task? And when you repay a debt, should you boast of it?

Avot 2:8b

חֲמִשָּׁה תַלְמִידִים הָיוּ לוֹ לְרַבָּן יוֹחָנָן
בֶּן זַכַּאי, וְאֵלוּ הֵן: רַבִּי אֱלִיעֶזֶר בֶּן
הֻרְקָנוֹס, וְרַבִּי יְהוֹשֻׁעַ בֶּן חֲנַנְיָה,
וְרַבִּי יוֹסֵי הַכֹּהֵן, וְרַבִּי שִׁמְעוֹן
בֶּן נְתַנְאֵל, וְרַבִּי אֶלְעָזָר בֶּן עֲרָךְ.
הוּא הָיָה מוֹנֶה שְׁבָחָם: רַבִּי אֱלִיעֶזֶר
בֶּן הֻרְקָנוֹס—בּוֹר סוּד שֶׁאֵין מְאַבֵּד
טִפָּה; רַבִּי יְהוֹשֻׁעַ בֶּן חֲנַנְיָה—
אַשְׁרֵי יוֹלַדְתּוֹ; רַבִּי יוֹסֵי הַכֹּהֵן—
חָסִיד; רַבִּי שִׁמְעוֹן בֶּן נְתַנְאֵל—
יְרֵא חֵטְא; רַבִּי אֶלְעָזָר בֶּן עֲרָךְ—
כְּמַעְיָן הַמִּתְגַּבֵּר. הוּא הָיָה אוֹמֵר:
אִם יִהְיוּ כָּל־חַכְמֵי יִשְׂרָאֵל בְּכַף
מֹאזְנַיִם, וֶאֱלִיעֶזֶר בֶּן הֻרְקָנוֹס בְּכַף
שְׁנִיָּה, מַכְרִיעַ אֶת־כֻּלָּם. אַבָּא שָׁאוּל
אוֹמֵר מִשְּׁמוֹ: אִם יִהְיוּ כָּל־חַכְמֵי
יִשְׂרָאֵל בְּכַף מֹאזְנַיִם, וֶאֱלִיעֶזֶר בֶּן
הֻרְקָנוֹס אַף עִמָּהֶם, וְאֶלְעָזָר בֶּן
עֲרָךְ בְּכַף שְׁנִיָּה, מַכְרִיעַ אֶת־כֻּלָּם.

Rabban Yochanan ben Zakkai had five disciples, and they were: Rabbi Eliezer ben Hyrcanus, Rabbi Joshua ben Chananiah, Rabbi Yosé the Priest, Rabbi Simeon ben Natanel, and Rabbi Elazar ben Arach. He would recount their virtues: Rabbi Eliezer ben Hyrcanus—a plastered well that never loses a drop; Rabbi Joshua—happy the woman who bore him; Rabbi Yosé—a pious man,[22] Rabbi Simeon ben Netanel—a man who fears sin; and Rabbi Elazar ben Arach—an overflowing spring.

He would say: Were all the sages of Israel on one side of a balance and Eliezer ben Hyrcanus on the other, he would outweigh them. Abba Saul says in his name: Were all the sages of Israel—including Rabbi Eliezer ben Hyrcanus—on one side of a balance and Rabbi Elazar ben Arach on the other, he would outweigh them.

a plastered well ... an overflowing spring—Of the two types of sage—the one who remembers everything he has learned, and the one from whom new insights are forever flowing—which is the greater? According to the Talmud (Berachot 64a) both are needed, but the former is greater. See also Talmud K'tubot 103b, Baba Metzia 85b. (Bunim, I, p. 175)

Avot 2:9a[23]

אָמַר לָהֶם: צְאוּ וּרְאוּ אֵיזוֹהִי דֶרֶךְ
יְשָׁרָה שֶׁיִּדְבַּק בָּהּ הָאָדָם.
רַבִּי אֱלִיעֶזֶר אוֹמֵר: עַיִן טוֹבָה.
רַבִּי יְהוֹשֻׁעַ אוֹמֵר: חָבֵר טוֹב.
רַבִּי יוֹסֵי אוֹמֵר: שָׁכֵן טוֹב.
רַבִּי שִׁמְעוֹן אוֹמֵר: הָרוֹאֶה אֶת־הַנּוֹלָד.
רַבִּי אֶלְעָזָר אוֹמֵר: לֵב טוֹב.
אָמַר לָהֶם: רוֹאֶה אֲנִי אֶת־דִּבְרֵי אֶלְעָזָר
בֶּן עֲרָךְ, שֶׁבִּכְלָל דְּבָרָיו דִּבְרֵיכֶם.

HE [Yochanan ben Zakkai] SAID to them: What is a right path for one to take?
Rabbi Eliezer says: A good eye.[24]
Rabbi Joshua says: A good friend.
Rabbi Yosé says: A good neighbor.
Rabbi Simeon says: Foresight.[25]
Rabbi Elazar says: A good heart.[26]
He said to them: I prefer the words of Elazar ben Arach, for his words include all of yours.

a right path—See comment to 2:1

--- One should adopt a single ideal to follow through to perfection. It is better to hold perfectly to one ideal than to be a spiritual 'jack of all trades.' And thus, having a firm footing, it is easier to reach out from there to other ideals.

--- To do one thing is purity of heart. (Søren Kierkegaard)

foresight—Those ruled by their appetites do whatever seems pleasant at the moment, and do not think of the long run. They might avoid much that is bitter, if only they looked ahead. (after Aknin)

A good heart—Such a person is generous, cultivates good companions (and is one), makes sure to seek out and dwell near good neighbors (and is one), and practices foresight, lest an impulsive act be the cause of harm. Such a person is at peace with God and with others. (after Duran)

Avot 2:9b

אָמַר לָהֶם: צְאוּ וּרְאוּ אֵיזוֹהִי דֶרֶךְ
רָעָה שֶׁיִּרְחַק מִמֶּנָּה הָאָדָם.
רַבִּי אֱלִיעֶזֶר אוֹמֵר: עַיִן רָעָה.
רַבִּי יְהוֹשֻׁעַ אוֹמֵר: חָבֵר רַע.
רַבִּי יוֹסֵי אוֹמֵר: שָׁכֵן רַע.
רַבִּי שִׁמְעוֹן אוֹמֵר: הַלֹּוֶה וְאֵינוֹ מְשַׁלֵּם.
(אֶחָד הַלֹּוֶה מִן הָאָדָם כְּלֹוֶה מִן
הַמָּקוֹם, שֶׁנֶּאֱמַר: לֹוֶה רָשָׁע וְלֹא
יְשַׁלֵּם, וְצַדִּיק חוֹנֵן וְנוֹתֵן.)
רַבִּי אֶלְעָזָר אוֹמֵר: לֵב טוֹב.
אָמַר לָהֶם: רוֹאֶה אֲנִי אֶת־דִּבְרֵי אֶלְעָזָר
בֶּן עֲרָךְ, שֶׁבִּכְלָל דְּבָרָיו דִּבְרֵיכֶם.

[And] he said to them: What is a wrong path that one should avoid?
Rabbi Eliezer says: A bad eye.[27]
Rabbi Joshua says: A bad friend.
Rabbi Yosé says: A bad neighbor.
Rabbi Simeon says: Who borrows and does not repay. (Who borrows from another person borrows, as it were, from the Omnipresent, who is blessed, as it is said (Psalm 37:21), *The wicked borrow and do not repay, but the righteous are gracious and give back.*)
Rabbi Elazar says: A wicked heart.[28]
He said to them: I prefer the words of Elazar ben Arach, for his words include all of yours.

Who borrows—Rabbi Simeon is the only one whose reply deviates from the obvious, since he does not merely put his previous reply into the negative, as do the others. And yet he seems to intend us to understand that his reply provides a concrete example of one who, though not wicked, does an injury. This comparison can only be sustained if we assume that failure to repay the debt resulted from improvidence, and not from wickedness. Then it becomes another example of the Law of Unintended Consequences. See the next comment. (CS)

foresight ... and borrowing—One may live without foresight and yet not follow a wrong path. Sometimes, however, our lack of foresight causes injury to others. Rabbi Simeon therefore provides us with a concrete example in which living without a care for the morrow is a "wrong path," for in this instance it amounts to living without a care for our neighbor. (CS)

Avot 2:10

הֵם אָמְרוּ שְׁלֹשָׁה דְבָרִים.

רַבִּי אֱלִיעֶזֶר אוֹמֵר:

יְהִי כְבוֹד חֲבֵרָךְ חָבִיב עָלֶיךָ כְּשֶׁלָּךְ;

וְאַל תְּהִי נוֹחַ לִכְעוֹס;

וְשׁוּב יוֹם אֶחָד לִפְנֵי מִיתָתָךְ.

(וֶהֱוֵי מִתְחַמֵּם כְּנֶגֶד אוּרָן שֶׁל חֲכָמִים,

וֶהֱוֵי זָהִיר בְּגַחַלְתָּן שֶׁלֹּא תִכָּוֶה.

שֶׁנְּשִׁיכָתָן נְשִׁיכַת שׁוּעָל, וַעֲקִיצָתָן

עֲקִיצַת עַקְרָב, וּלְחִישָׁתָן לְחִישַׁת

שָׂרָף. וְכָל־דִּבְרֵיהֶם כְּגַחֲלֵי אֵשׁ.)

THEY SAID three things [each]. Rabbi Eliezer[29] says:
Let your friend's honor be as dear to you as your own.[30]
Do not be easily angered.
Return [to God][31] one day before you die.
(And warm yourself by the fire of the sages, but beware of their coals, lest you be burnt. Their bite is [like] the bite of a fox, their sting is [like] the sting of a scorpion, and their hiss is [like] the hiss of a snake. And all their words are like fiery coals.)

your friend's honor—If you don't want others to speak ill of you, don't speak ill of them. (ARN)

--- *Love your neighbor as yourself* (Leviticus 19:18). The sages laid it down as a principle: "What is hateful to you, do not do to anyone else." (Talmud Shabbat 31a) (Aknin) [see 1:12, commentary]

--- "Who rises by humiliating a neighbor has no share in the world–to–come." (Midrash Genesis Rabbah 1:7; Jerusalem Talmud Chagigah 2:1)

easily angered—"One who falls into a rage is like one who is worshipping an idol." (Talmud Shabbat 105b)

--- "People reveal themselves through their wallet, their wine, and their wrath." (Talmud Erubin 65b)

Return one day—His disciples asked Rabbi Eliezer, "Do we know the day of our death? He answered: Let us then repent every day. (Abridged from ARN)

--- It is well that the day of our death is concealed, for if we knew our death was imminent we might stop doing anything useful to the world; and if we knew our death was far off we might not do good works, saying, "There is still time." (Nachmias)

but beware of their coals—Eliezer's words have a dark side to them; does that reflect his biography? See pages 82-84. He reminds us forcibly that fire is as likely to burn as it is to warm. (CS)

Insult and Shame

1. Why do scholars rarely have children who are scholars? Rav Ashi answered: Because they [tend to] look down on others and insult them. (Talmud Nedarim 91a)

2. They said in the name of Rabbi Yosé of Hutzal: How is it known that I must honor a colleague who is superior to me even in a single thing? It is said (Daniel 6:4), *because a superior spirit was in him, the king planned to set him over the whole kingdom.* (Talmud Pesachim 113b)

3. Shame no one—and you will not shame yourself. (Talmud Mo'ed Katan 9b)

4. If you spit upward you get it on your own face. (Midrash Ecclesiastes Rabbah 7)

5. A sage taught before Rabbi Nachman bar Yitzchak: "One who shames[32] his friend in public is like who sheds blood." "That is well said," remarked Rabbi Nachman, "for his complexion was ruddy, and now it is pale!" (Talmud Baba Metzia 58b) [See, also, 3:11]

6. Rabbi Chanina said: "To slap a friend's face is tantmount to slapping the face of the Shechinah."[33]

Resh Lakish said: "If you raise your hand against another you are called wicked even if you don't strike a blow, as it is said (Exodus 2:13), *He said to the evildoer, 'Why are you smiting your fellow?'* It does not say, Why have you smitten... Although he has not yet hit him he is called wicked." (Talmud Sanhedrin 58b)

7. Rabbi Pinchas B. Ya'ir was on his way to redeem some captives,[34] when he came to the Ginnai River.

He said: "Ginnai, part for me, I need to get through."

The river retorted: "You are doing your Creator's will and so am I; you may succeed in your enterprise, and you may fail—but I am sure to succeed."

"If you do not part," threatened Rabbi Pinchas, "I will see to it that your waters will fail."

It parted for him.

There was a man with a load of wheat for Passover. Rabbi Pinchas ben Ya'ir told the river to part for him: "He is engaged in doing a Mitzvah; let him through."

It did.

An Arab had joined them along the way. Rabbi Pinchas said to the river: "Part for this one, too. Let no one say, 'This you do to your travelling companions!'"

It parted a third time.

His disciples then asked him: "Can we get through?"

Rabbi Pinchas ben Ya'ir said to them: "Any one of you who has never shamed another Jew will get through unharmed." (Jerusalem Talmud Demai 1:3; Midrash Deuteronomy Rabbah 3)

Avot 2:11

רָבִּי יְהוֹשֻׁעַ אוֹמֵר:	RABBI JOSHUA[35] says:
עַיִן הָרַע	The bad eye,[36]
וְיֵצֶר הָרַע	the *Yetzer Hara*,
וְשִׂנְאַת הַבְּרִיּוֹת	and hatred of others
מוֹצִיאִין אֶת־הָאָדָם מִן הָעוֹלָם.	drive one out of the world.[37]

the Yetzer—Translated in various ways: "The Evil Impulse," "The Will to Evil," 'The Evil Inclination.' The term derives ultimately from Genesis 8:21 (See, also, Genesis 6:5), and sometimes, without the modifier, יֵצֶר, *Yetzer*, means, simply, 'human nature.' See, for example, Deuteronomy 31:21, Psalm 103:14. Its root, יָצַר, *Yatzar*, means 'create, fashion, form.' Here, it may be rendered 'wrongful, illicit desires.' More often than not, in rabbinic literature, it is associated with sexual desire, though sometimes it is used to refer to our passional nature in a broader sense—in fact, to those things that drive us not only to destroy but also to create. The rabbis also utilize an opposite term in reference to energies that have their approval, namely, יֵצֶר הַטּוֹב, *Yetzer Hatov*, "The Good Inclination." (CS)

--- is thirteen years older than the will to good, since it comes into being at birth. (ARN)

--- Rabbi Simeon ben Elazar says: An iron bar in a smithy—as long as it is in the flame you may mold it into any implement you like; so with the Yetzer—the only way to mold it is through the words of Torah, which are like fire. (ARN)

--- When you encounter the Yetzer, pull it into the House of Study: if it is stone, it will dissolve; if it is iron, it will shatter. (Talmud Sukkah 52b, Kiddushin 30a)

--- At first the Yetzer is like the thread of a spider's web; in the end it is as thick as wagon-rope. (Talmud Sukkah 52a)

--- Rabbi Samuel bar Nachman said in the name of Rabbi Jonathan: The Yetzer seduces you in this world and then bears witness against you in the world-to-come. (Talmud Sukkah 52b)

--- The power of the Yetzer is overwhelming, and few of any generation escape from its evil effects. Those few are the only ones who are truly free, who are not slaves but masters of their passions. (Aknin) [see 4:1]

hatred—Hatred is the evil spirit, the sickness of melancholy that leads you to despise the sight of your own kind and to hate all things. One then prefers the society of animals, prefers places without habitation. Without doubt this shortens a person's life. (Maimonides)

The bad eye—One who always yearns for what others have.

The Passions

1. Rabbi Yudan said in the name of Rabbi Aibu: None leave the world with half their desires gratified. If I have a hundred I want to make them two hundred, and if I have two hundred I want to make them four hundred. (Midrash Kohelet Rabbah 1)

2. The Holy One said: Show me passion, for without it the world could not stand: no one would build a house or plant a vineyard or marry. (Midrash Socher Tov 37)

Oppression, Dishonesty

1. Rav Chisda said: All the gates [of Heaven] are shut, except the gate of anguish [caused by oppression].[38]

Rabbi Elazar said: All [divine] punishment is effected [indirectly] by way of a messenger—except [for the punishment due] oppression.

Rabbi Abahu said: The veil [in front of the Throne of Glory] is never shut for these three things: oppression, robbery, and idolatry.[39] (Talmud Baba Metzia 59a)

2. Our sages taught: Whence do we know that where they customarily give a heaping measure it is forbidden to give a flat one? Scripture says (Deuteronomy 25.15), *a full measure*. And whence do we know that one may not say, "I will flatten where they heap up and charge less," or "I will heap up where they flatten and charge more"? Scripture says (ibid.), *You shall have a full and just measure*. (Talmud Baba Metzia 89a)

3. *Your silver has turned to dross, your wine mixed with water.* (Isaiah 1:22). One hears the smith tell a worker to adulterate the silver; another hears the wine merchant tell a clerk to dilute the wine. That's what this verse means: *Your silver has turned to dross, your wine mixed with water.* (Midrash Pesikta 15)

4. *Do not place a stumbling-block before the blind.* (Leviticus 19:14). This is meant metaphorically. Here are some examples: If someone asks you whether a particular woman may marry a priest, do not say "Yes" when you know the answer is "No." If someone asks your advice, do not give counsel that is inappropriate. Do not say: "Go out early," when [you have reason to know] there are robbers about; do not say: "Go out at noon," when the heat is oppressive; and do not say: "Sell your field and buy a donkey," when your [secret] intention is to get that field by guile. You may claim that all you're doing is giving good advice, but this matter goes to your heart,[40] as it says (ibid.), *and you shall revere your God; I am the Eternal.* Whenever a matter concerns the heart these words appear: *you shall revere your God.* (Midrash Sifra, Kedoshim; Talmud Kiddushin 32b)

5. There are seven types of thief, and the chief among them is one who steals the mind.[41] (Midrash Mechilta, Mishpatim)

6. Our sages taught: *You shall not wrong one another.* (Leviticus 25:17). The verse is talking about wronging with words.

[An objection is raised:] You say it refers to wronging with words, but isn't it really about wronging in money matters?

No, for it says (ibid., 25:14), *If you sell to your neighbor or buy from your neighbor, you shall not wrong one another.* That refers to money matters. So [the repetition of] *You shall not wrong one another* would be redundant unless it had to do with words. How so? One must not say to a penitent, "Remember your former deeds." One must not say to a convert, "Remember the deeds of your ancestors." One must not say to a convert who has come to study Torah, "A mouth that has eaten forbidden, loathesome foods wants to say the words of Torah that have come from the mouth of the Holy One!?" One beset by afflictions, laid low by illnesses, or whose children have died, must not be spoken to as Job was by his friends, who said (Job 4:7), *Think now, who, being innocent, ever perished?* And if donkey–drivers come seeking to buy grain from your neighbor, do not send them elsewhere.

Rabbi Judah adds: Moreover, do not look at something as though you were going to buy it when in your heart you know you [aren't going to buy it because you] haven't any money. All matters concerning the heart are referred to by the words (Leviticus 25:17), *you shall revere your God.*

Rabbi Yochanan said in the name of Rabbi Simeon bar Yochai: Wronging with words is worse than wronging with money, for only in regard to the former is it written (Leviticus 25:17), *you shall revere your God*; and Rabbi Elazar says: With words you wrong the person; in the other case, only the person's money. Rabbi Samuel bar Nachmani said: In the one case (money) restitution is easy; in the other, not so. (Talmud Baba Metzia 58b) [This passage is repeated in Section 3:3, on Rabbi Simeon bar Yochai]

Avot 2:12

רַבִּי יוֹסֵי אוֹמֵר:

יְהִי מָמוֹן חֲבֵרְךָ חָבִיב עָלֶיךָ כְּשֶׁלָּךְ.

וְהַתְקֵן עַצְמְךָ לִלְמוֹד תּוֹרָה, שֶׁאֵינָהּ

יְרֻשָּׁה לָךְ;

וְכָל־מַעֲשֶׂיךָ יִהְיוּ לְשֵׁם שָׁמַיִם.

RABBI YOSÉ[42] says:
Let your friend's property be as dear to you as your own.[43]
Discipline yourself to learn Torah, for it is not something you inherit.
And let your every deed be for the sake of Heaven.

Discipline yourself to learn Torah—If someone says, "I have labored but I have not achieved," do not believe it. If someone says, "I have not labored but I have achieved," do not believe it. If someone says, "I have labored and achieved," believe · it. (Talmud Megillah 6b)

--- Before you can begin to learn Torah you must prepare your heart. (Midrash Shemuel)

--- Rabbi Leib son of Sarah, the hidden saint who wandered the earth and its hills and valleys redeeming dead and living souls, said this: "I went to the Great **Maggid** not to hear him say Torah, but to see his way of unlacing his boots and lacing them up again." (See Buber, *Or ha–Ganuz*, p. 114)

inheritance—It was Joshua, not Moses' son Gershom, who succeeded Moses.

--- No one is born to be good or bad; no one is born to ply a particular trade. You may be born with a potentiality toward good or evil, and find it easier to do the one and harder to do the other; and you may be born with a talent for a particular craft, but you will still require training. (Aknin)

--- O the seas that have run dry! O the stones that have brought forth water! Your ancestors may have been sages, they may have been illiterate: which one you will be depends on you. (after Meiri)

for the sake of Heaven—Greater is sin for the sake of the good, than the good not for its own sake. (Talmud Nazir 23b) [Note that the form is comparative.]

Private Property

One of the sages observed a man taking stones out of his own field and dumping them on public land.

"Why are you taking stones from property that isn't yours and putting them on land that does belong to you?"

The man did not understand his admonition and laughed: "Fool! It's just the other way around!"

He had been removing the stones so that the field might fetch more money, and a few months later he sold it.

As he walked along the public road leading from that field, he stumbled over some stones he had thrown there, and bruised his leg.

"I am the fool, twice over," he reflected. (Talmud Baba Kamma 50b)

Avot 2:13

רַבִּי שִׁמְעוֹן אוֹמֵר:

הֱוֵי זָהִיר בִּקְרִיַּת שְׁמַע וּבִתְפִלָּה.

וּכְשֶׁאַתָּה מִתְפַּלֵּל, אַל תַּעַשׂ תְּפִלָּתְךָ

קֶבַע, אֶלָּא רַחֲמִים וְתַחֲנוּנִים לִפְנֵי

הַמָּקוֹם בָּרוּךְ הוּא. שֶׁנֶּאֱמַר: כִּי־חַנּוּן

וְרַחוּם הוּא, אֶרֶךְ אַפַּיִם, וְרַב־חֶסֶד,

וְנִחָם עַל־הָרָעָה.

וְאַל תְּהִי רָשָׁע בִּפְנֵי עַצְמֶךָ.

RABBI SIMEON[44] says:
Be careful in reciting the Shema and the T'fillah.[45]
And when you pray, never let your prayer be routine,[46] but [let it be] a plea for compassion and grace from the Blessed Presence,[47] as it is said (Joel 2:13), *For [God] is gracious and compassionate, slow to anger, abounding in lovingkindness, and repents of the evil.* And never regard yourself as wicked.[48]

... as it is said—What does the quotation from Joel add? It adds nothing to the main point of praying with passion, but it assures us that when we pray for compassion and grace we have the right address. Of course, this speaks only of prayer as petition. (CS)

never regard yourself as wicked—Do not do something today for which you won't be able to face yourself tomorrow. (Rashi) [translating this as "do not see yourself as wicked"]

--- Do not do something that you yourself know to be evil, though others may not recognize it as such. (Vitry)

--- Do not sin by yourself: do not think a sin is no sin if there is none to see it done. (TH)

--- Do not regard yourself as wholly evil, so that you give up hope of improvement. You are not beyond redemption: exaggerate neither your virtues nor your faults. (Maimonides)

--- When I have a low opinion of myself, any meanness I am guilty of does not seem surprising or outrageous to me. (Maimonides)

Prayer

1. The Holy One says to Israel: I bade you pray in the synagogue of your city, but if you cannot pray there, pray in your field, and if you cannot pray there, pray on your bed, and if you cannot pray there, then meditate in your heart and be still. (Midrash Pesikta de Rav Kahana 158a)

2. When the Holy One said to Moses (Exodus 25:8), *Let them make Me a sanctuary, that I may dwell among them,* Moses said: Who can do that? It is written (Jeremiah 23.:4), *Do I not fill heaven and earth?* and (Isaiah 66:1), *The heaven is My throne, and the earth is My footstool.* Then the Holy One said: I do not ask according to My

capacity, but according to theirs, for all the world cannot contain My glory. (Midrash Numbers Rabbah, Naso, 12:3)

3. Rabbi Judah said in the name of Rav: if you are walking when the time has come to say the Sh'ma, stand still and receive the Kingdom of Heaven. And what is the Kingdom of Heaven? *The Eternal One is our God, the Eternal God is One.* (Midrash Deuteronomy Rabbah, Va–etchanan, 2:31)

4. Rabbi Abin said: Jacob, of the village of Neboria near Tyre, would say (Psalm 65:1), *To You silence is praise.* Silence is a sovereign remedy, a priceless jewel that cannot be overvalued... (Midrash to Psalms on 19:1)

Avot 2:14

רַבִּי אֶלְעָזָר אוֹמֵר:
הֱוֵי שָׁקוּד לִלְמֹד תּוֹרָה.
וְדַע מַה שֶּׁתָּשִׁיב לְאַפִּיקוֹרוֹס.
וְדַע לִפְנֵי מִי אַתָּה עָמֵל, וְנֶאֱמָן הוּא
בַּעַל מְלַאכְתָּךְ שֶׁיְשַׁלֶּם לָךְ שְׂכַר
פְּעֻלָּתָךְ.

RABBI ELAZAR[49] says:

Be eager to learn Torah.[50]

Know how to answer a skeptic.[51]

And know before whom you labor, for your employer can be relied on to pay you your wages for your labor.

skeptic (Epicurean)—The unbelief of the Hellenistic world in which the Rabbis lived. They had to confront this and know how to answer. This meant knowing the 'Torah' of the Greco–Roman world. Their refusal to isolate themselves was an act of courage. (Neusner)

--- To be a Jew is an act of affirmation, an act of faith, an act of hope. It is not a ratification of how things really are. To know what to answer the unbeliever is to know how to live in the world as it is. To maintain the faith of Israel is to know how to live in the world as it should be; and, we believe, as in God's own time, it will be. (Neusner)

know how to answer—This might be translated, "know what to answer," in the sense: know what question you ought to answer—and, in turn, that might depend on who is asking the question and on how it is being asked. See, also, Proverbs 26.4–5: *Do not answer fools according to their folly, lest you become like them. Answer fools according to their folly, lest they be wise in their own eyes.* The sages (Talmud Shabbat 30b) explain: When the question concerns Torah, answer; otherwise, hold your tongue. Answer concerning Torah, so that you do not give the fool—and others who may be listening—the impression that there is no answer; otherwise, silence is the best answer to a foolish question.

your wages—"In this world there is no reward for a Mitzvah." (Talmud Kiddushin 39b)

Reproof

1. Rabbi Yosé bar Chanina said: Reproof leads to love, as it is said (Proverbs 9:8), *Reprove the wise, and they will love you.*

Resh Lakish said: Reproof leads to peace. (Midrash Genesis Rabbah 54)

2. Rabbi Illai said in the name of Rabbi Elazar son of Rabbi Simeon: As it is a Mitzvah to speak [in reproof] what will be accepted, it is a Mitzvah not to say what will not be accepted. Rabbi Aba said: It is a fault [to offer reproof one knows will be

rejected], as it is said (Proverbs 9:8), *Do not reprove scoffers, or they will hate you.* (Talmud Yebamot 65b)

3. Love the one who reproves you and despise the one who lauds you. (ARN 29)

4. Rabbi Chanina said: Jerusalem was destroyed only because people failed to reprove each other. Rabbi Tarfon said: It would surprise me to find anyone in this generation who knows how to give reproof rightly,[52] or how rightly to receive it. If one says to another, "Take the splinter out of your eye," the other replies, "Take the beam out of yours!" (Talmud Arachin 26b; Shabbat 119b)

5. Rabbi Yochanan ben Nuri said: Let heaven and earth bear witness how often I punished Akiba, bringing him before Rabban Gamaliel. Yet he always responded with love, fulfilling what is said (Proverbs 9:8), *Reprove the wise, and they will love you.* (Talmud Arachin 16b)

6. *Bring yourselves together and call an assembly.* (Zephaniah 2:1) Resh Lakish said: This means, Correct yourself first, and then correct others.[53] (Talmud Baba Metzia 107b)

7. Rabbi Nathan said: Do not project your own fault onto your friend. (Talmud Baba Metzia)

Avot 2:15

רַבִּי טַרְפוֹן אוֹמֵר:	RABBI TARFON[54] says:
הַיּוֹם קָצָר,	The day is short,
וְהַמְּלָאכָה מְרֻבָּה,	the work heavy,
וְהַפּוֹעֲלִים עֲצֵלִים,	the workers lazy,
וְהַשָּׂכָר הַרְבֵּה,	the wages high,
וּבַעַל הַבַּיִת דּוֹחֵק.	the employer pressing.

the work—The measure has no limit, the work has no end; keep at it. A parable: A man was hired to draw water from the sea and pour it onto the land. The sea was not diminished, the land was not flooded. At length he grew impatient and was told, "Wretch! Why do you grow impatient? Every day take your wages!" (after ARN) --- During his forty days on Mt. Sinai Moses did not sleep a wink. A parable: A king said to his servant, "Count gold pieces from now until tomorrow, and you may keep all that you can count." How could he sleep? He would be losing a fortune! So Moses said, "How many precious words of Torah I would lose should I go to sleep!" And this applies to all of us. (Rabbi Jonah ben Abraham)

Avot 2:16

הוּא הָיָה אוֹמֵר:

לֹא עָלֶיךָ הַמְּלָאכָה לִגְמוֹר,

וְלֹא אַתָּה בֶן־חוֹרִין לִבָּטֵל מִמֶּנָּה.

אִם לָמַדְתָּ תּוֹרָה הַרְבֵּה,

נוֹתְנִים לָךְ שָׂכָר הַרְבֵּה.

וְנֶאֱמָן הוּא בַּעַל מְלַאכְתְּךָ שֶׁיְשַׁלֵּם

לָךְ שְׂכַר פְּעֻלָּתֶךָ. וְדַע שֶׁמַּתַּן שְׂכָרָן

שֶׁל צַדִּיקִים לֶעָתִיד לָבֹא.

HE WOULD say:

You are not required to complete the work, but you are not free to abandon it.

If you have learned much Torah, you will be given a good reward.

Your employer can be relied on to pay you your wages for your labor.

And know that the reward of the righteous is in the time to come.

your wages—See comment, at 2:14. Note that Tarfon's words here are identical to those of Elazar. (CS)

complete the work—You don't have to take the whole Torah on yourself to complete. (ARN)

--- Though there is much to do, and though your days fly swifter than flight itself, do not drive yourself the way workers do who have a fixed task [and a limited time in which to complete it]. If you try to do more than you can you will finally do less, because you will wear out your body, dull your mind's edge, lose enthusiasm and grow limp. And having been worn out, you will quit altogether. (after Aknin)

in the time to come—Like the preceding two statements, this refers to the judgment that is to come after death. (CS)

Sages 2

The following section supplements Pirké Avot, by adding passages from the rabbinic literature that either quote or tell about the sages of Avot.

2:1

Rabbi [Judah the Prince]

1. At the very moment of Rabbi Akiba's death, Rabbi was born. (Talmud Kiddushin 72b)

2. The government had forbidden the circumcision of Jewish boys at the time of the birth of our holy Rabbi. His father, Rabban Simeon ben Gamaliel, thought it better to obey the decree of the Holy One than that of those evildoers. The city's governor summoned him and told him: "I grant you much honor as the leader of your folk, but I cannot overlook this; it is the king's decree. I will send you to the king; let him do as he wills."

All day they journeyed to the capital. They reached the royal dwelling around the time of Antoninus' birth. Rabbi's mother went in to Antoninus' mother.

She asked: "How are you?"

"Not well," was the reply. "A decree has been issued forbidding circumcision, and I circumcised my son. Now they are taking all of us to the king."

The queen said: "Take my son instead—he's not circumcised. I'll keep yours with me."

She did this and left. Later the governor brought her to the king. At the king's command they examined the infant and discovered that he was uncircumcised. The king was furious at the governor: "My decree was about the circumcised, and you bring me an uncircumcised child!" Turning to his guards he said: "Have this fool put to death! And let these Jews go free!"

They returned to the queen's chamber. The queen said to Rabbi's mother: "The Holy One has worked a miracle for you through me, and for your son through mine; let them be friends forever!" (Jellinek, Bet Hamidrash, Part 6)

3. Rabbi Chiya and Rabbi Simeon, Rabbi's son, were sitting learning, and one of them said: "One who prays should look downward,[55] for it says (I Kings 9:3), *My eyes and My heart will be there.*"[56] The other said: "One should look upward,[57] for it says (Lamentations 3.41), *Let us lift our hearts and hands to heaven.*"

As they were debating, Rabbi Ishmael, son of Rabbi Yosé, came along. He said: "What have you been discussing?" "[The proper attitude in] prayer," they told him. "This is what father said," he told them. 'Direct your eyes upward and your heart downward. Then you will fulfill both these verses.'"

Meanwhile Rabbi arrived at the Session. Rabbi Chiya and Rabbi Simeon, who were slim, reached their usual places without difficulty and sat down. Rabbi Ishmael, son of Rabbi Yosé, was bulky, and had to push his way through the crowd of students to get a place. Rabbi Yudan noticed this and said: "Who is this that treads on the heads of holy folk?"

He answered: "I am Ishmael, son of Rabbi Yosé. I have come to learn Torah from Rabbi."

"And you are fit to learn Torah from Rabbi?"

"Was Moses fit to learn Torah from the Holy One?"

"And you are Moses?"

"And your master is God?" (Talmud Yebamot 105b)

4. Elijah frequented Rabbi's Academy. Once, on the New Moon, he was late in coming. Rabbi said to him: "Why was the Master late today?" "Until I woke Abraham, and washed his feet, and he prayed, and had him lie down, and then Isaac, and then Jacob..."

"And could not the Master have gotten them up all at one time?"

"I was afraid to, lest they combine their strength in prayer and bring the Messiah before the destined time."

Then Rabbi said: "Are their equals to be found in this world?"

"Yes," answered Elijah, "Rabbi Chiya and his sons."

Rabbi then declared a fast–day, and they placed Rabbi Chiya and his sons [to lead prayers] before the Ark. When they said "He makes the wind to blow," the wind blew; when they said "He causes the rain to fall," the rain fell; and when they reached the words "He gives life to the dead," the world began to shake.

They asked in Heaven: "Who has revealed this secret to the world?"

"Elijah!" was the answer.

They brought Elijah and scourged him with 60 straps of fire, so he went back and appeared to them as a fiery bear. He ran among them and dispersed them. (Talmud Baba Metzia 85b)

5. Judah and Hezekiah, sons of Rabbi Chiya, were at a feast in Rabbi's home and were silent.

He said to his retainers: "Give the lads more wine; it will loosen their tongues."

They became drunk and spoke up, saying: "The son of David will not come until the two great houses[58] of Israel come to an end—the Exilarch in Babylon and the Patriarch in Israel, as it says (Isaiah 8:14), *He will become a sanctuary, and a stone of offense, and a rock of stumbling to both houses of Israel.*"

"My sons," cried Rabbi, "You are throwing thorns into my eyes!"

"Do not take it amiss, Rabbi," said Rabbi Chiya. "The numerical value of 'wine' [יין, *yayin*] is 70, and that of 'secret' [סוד, *sod*] is 70: when wine enters, secrets exit." (Talmud Sanhedrin 38a)

6. The people of Simoniah asked Rabbi to appoint someone who would be for them an expositor, a judge, a teacher, a scribe, a jack-of-all-trades in Torah. He gave them Levi ben Sissi.

They made a platform for him and set him up above them. When they came to ask him the Halachah he had no answers, so they thought: Perhaps he is not an expert in law. They then asked him to teach them Agadah; again he had no answers.

They went back to Rabbi and complained: "Is this what we asked of you?" He said to them: "By God, I sent you a man like myself!" So Rabbi summoned him and examined him in Halachah, and he answered. He then questioned him on Agadah, and he answered. "Why then didn't you answer them?" he asked. "Because they set me up on a large platform and seated me high up, higher than they were. I was filled up with pride and the words of Torah vanished from my mind." Rabbi then applied these words to him (Proverbs 30:32), *"If you have been foolish, exalting yourself, or if you have been devising evil, put your hand on your mouth...* Who forced you to make a fool of yourself through the Torah? You did it to yourself, by using it to exalt yourself!" (Jerusalem Talmud Yebamot 2:5)

7. Rabbi once visited Rabbi Tarfon's home town. He asked the residents: "Does a son survive to that saint who always swore to teach his sons wisdom?" "No," they told him, "but there is a grandson. And if a whore's pay is two gold pieces, he gets four."

They brought him to Rabbi, who said to him: "If you return [to God], I will let you have my daughter to marry." He returned [to God].

Some say: He married and divorced her.

And others say: He didn't marry her at all, so that people should not say: He returned on her account. (Talmud Baba Metzia 85a)

8. There was a drought and Rabbi opened the storehouse, saying: "Let those versed in Scripture, Mishnah, Talmud, Halachah, and Agadah enter, but not the ignorant."

Rabbi Yonatan ben Amram knocked and was allowed to enter.

He said: "Rabbi, give me sustenance!"

"Have you learned Scripture, my son?"

"No."

"Mishnah?"

"No."

"In that case, why should I sustain you?"

"Feed me as you would a dog or a bird."

He gave him food.

Afterward, Rabbi regretted it and said: "Why did I give food to an ignoramus?"

Rabbi Simeon his son then said to him: "Perhaps that was your disciple Yonatan ben Amram, who has never allowed himself to benefit from his Torah-learning in his life." They investigated and found it to be so.

Rabbi then said: "Let everyone enter." (Talmud Baba Batra 8a)

9. Rabbi Judah asked Rabbi Joshua ben Korchah: "What [merit] has given you such long life?"

"Does it disturb you?"

"No, but it is Torah and I need to learn it."

"I never met a wicked man," was his answer.

As Rabbi Joshua lay dying, Rabbi said to him: "Bless me."

"May you live half as long as I have."

"And not as long?"

"Do you want your [would-be] successors to tend cattle?" (Talmud Megillah 28a)

10. Antoninus asked our Holy Rabbi: "What is your rule about hourly prayer?"

"It is forbidden," Rabbi told him.

"Why is it forbidden?"

"It is frivolous to address the Holy One so frequently."

Antoninus expressed his disagreement.

On the following morning, Rabbi got up early and went to see Antoninus. Arriving, he called out: "Greetings to the king!" An hour later he returned and proclaimed in a loud voice: "Great Caesar!" After another hour he returned and said: "A good day to you, Emperor!"

Antoninus said to him with irritation: "Why are you making light of the crown?"

"Let your ears hear what your mouth is saying!" responded Rabbi. "You are flesh-and-blood, and yet you think that one who greets you every hour is making light of you! How much more then the Sovereign who is supreme over all!" (Midrash Tanchumah, Mikeitz)

11. Our Rabbi once invited Antoninus to a meal on the Sabbath, and had him served cold dishes. Another time the emperor invited him to a meal on a weekday; this time they were served hot dishes.

Antoninus said: "I liked the other meal—the one you served me—better than this one."

"This one lacked an ingredient," Rabbi observed.

"What is it that the stores of the emperor could possibly lack?"

"One thing is missing: the Sabbath." (Midrash Genesis Rabbah 11)

12. As Rabbi lay dying the sages decreed a fast and began to plead for mercy. Rabbi's servant went up to the roof, thinking: "They want Rabbi above and below: may the ones below overcome the ones above." When she saw that he was in great pain, she thought: "May the ones above overcome," but the sages did not cease to pray for mercy. She then took a pitcher and threw it down from the roof. The sages were startled into silence, and Rabbi's soul departed. (Talmud K'tubot 103b–104a)

The Circle of Rabbi [Judah the Prince]

1. Resh Lakish said: "I speak in praise of Rabbi Chiya and his sons: Once when the Torah was forgotten in Israel, Ezra came up from Babylonia and restored it; it was forgotten another time, and Hillel the Babylonian came up and restored it; it was forgotten a third time, and Rabbi Chiya and his sons came up and restored it." (Talmud Sukkah 20a)

2. Rabbi Chiya the Great and Rabbi Simeon ben Chalafta was sitting learning Torah in the Great House of Study in Tiberias on the eve of Pesach [and some say, on the eve of Yom Kippur]. They heard the raised voices of people outside. Rabbi Simeon said to Rabbi Chiya: "What are those people doing?" He answered: "Who has [money] is buying what he needs for the festival; who hasn't any is getting some from his employer." Rabbi Simeon then said: "If that is so, then I too will go and get what I need from my Employer."

Rabbi Simeon went to a particular cave outside Tiberias to pray. A hand reached down and handed him a pearl, and he took it to Rabbi. "Where did this come from?" he inquired. "It's valuable. Take three dinarii meantime to honor the day; after the festival we'll hawk it and see what you can get for it." He took the three dinarii and bought food and came home. His wife said: "Simeon, have you become a thief? All your property adds up to a hundred ma'in, so how did you get all this stuff?" "The Holy One gave it to me." "I won't taste a morsel unless you tell me where you got it." He told her what had happened: "So I prayed and the Holy One gave it to me from Heaven." "Do you want your Chuppah[59] in the world–to–come to have one pearl less than those of your colleagues?" "What do you want me to do?" "Bring back what you bought to their owners, the dinarii to their owners, and the pearl to its owner."

When Rabbi heard of Rabbi Simeon's distress, he summoned Simeon's wife. "Why are you giving this saint so much grief?" he asked. She replied: "Do you really want his Chuppah in the world–to–come to have one pearl less than that of all the rest of you?" "If anything is missing, won't we be able to make up the difference?" "Rabbi, we may never have the good fortune to see you in the world–to–come! Doesn't each saint have a separate dwelling there? Don't we each one have our world to ourselves, as it is said (Ecclesiastes 12:5), *Humans goes to their long home?*"[60] He conceded the point.

When Rabbi Simeon heard this, he went back to the cave. An angel descended and took the pearl the instant he stretched out his hand to return it.

Our sages said: "The second miracle was greater than the first. It is the way of the upper world to give, not to take." (Midrash Ruth Rabbah 3; Exodus Rabbah 52:3)

2.8

Rabban Yochanan ben Zakkai

1. They said of Rabban Yochanan ben Zakkai: He never engaged in idle chatter. He never walked four cubits without Tallit and Tefillin. No one ever preceded him to the House of Study. He never slept in the House of Study. He never brought someone to the House of Study and left. He never while meditating on Torah set foot in a filthy place. One ever found him sitting and learning, not in silence. He and he alone opened the door to admit his disciples. He taught only what he had heard from his master's lips. He never said: "It is time to leave the House of Study," save for the eve of Pesach and the eve of Yom Kippur. And Eliezer his disciple modeled himself after him. (Talmud Sukkah 28a)

2. They said of Rabban Yochanan ben Zakkai: No one ever greeted him first, not even a foreigner in the marketplace. (Talmud Berachot 17a)

3. When Rabban Yochanan ben Zakkai sickened, his disciples came to visit him. Seeing them, he began to weep. They said: "Master, Light of Israel, Upright Column, Mighty Hammer, why are you crying?" "Were they bringing me [for judgment] to a mortal king, one here today and tomorrow in the grave, whose anger does not last, whose rejection does not endure, who can kill me only in this world, who can be appeased with words and bribed with money—still I would weep. Now they are bringing me before the Sovereign who is supreme over all, the Holy One, ever to be praised, who lives and endures to all eternity, whose anger might be eternal, whose rejection might be eternal, who can kill me for eternity, and who cannot be appeased with words nor bribed with money. What is more, two roads stand before me—one to Eden, the other to Gehenna, and I don't know which one is mine: should I not weep?" "Rabbi," they said to him, "bless us." He said: "May your fear of Heaven be as great as your fear of flesh and blood." "No more than that, Rabbi?" "Would that it were that much! When we transgress we say, 'If only no one sees me!'" (Talmud Berachot 28b)

4. His disciples asked Rabban Yochanan ben Zakkai: "Why is the Torah harsher with a thief than a robber?" He answered them: "Because the thief shows less respect for the honor of God than does a robber. The [robber acts openly, but the] thief acts in stealth as if he were neither seen nor heard by the Above, as it is said (Isaiah 29:25), *Woe to those who hide deep from the Eternal One their intent, whose deeds are in the dark, and who say, 'Who sees us? Who knows us?'*"

Rabbi Meir said: They give an example in the name of Rabban Gamaliel: Two men held feasts. One invited all the townspeople but not the royal family; the other invited neither the townspeople nor the royal family. Who received the more severe punishment? Surely the one who invited the townspeople but not the royal family! (Talmud Baba Kama 79b)

5. ...*his master shall bore his ear through with an awl* (Exodus 21:6). Rabban Yochanan ben Zakkai's exposition of this verse was a gem:

What makes the ear different from the rest of the body?

The Holy One said: The ear that heard my voice at Sinai saying (Leviticus 25:55), *For to Me the people of Israel are servants; they are My servants.*—and not servants to servants —yet this one went and bought a master: let him be pierced through it!

*He shall bring him to the door or the doorpost...(Exodus 21:6). Rabbi Simeon son of Rabbi's exposition of this verse was a gem:

What makes the door and doorpost different from the rest of the house? [Why use the doorpost?]

The Holy One said: The door and the doorpost were witnesses in Egypt when I skipped over the lintel and the doorposts, saying (Leviticus 25:55), *For to Me the people of Israel are servants.*—and not servants to servants. I brought them from bondage to freedom, yet this one went and bought himself a master: let him be pierced through them! (Talmud Kiddushin 22b)

6. Rabban Yochanan ben Zakkai would say: If you are holding a plant and you hear them tell you the Messiah has come, plant it first. You can go greet the Messiah later. (Midrash Leviticus Rabbah 25)

2:8

Eliezer ben Hyrcanus

1. Our sages taught: Rabbi Eliezer was living in the Upper Galilee and they asked him thirty questions on the Halachah of Sukkot. Twelve he answered, saying: "I have heard [an answer from my teachers]." On eighteen he said: "I have not heard." Rabbi Yosé son of Rabbi Judah says that it was the other way around: on eighteen he averred that he had heard an answer, and on twelve, that he had not heard. They said to him: "Master, are your answers only what you have heard [from your teachers]?" He replied: "Now you force me to say something that I did not hear from my teachers: No one ever preceded me to the House of Study; I never went to sleep or fell asleep in the House of Study; I never left the House of Study before anyone else; I never indulged in idle chatter; and I never taught anything that I did not learn from my teachers." (Talmud Sukkah 28a)

2. One of his disciples expounded Torah in the presence of his master, Rabbi Eliezer. He said to his honorable wife: "Woe to the wife of this man! He won't live past the Sabbath." Nor did he. The sages approached him and his disciples said: "Are you a prophet, Master?" "Neither a prophet nor the son of a prophet, but this I have learned: If you teach Halachah in your own teacher's presence, you deserve to die." (Jerusalem Talmud Gittin 1:2; Midrash Leviticus Rabbah 20)

3. We have been taught: If an oven was cut up into sections and sand placed between each one, Rabbi Eliezer says: "Such an oven can never become impure." But the sages say: "It can."

On that day, Rabbi Eliezer employed every conceivable argument, and yet the sages were not convinced: they would not yield.

He then said: "If I am right, this carob tree will prove it." And the carob tree moved a distance of one hundred cubits. (Others say: four hundred.)

The sages replied: "Carob trees prove nothing."

He then said: "If I am right, this stream of water will prove it." And the stream began to flow backwards.

The sages replied: "A stream of water proves nothing."

He then said: "If I am right, the walls of this house of study will prove it." The walls began to cave in.

Rabbi Joshua rose at this point and rebuked the walls: "When sages debate the law, what business is it of yours?!"

The result was that, out of respect for Rabbi Joshua, the walls did not cave in, but out of respect for Rabbi Eliezer, the walls did not return to their original position. Thus do they remain inclined, to this very day!

Eliezer then said to his colleagues: "If I am right, Heaven (itself) will prove it!" And a voice from Heaven was heard to say: "Why do you reject Rabbi Eliezer? The law has always been as he says."

Rabbi Joshua now rose and exclaimed: "*It is not in heaven.*[61] When we decide the law, we take no notice even of a voice from heaven, for it is already written in the Torah (Exodus 23:2): *The majority view must be followed.*"[62]

One day Rabbi Nathan encountered Elijah the Prophet and asked him: "What did the Holy One do when all this happened?"

Elijah answered: "God laughed and said: 'My children have overcome Me, My children have overcome Me!'" (Talmud Baba Metzia 59a)

4. Rabbi Eliezer was a stubborn man. He would not accept the decision of the sages, though they had decided the matter and voted on it. He continued to maintain his view, and the sages felt obliged to put him under the ban. [He would be barred from their discussions until he submitted.] But who among them would dare take it on himself to tell him? Rabbi Akiba offered, explaining: "If the wrong man tells him, it could endanger the whole world."

Akiba prepared himself by wearing black. He went and sat four cubits away from the venerable sage, who had in time past been his master.

Observing him thus, Eliezer said: "Akiba, how is this day different from all other days?"

"Master," he replied, "it seems your colleagues have separated themselves from you."

At these words Eliezer did what all do who are banned: he tore his clothes, took off his shoes, and sat on the ground, like one in mourning. And he began to weep. This grief of his brought much suffering upon the world—a blight destroyed a third of the olive crop, and a third of the wheat and barley. Moreover, his burning glance consumed all that it happened to fall upon.

Just then Rabban Gamaliel was taking a journey by sea. A tremendous wave rose up, imperilling the ship, its passengers and crew. He thought: "This must be the work of Rabbi Eliezer!" Standing up, he cried: "Ruler of the world, did I act out of selfish motives? For the glory of my family? Was it not rather for Your glory, for the unity of the House of Israel?"

The sea grew calm.

Rabbi Eliezer's wife was the sister of Rabban Gamaliel. From that time onward she would not allow Rabbi Eliezer to prostrate himself when praying. A poor man came once and stood at the threshhold. She fetched the man a loaf. [Returning,] she found him prostrate. "Get up!" she shouted. "You've already killed my brother!" Just then the shofar sounded from Rabban Gamaliel's house, announcing his death. Rabbi Eliezer said to her: "How did you know?" She answered: "This I learned in

83

grandfather's house: All the gates (of prayer) are shut, except the gates of anguish."
(Talmud Baba Metzia 59a)

2:8

Joshua ben Chananiah

1. Hadrian, emperor of Rome, said to Rabbi Joshua ben Chananiah: "How hard it is for a sheep whose shepherd is surrounded by 70 wolves." He answered: "How strong the keeper who saves her from them all." (Midrash Yalkut Shimoni, Kohelet, 9)

2. Rabbi Joshua ben Chananiah said: "Only three times has anyone gotten the better of me. One of them was a young girl, another was a young boy: I was walking one day when I came upon a boy sitting at a crossroads. I said to him: 'Son, which road leads to town?' He answered: 'This one is short but long and that one is long but short.' So I took the first one. When I got near the town I found myself blocked by a ring of gardens and orchards and I had to turn back. The boy was still there at the crossroads, and I said to him: 'Didn't you say, son, that this road is the short one?' He answered: 'Master, didn't I also say *but long*?' I kissed his head and said to him: 'Happy are you, O Israel, whose young and old alike are clever!'" (Talmud Erubin 53b; Midrash Yalkut Shimoni, Kohelet, 9)

3. Rabbi Joshua ben Chananiah told how a little girl had bested him. "I was walking and came upon a path that led through a field, so I took it. A little girl called out to me: 'Isn't the path you're on part of the field, sir?' 'It looks like a public path; the ground is beaten down,' I said. 'Yes," she said, "and robbers like you have made it like that!" (Talmud Erubin 53b)

4. The emperor's daughter said to Rabbi Joshua ben Chananiah: "How can such great wisdom as yours reside in such an ugly vessel?"
"Does your father keep wine in clay jugs?" That was his response.
"Yes," she said. "What else should he keep wine in?"
"People of your standing ought to keep their wine in gold and silver containers."
When she told this to her father, he ordered gold and silver containers for his wine. Before long the wine had turned sour.
This was reported to the emperor, who asked his daughter: "Who told you to keep wine in gold and silver vessels?"
She said to him: "Rabbi Joshua ben Chananiah."
The emperor summoned him and demanded to know why he had so advised her.
"I told her to follow her own way of thinking."
"Are there no handsome sages, then?"
"They would be wiser still were they ugly." (Talmud Nedarim 50b; Ta'anit 7a)

5. When the Temple was destroyed, the number of ascetics in Israel multiplied. They ate no flesh and drank no wine. Rabbi Joshua wanted to know why they were doing this, and they explained that flesh had been offered on the altar and wine used in libations. All that had now ceased.

"In that case," he said, "we should not eat bread, because the meal offerings have also ceased." "We can live on fruit, then," they said. "But the offering of the firstfruits, too, has come to an end," he objected. "Then we will eat only of those fruits that were not offered as firstfruits." "And as water was used in the libations, we should abstain from drinking it," he urged. They were silent.

"What has happened has happened," he counseled, "and it is impossible not to mourn at all. But we may not mourn excessively either, for a practice must not be imposed that a majority of the community cannot bear." (Talmud Baba Batra 60b)

6. Rabbi Joshua ben Chananiah was standing once on the slope of the Temple Mount when Ben Zoma came along. Though he approached quite near, Ben Zoma did not greet him, and he said to Ben Zoma: "Whence and where, Ben Zoma?" He answered: "I was gazing at the Work of Creation,[63] and between the Upper and Lower Waters there is a width of only three fingers, as it is said (Genesis 1:2), ...and the spirit of God hovered over the face of the waters.—as a dove hovers over her young, touching yet not touching."

Rabbi Joshua said to his disciples: "Ben Zoma is already outside."[64] Only a few days later Ben Zoma passed on. (Talmud Chagigah 15a; Tosefta Chagigah 2)

7. But where can wisdom be found? (Job 28:12)

Solomon was seeking the place from which wisdom emanates.

Rabbi Eliezer says: The head.

Rabbi Joshua says: The heart. That is why it is said (Psalm 4:8), You have put joy in my heart, and (Proverbs 27:11), Grow wise, my son, and gladden my heart. (Midrash Proverbs 1)

8. The emperor said to Rabbi Joshua ben Chananiah: "You claim to be great sages; tell me what I will dream about."

He replied: "You will see the Persians coming. They will subjugate and despoil you; strangers will tend your flocks with golden rods."

He pondered this all that day; at night he saw. (Talmud Berachot 56a)

2:8

Elazar ben Arach

1. As long as Rabban Yochanan ben Zakkai lived, his five disciples remained with him. Upon his death they went to Yavneh, but Elazar ben Arach went to his wife in Demsit, a place of good waters and scenic beauty. He invited them to come to him, and when they refused he wanted to go to them, but his wife did not let him. She

said: "Who is obliged to whom?" "They are obliged to me," was his reply. "Cheese and mice: do the mice go to the cheese, or does the cheese go to the mice?" He heeded her and remained there until he had forgotten his learning.

Some time later they came to him and asked him questions on the Torah. He was unable to answer. (ARN 14; Midrash Ecclesiastes Rabbah 7)

2:15

Rabbi Tarfon

1. Rabbi Tarfon was like a heap of nuts. When one removes a nut from the pile the rest rattle against one another. So, when a scholar came and said to him: "Teach me!" he would bring forth Scripture and Mishnah, Midrash, Halachot, and Agadot.[65] One left his presence full of blessing and well-being. (ARN 18)

2. Rabbi Tarfon once went down to his grove. took some figs and started to eat them. The steward found him thus and, not recognizing him, said: "Here's the man who's been poaching all year!" He struck him and put him into a sack, intending to throw him into the river. When Rabbi Tarfon saw his peril he said: "Tell the people of Tarfon's household to prepare shrouds for him." The man was stunned and mortified and begged forgiveness. Tarfon said: "I swear that I forgave you each time you struck me!"

They said in the name of Rabbi Chananiah ben Gamaliel: That saint grieved over this all his life. He said: "Woe is me! I made [personal] use of the crown of Torah."[66] (Talmud Nedarim 62a)

3. They said of Rabbi Tarfon that he was a very rich man who did not give many gifts to the poor. Rabbi Akiba once chanced upon him and said: "Rabbi, would you like me to acquire a village or two for you?" Rabbi Tarfon agreed and handed him four thousand gold dinarii. Rabbi Akiba took them and distributed them to poor scholars. A few days later Rabbi Tarfon asked him: "Where are the villages you acquired for me?" Akiba took him by the hand and led him to the House of Study. He then brought a child over, who was holding a copy of the Psalms. He recited it until he reached this verse (Psalm 112:9): *He gives freely to the poor; his righteousness endures for ever.* And he said: "This is the village I acquired for you." Rabbi Tarfon arose and kissed him, saying: "My Master and Mentor—my master in wisdom, my mentor in right action!"—and he gave him still more money to distribute. (Talmud Kallah 2)

4. Rabbi Tarfon would bend down and let his mother step on him when she wanted to go up on to her bed. He boasted of this in the synagogue, and they said to him: "You have not done even half your duty! Has she thrown your purse into the sea before your eyes without you putting her to shame?"

When Rabbi Joseph heard his mother's footsteps, he would say, "I rise before the approaching Shechinah. (Talmud Kiddushin 31b;)

In Sum

The basic message of chapter 2 is: Live each day as though it were your last... and remember the world–to–come. (Neusner)

•••••••

Notes

[1]Rabbi Judah the Prince, compiler of the Mishnah (135–219 CE).

[2]See, also, 2:9.

[3]See, also, 2:7, 3:10, 4:13.

[4]See, also, 4:2.

[5]2nd–3rd C. CE.

[6]This translation seems demanded by the context. דרך ארץ, *derech eretz*, is, literally, the "way of earth." It usually means 'good manners, graciousness, civility.'

[7]See, also, 2:5, 3:17, 4:10.

[8]Or, 'congregation.' See, also, 5:18.

[9]Or, be sold as slaves.

[10]See, also, 1:10.

[11]This mishnah has been divided into two sections for the sake of clarity.

[12]This mishnah has been divided into two sections for the sake of clarity.

[13]Joseph Hertz, in his commentary to Avot, suggests another possible translation or paraphrase: "Divulge nothing that ought to be kept secret, on the plea that in the end all things are sure to become public knowledge."

[14]That is, in displaying one's fear of Heaven.

[15]Or, "Not everyone who is steeped in business can grow wise." See, also, 2:1, 3:17, 4:10.

[16]The rest of the passage is in Aramaic.

[17]ישיבה, *Yeshivah*, literally 'sitting,' that is, sitting in an academy of learning, The word to this day denotes a school devoted primarily to Jewish learning, but it is often restricted to denote a preparatory school, followed by attendance at a *Metivtah*, its Aramaic equivalent.

[18]The remaining Hebrew is in the 3rd masc. singular.

[19]Literally, "words."

[20]The Mishnah has been divided for the sake of convenience.

[21]1st. C. CE (died 80 CE). He was a leader among the Pharisees and played a major role in ensuring the continuation of Judaism after the destruction of the Temple. This mishnah is unique in Avot, in that it characterizes some of the sages. Rabbi Eliezer, here praised, achieved great eminence. Rabbi Elazar ben Arach, who receives higher praise still, is little known.

[22]Or, 'a saint.' See 2:5.

[23]See, also, 2:1.

[24]Or, 'A generous spirit,' 'Freedom from envy.'

[25]Or, 'Learning from experience.' See, also, Talmud Tamid 32a: "Who is wise? One who foresees the consequences of things."

[26]Or, 'Good will.'

[27]Or, 'An ungenerous spirit,' 'Envy.' See Deuteronomy 15:9. The 'bad eye,' (עין הרע,

ayin hara) came in time to mean the 'evil eye.'

[28]Or, 'Ill Will.'

[29]Ca. 45–117 CE.

[30]See, also, 2:12, 4:12.

[31]That is, 'repent,' 'do Teshuvah.' תשובה, *Teshuvah,* is the noun usually translated by 'repentance' or 'penitence.' Literally, however, it means '(re)turning.' See 4:16.

[32]humiliates; Literally, 'whitens.'

[33]the Divine Presence.

[34]This Mitzvah has priority over most others, and Jewish history has afforded ample opportunity for its fulfilment.

[35]Ca. 50–130 CE.

[36]I.e, 'An ungenerous spirit,' 'Envy.' See Note at 2:9, where it is Rabbi Eliezer, not Rabbi Joshua, who speaks of the 'bad eye' as the path to be avoided.

[37]That is, "exclude one from human society."

[38] Therefore supplications can always enter through this gate.

[39]The Holy One is always concerned with these .

[40]That is, one's innermost thoughts and intentions.

[41]That is, who engages in deception.

[42]1st–2nd C. CE.

[43]See, also, 2:10, 4:12.

[44]1st–2nd C. CE.

[45]The basic daily prayers.

[46]See, also, 1:15.

[47]Literally, "before the Omnipresent who is blessed for compassion and grace." See Note at 2:9.

[48]Literally, "Never be wicked before yourself." Or, "Never be evil in your own eyes." See, also, Talmud Kiddushin 40b: "Always regard yourself as half–righteous, half–wicked; by one good deed you then place yourself and the whole world on the scale of merit (and vice–versa)."

[49]1st–2nd C. CE.

[50]See, also, 1:15, etc. The learning of Torah is examined again and again in Avot: variations on a theme.

[51]Or, 'heretic,' 'unbeliever.' From 'Epicurean.'

[52]That is, without shaming the one being reproved.

[53]This depends on a pun and on the fact that the first verb in the text is reflexive.

[54]Ca. 46–117 CE.

[55]That is, wherever one dwells.

[56]In the Temple, on earth.

[57]That is, towards the land of Israel. The debate, then, has to do with the diaspora vs. the land of Israel.

[58]"fathers' houses": dynasties

[59]The Chuppah referred to here is not the marriage–canopy of modern times but a chamber or dwelling in which the blessed enjoy Paradise. What is given in this world must be taken from the next.

[60]The passage from Ecclesiastes can be translated as 'Humans go to the house of their world,' That is, all have their own individual houses.

[61]Deuteronomy 30:12. That is, the Torah is not in Heaven but on earth, and entrusted to the Sages to interpret and decide.

[62]A deliberate and bold 'misinterpretation' of the verse in Exodus, which in fact is an injunction <u>not</u> to follow the majority to do wrong. Here, it is used to affirm the principle of majority rule in the determination of the Halachah.

[63]מעשה בראשית, ma'asei b'reishit, the Work(s) of Creation, is a term used in rabbinic literature for mystical speculation.

[64]this world.

[65] That is, all the sources of law and lore.

[66] See Avot 1:13 (and 4:15).

Avot 3

A Note

The authors cited in chapter 3 lived between 70–132 CE—between the two great wars against Rome. This was a time to look back with hope of restoration (as after the destruction of the First Temple, during the Babylonian Exile). The messianic hope was strong; the calamity had been great, but hopes were high. Both Akavia and Chananiah (3:2) had seen the Temple destroyed. They could face the darkness of life and human nature because God gives light. (Neusner)

•••••••

Additional readings on the sages whose sayings are featured in this chapter begin on page 118.

Avot 3:1

עֲקַבְיָא בֶּן מַהֲלַלְאֵל אוֹמֵר:
הִסְתַּכֵּל בִּשְׁלשָׁה דְבָרִים וְאִי אַתָּה
בָא לִידֵי עֲבֵרָה: דַּע מֵאַיִן בָּאתָ,
וּלְאָן אַתָּה הוֹלֵךְ, וְלִפְנֵי מִי אַתָּה
עָתִיד לִתֵּן דִּין וְחֶשְׁבּוֹן.
מֵאַיִן בָּאתָ? מִטִּפָּה סְרוּחָה. וּלְאָן אַתָּה
הוֹלֵךְ? לִמְקוֹם עָפָר, רִמָּה וְתוֹלֵעָה.
וְלִפְנֵי מִי אַתָּה עָתִיד לִתֵּן דִּין וְחֶשְׁבּוֹן?
לִפְנֵי מֶלֶךְ מַלְכֵי הַמְּלָכִים, הַקָּדוֹשׁ
בָּרוּךְ הוּא.

AKAVIA BEN Mehalalel[1] says:
Keep your eye on three things and you will not fall into the grip of sin:[2]
Know where you come from,
and where you are going,
and before whom you are destined to give a full account.
Where you come from—a putrid drop.
And where you are going—to a place of dust, worms, and maggots.
And before whom you are destined to give a full account—before the Sovereign who is supreme over all, the Holy One, ever to be praised.

Know where you come from—We may seem as nothing, but we are God's. 3:1 and 3:7 are in counterpoint. (Neusner)

If "we are God's," our attachment to the Infinite "endows us with abiding worth" (prayerbook). Akavia's humility is not self-abasement but self-knowledge. (CS)

--- With this in mind, it should not occur to you to seek a crown or to think yourself exempt from the commandments. Still, if your Yetzer remains overpowering, consider before whom you are going to have to give a full account of yourself. (Vitry)

Avot 3.2a[3]

רִבִּי חֲנַנְיָה סְגַן הַכֹּהֲנִים אוֹמֵר:
הֱוֵי מִתְפַּלֵּל בִּשְׁלוֹמָהּ שֶׁל מַלְכוּת,
שֶׁאִלְמָלֵא מוֹרָאָהּ, אִישׁ אֶת־רֵעֵהוּ
חַיִּים בְּלָעוּ.

RABBI CHANANIAH,[4] Prefect[5] of the Priests, says:
Pray for the welfare of the government, because, were people not afraid of it, they would swallow each other alive.

the welfare of the government—One should pray for the welfare of the whole world and share in the grief of others. We are not permitted to pray only for our own needs. (Rabbi Jonah ben Abraham)
--- See, also, 1:10, 2:3, 2.10, and see Jeremiah 29:7: *Seek the welfare of the city...* The Talmud (Gittin 10b, Nedarim 28a, etc.) adds: "The civil law of the state is the law [which the Jew is duty–bound to observe]." (CS)
people would swallow—"You cry against the noble senate who...keep you in awe, which else would feed on one another." (Shakespeare, Coriolanus I:1, 188–192)

Avot 3.2b[6]

רַבִּי חֲנַנְיָה בֶּן תְּרַדְיוֹן אוֹמֵר: שְׁנַיִם
שֶׁיּוֹשְׁבִין וְאֵין בֵּינֵיהֶן דִּבְרֵי תוֹרָה,
הֲרֵי זֶה מוֹשַׁב לֵצִים, שֶׁנֶּאֱמַר:
[אַשְׁרֵי־הָאִישׁ אֲשֶׁר לֹא הָלַךְ בַּעֲצַת
רְשָׁעִים וּבְדֶרֶךְ חַטָּאִים לֹא עָמָד]
וּבְמוֹשַׁב לֵצִים לֹא יָשָׁב.
אֲבָל שְׁנַיִם שֶׁיּוֹשְׁבִין וְיֵשׁ בֵּינֵיהֶן דִּבְרֵי
תוֹרָה, שְׁכִינָה שְׁרוּיָה בֵּינֵיהֶם, שֶׁנֶּאֱמַר:
אָז נִדְבְּרוּ יִרְאֵי יהוה אִישׁ אֶת־רֵעֵהוּ,
וַיַּקְשֵׁב יהוה וַיִּשְׁמָע, וַיִּכָּתֵב סֵפֶר
זִכָּרוֹן לְפָנָיו, לְיִרְאֵי יהוה וּלְחֹשְׁבֵי
שְׁמוֹ.
אֵין לִי אֶלָּא שְׁנַיִם. מִנַּיִן שֶׁאֲפִילוּ אֶחָד
שֶׁיּוֹשֵׁב וְעוֹסֵק בַּתּוֹרָה, שֶׁהַקָּדוֹשׁ
בָּרוּךְ הוּא קוֹבֵעַ לוֹ שָׂכָר? שֶׁנֶּאֱמַר:
יֵשֵׁב בָּדָד וְיִדֹּם, כִּי נָטַל עָלָיו:

RABBI CHANANIAH ben T'radion[7] says:
When two are sitting[8] and words of
Torah do not pass between them, why,
this is a "seat of cynics," as it is said
(Psalm 1:1), [Happy is the one who does
not walk in the counsel of the wicked, nor
stands on the path of sinners,] nor sits in
the seat of cynics.

But when two are sitting and words of
Torah do pass between them, the
Shechinah is with them, as it is said
(Malachi 3:16), Then those who feared
God[9] spoke to one another, and God
hearkened and heard, and a book of remembrance was written before God, for
those who feared the Eternal One and
gave thought to the divine name.

We see that this applies to two. How do
we know that the Holy One, ever to be
praised, sets aside a reward even for one
who sits engaged in Torah? For it is said
(Lamentations 3:28), Let him sit alone
and keep silent, for God has laid it on
him.[10]

and words of Torah pass between them—This may be applied to our everyday
business and social dealings. To speak of actual Torah texts is commendable; to
apply Torah values when we talk or negotiate with one another is an even higher
obligation.

N.B.: This is the first passage in Avot to cite Scripture.[11] Many others will come
along and do so. Since Avot is also Torah, what purpose is served by this practice?
Not merely to prove that the opinion stated is true, since the opinion at hand also
comes from Sinai: Torah is Torah, whatever its source or date. Judaism is not a
religion that stopped the day it started, so to speak, with one authoritative Torah,
the written one. The quotation serves two purposes: it illustrates Chananiah's
words, and Chananiah's words illustrate Scripture. The direction of the exchange is
not important. Chananiah both learns and teaches Torah. The passage of the written
Torah is cited to do two things: first, to prove that we teach Torah; and so, second, to
demonstrate that Torah teaches Israel, also, through us. God speaks to each

generation. Judaism is the religion of the ongoing revelation, the religious experience of Torah. (Neusner)

Avot 3:3

רַבִּי שִׁמְעוֹן אוֹמֵר:

שְׁלֹשָׁה שֶׁאָכְלוּ עַל שֻׁלְחָן אֶחָד

וְלֹא אָמְרוּ עָלָיו דִּבְרֵי תוֹרָה,

כְּאִלּוּ אָכְלוּ מִזִּבְחֵי מֵתִים, שֶׁנֶּאֱמַר:

כִּי כָּל־שֻׁלְחָנוֹת מָלְאוּ קִיא צֹאָה,

בְּלִי מָקוֹם.

אֲבָל שְׁלֹשָׁה שֶׁאָכְלוּ עַל שֻׁלְחָן אֶחָד

וְאָמְרוּ עָלָיו דִּבְרֵי תוֹרָה, כְּאִלּוּ אָכְלוּ

מִשֻּׁלְחָנוֹ שֶׁל מָקוֹם, שֶׁנֶּאֱמַר: וַיְדַבֵּר

אֵלַי: זֶה הַשֻּׁלְחָן אֲשֶׁר לִפְנֵי יהוה.

RABBI SIMEON[12] says:
Three who have eaten together[13] and have not spoken words of Torah are as though they have eaten of sacrifices to the dead, as it is said (Isaiah 28:8), *For all tables are full of vomit and filth, so that there is no place left.*[14]

But three who have eaten together and have spoken words of Torah are as though they have eaten at the table of the Omnipresent who is blessed, as it is said (Ezekiel 41:22), *And he said to me: This is the table that is before the Eternal.*

the table of the Omnipresent—If, when left to our own devices, we would eat each other up alive (3:2), we can, through Torah, eat in God's presence. (Neusner)

sacrifices—That is, an idolatrous offering. Now, with the Temple gone, our own table is called an altar, and the food on it is regarded as an offering. So the question becomes, "To whom is the offering made?" When words of Torah are not spoken, the offering cannot be to God, and must therefore be idolatrous. By the same token, now that there is no Temple, we achieve atonement by means of our own tables, by giving food and drink to the poor. (Vitry)

Avot 3.4[15]

רִבִּי חֲנַנְיָה בֶּן חֲכִינָאִי אוֹמֵר:

הַנֵּעוֹר בַּלַּיְלָה,

וְהַמְהַלֵּךְ בַּדֶּרֶךְ יְחִידִי

וּמְפַנֶּה לִבּוֹ לִבְטָלָה:

הֲרֵי זֶה מִתְחַיֵּיב בְּנַפְשׁוֹ.

RABBI CHANANIAH ben Chachinai[16]
says:
Who get up at night,
who walk about alone
and turn their hearts[17] to emptiness:[18]
such people are their own worst
enemies.[19]

alone—These were dangerous times, and this may be a warning that solitary walkers risked physical harm. (CS)

night...alone...emptiness—The demons of solitude, the emptiness of night, when we talk to none but ourselves. (Neusner)

turn their hearts—Do nothing that will put your heart to sleep or numb your mind. (Meiri)

Avot 3.5

רַבִּי נְחוּנְיָא בֶּן הַקָּנָה אוֹמֵר:
כָּל־הַמְקַבֵּל עָלָיו עֹל תּוֹרָה
מַעֲבִירִין מִמֶּנּוּ עֹל מַלְכוּת וְעֹל דֶּרֶךְ
אֶרֶץ. וְכָל־הַפּוֹרֵק מִמֶּנּוּ עֹל תּוֹרָה
נוֹתְנִין עָלָיו עֹל מַלְכוּת וְעֹל דֶּרֶךְ אֶרֶץ.

RABBI N'CHUNIA ben Hakana[20] says:
If you take on the yoke of Torah, you will be spared the yoke of the State and the yoke of earning a living.[21]
But if you throw off the yoke of Torah, you will have to bear the yoke of the State and the yoke of earning a living.

the yoke of Torah—Taking on the yoke of Torah enables us to bear the afflictions of life; to the extent that we do, we lighten our burdens. Our strength is ultimately spiritual. (CS)

--- Torah has the power to change our work, to lift it beyond the mere struggle for existence. (CS)

the yoke of the State—This probably refers to the ordinary burdens of citizenship. (CS)

the yoke of Torah—The discipline of study, attendance upon sages, diligence in carrying out Mitzvot, avoidance of transgression. (Aknin)

--- Making one's study of Torah primary and one's other needs secondary. (Rabbi Jonah ben Abraham)

one who throws off the yoke of Torah—Refusal to submit to it, by one who acknowledges its divine origin. (Maimonides)

Where Torah is Given

1. The Torah was given in fire,
The Torah was given in water,
The Torah was given in wilderness.
In fire: And Mount Sinai was wrapped in smoke... (Exodus 19:18)
In water: The clouds dropped water... (Judges 5:4)
In wilderness: And the Eternal One spoke to Moses in the wilderness of Sinai... (Numbers 1:1)
And why?
As these three are a free gift to all who dwell on earth,
So are the words of Torah a free gift,
as it is said (Isaiah 55:1),
Ho, every one who thirsts, come to the waters,
and the one who has no money, come, buy and eat!
Come buy wine and milk

without money and without cost.

•

Another interpretation: "in the wilderness of Sinai... "—
Make yourself free as the wilderness: and acquire wisdom and Torah. (Midrsah Numbers Rabbah, B'midbar, 1:7)

2. The Torah was given in public, in the open, in a place belonging to none. Had it been given in Israel, the nations could have said: "We have no portion in it." Therefore was it given in the wilderness, in public, in the open, in a place belonging to none. Whoever wants to receive it can come and receive it. (Midrsah Mechilta, Bachodesh, Yitro, 1)

3. Why was the Torah given in the desert? To teach you that those who do not make themselves free to all as the desert[22] are not worthy to receive the Torah.

And as the wilderness has no limit, so the words of Torah have no limit, as it is said (Job 11:9), *Its measure is larger than the earth and broader than the sea.*

And as the words of the Torah are without limit, so is their reward without limit, as it says (Psalm 31:19), *How great is Your goodness You have laid up for those who revere You.* (Midrash Pesikta de Rav Kahana 107a)

Avot 3:6[23]

RABBI CHALAFTA[24] of K'far Chananiah says:

When ten sit and occupy themselves with Torah, the Shechinah abiides with them, as it is said (Psalm 82:1), *God stands in the congregation of God.*

And how do we know this even of five? For it is said (Amos 9:6), *He has founded his group upon the earth.*

And how do we know this even of three? For it is said (Psalm 82:1), *God judges among the judges.*

And how do we know this even of two? For it is said (Malachi 3.:6), *Then those who feared God spoke to one another, and God hearkened and heard.*

And how do we know this even of one? For it is said (Exodus 20:24), *In every place where I cause My name to be remembered I will come to you and bless you.*

רַבִּי חֲלַפְתָּא, אִישׁ כְּפַר חֲנַנְיָה, אוֹמֵר:
עֲשָׂרָה שֶׁיּוֹשְׁבִין וְעוֹסְקִין בַּתּוֹרָה,
שְׁכִינָה שְׁרוּיָה בֵּינֵיהֶם, שֶׁנֶּאֱמַר:

אֱלֹהִים נִצָּב בַּעֲדַת־אֵל.

וּמִנַּיִן אֲפִילוּ חֲמִשָּׁה? שֶׁנֶּאֱמַר:

וַאֲגֻדָּתוֹ עַל־אֶרֶץ יְסָדָהּ.

וּמִנַּיִן אֲפִילוּ שְׁלֹשָׁה? שֶׁנֶּאֱמַר:

בְּקֶרֶב אֱלֹהִים יִשְׁפֹּט.

וּמִנַּיִן אֲפִילוּ שְׁנַיִם? שֶׁנֶּאֱמַר:

אָז נִדְבְּרוּ יִרְאֵי יְהוָה אִישׁ אֶת־רֵעֵהוּ,
וַיַּקְשֵׁב יהוה וַיִּשְׁמָע,

וּמִנַּיִן אֲפִילוּ אֶחָד? שֶׁנֶּאֱמַר:

בְּכָל־הַמָּקוֹם אֲשֶׁר אַזְכִּיר אֶת־שְׁמִי
אָבוֹא אֵלֶיךָ וּבֵרַכְתִּיךָ.

ten—A group of ten is called a "congregation." (Vitry) [In numbers 14:27 the 12 spies, minus Joshua and Caleb, are called עדה, *eidah*, "congregation." Hence, ultimately, "Minyan," the quorum of ten required for public prayer. See Talmud Megillah 23b. (CS)]

N.B.: The point of the lesson is not in the fact of the divine presence, for that is assumed, but in the haggadic interpretation which finds scripture proof for that unquestioned truth. (TH)

five—אגדה, *Agudah*, the word for "group," is related to the verb אגד, *agad*, "gather," as in the expression, "when a man gathers into one of his hands." Since a hand has five fingers, the sum of these fingers makes a group. (Maimonides)

three—The minimum numbers of judges in a court is [ordinarily] three. (Rabbi Jonah ben Abraham)

Avot 3:7[25]

רבי אֶלְעָזָר, אִישׁ בַּרְתּוֹתָא , אוֹמֵר:

תֶּן לוֹ מִשֶּׁלּוֹ, שֶׁאַתָּה וְשֶׁלְּךָ שֶׁלּוֹ.

וְכֵן בְּדָוִד הוּא אוֹמֵר:

כִּי־מִמְּךָ הַכֹּל, וּמִיָּדְךָ נָתַנּוּ לָךְ.

רבי שִׁמְעוֹן אוֹמֵר:

הַמְהַלֵּךְ בַּדֶּרֶךְ וְשׁוֹנֶה, וּמַפְסִיק

מִמִּשְׁנָתוֹ וְאוֹמֵר, מַה נָּאֶה אִילָן

זֶה, מַה נָּאֶה נִיר זֶה, מַעֲלִין

עָלָיו כְּאִלּוּ מִתְחַיֵּב בְּנַפְשׁוֹ.

RABBI ELAZAR[26] of Bartota says:
Give God what is God's, for you and yours belong to God. And so is it said by David (I Chronicles 29:14), *For all things come of You, and of Your own (hand) have we given You.*

RABBI SIMEON[27] says:
If you[28] walk along the road reviewing Torah and interrupt your study to say, "How beautiful this tree is, how beautiful this field is"—Scripture regards it as though you had destroyed yourself.[29]

Give God what is God's—Be ungrudging in giving charity. (Rabbi Jonah ben Abraham)

--- The sages have said, "If you have done much good, let it be little in your eyes; and do not say, 'I have done good out of what is mine'—say, rather, 'out of what was mercifully given to me.'" (Nachmias)

How beautiful this tree is—The traditional blessing recited upon seeing a natural beauty is: "We praise You, Eternal One, Sovereign of the universe, whose world is filled with beauty." It is but one of many blessings ordained to be recited on beholding and experiencing natural wonders. See *On the Doorposts of Your House*, pp. 27-28 [CCAR Press, 1995, Chaim Stern, editor] (CS)

destroyed yourself—Why such severe condemnation? Because by nature we are drawn to vain and useless things; if we do not resist, we will end up giving Torah short shrift and throwing off its yoke altogether. (Meiri)

--- The Torah is life to those who study it, so one who breaks away from study withdraws from life. We read in the Talmud (Avodah Zarah 3b): "What does the verse (Habakkuk 1:14) mean, *You make mortals as the fishes of the sea?* As fish die the moment they come on dry land, so human beings die the moment they withdraw from the words of the Torah." The passage gives one example among many, for its point is that people who walk along a road are easily distracted by the sights and sounds that surround them. (Duran)

Avot 3:8[30]

רַבִּי דוֹסְתַּאי בַּר יַנַּאי, מִשּׁוּם רַבִּי
מֵאִיר, אוֹמֵר:
כָּל־הַשּׁוֹכֵחַ דָּבָר אֶחָד מִמִּשְׁנָתוֹ
מַעֲלֶה עָלָיו הַכָּתוּב כְּאִלּוּ מִתְחַיֵּב
רַק הִשָּׁמֶר לְךָ וּשְׁמֹר נַפְשְׁךָ מְאֹד
בְּנַפְשׁוֹ, שֶׁנֶּאֱמַר: פֶּן־תִּשְׁכַּח
אֶת־הַדְּבָרִים אֲשֶׁר־רָאוּ עֵינֶיךָ.
יָכוֹל אֲפִילוּ תָּקְפָה עָלָיו מִשְׁנָתוֹ.
תַּלְמוּד לוֹמַר: וּפֶן־יָסוּרוּ מִלְּבָבְךָ
כָּל יְמֵי חַיֶּיךָ. הָא אֵינוֹ מִתְחַיֵּב בְּנַפְשׁוֹ
עַד שֶׁיֵּשֵׁב וִיסִירֵם מִלִּבּוֹ.

RABBI DOSTAI bar Yannai,[31] in the name of Rabbi Meir,[32] says:

Scripture regards it as though we have forfeited our lives[33] if we forget a single thing of what we have learned, as it is said (Deuteronomy 4:9): *Only be very careful to make certain, lest you forget the words that your eyes have seen.*

We might suppose this to be true even if our learning had become too difficult for us. Scripture therefore says (ibid.), *Lest they depart from your heart all the days of your life.* Thus [we learn that] we are not liable unless we deliberately remove [our learning] from our hearts.

deliberately remove—"Forsake Me a day, I will forsake you two." (Jerusalem Talmud Berachot 9.14)

--- Reviewing is the essence of learning. (Vitry, et al)

N.B.: Read together, 3:7–8 demand uninterrupted devotion to Torah. That is to say, at least, that when it is time for Torah, do not turn away from it. The passages are aimed at deliberate negation of Torah, which results in self–negation, for Torah is our Tree of Life, not to be forsaken. (after Neusner)

Avot 3:9[34]

רַבִּי חֲנִינָא בֶּן דּוֹסָא אוֹמֵר:
כָּל־שֶׁיִּרְאַת חֶטְאוֹ קוֹדֶמֶת לְחָכְמָתוֹ,
חָכְמָתוֹ מִתְקַיֶּמֶת. וְכָל־שֶׁחָכְמָתוֹ
קוֹדֶמֶת לְיִרְאַת חֶטְאוֹ, אֵין חָכְמָתוֹ
מִתְקַיֶּמֶת.
הוּא הָיָה אוֹמֵר: כָּל־שֶׁמַּעֲשָׂיו מְרֻבִּין
מֵחָכְמָתוֹ, חָכְמָתוֹ מִתְקַיֶּמֶת.
וְכָל־שֶׁחָכְמָתוֹ מְרֻבִּין מִמַּעֲשָׂיו,
אֵין חָכְמָתוֹ מִתְקַיֶּמֶת.

RABBI CHANINA ben Dosa[35] says: If you fear sin more than you covet wisdom, you will acquire enduring wisdom. But if you covet wisdom more than you fear sin, you will not acquire enduring wisdom.[36]

He would say: If your deeds are greater than your wisdom, you will acquire enduring wisdom. But if your wisdom is greater than your deeds, you will not acquire enduring wisdom.

fear of sin ... wisdom—Wisdom may be understood as "skill," "mastery of technique," "science." The passage thus construed becomes a teaching that morality should inform skill, a warning against the use of "wisdom" for destructive purposes, and praise for its constructive use. (CS)

--- Rabbi Yochanan ben Zakkai was asked, "The wise who fear sin, what are they like?" He replied, "Like artisans with the tools of their craft in hand." They then asked, "The wise who do not fear sin, what are they like?" He replied, "Like artisans without the tools of their craft in hand." "And what of they who fear sin but are not wise?" He replied, "They may not be artisans, and yet the tools of the craft are in their hands." (ARN)

--- This 'before' cannot mean precedence in time, since without wisdom, one cannot fear sin.[37] We have already learned (2:5) that "A boor does not fear sin." The precedence, therefore, is logical, that is, "One who in the first place is wise enough to fear sin, will then acquire additional wisdom." A comparison: People say, "Planning this house came before its building." Had there been no thought of a residence, the house would not have been built. What begins in thought ends in action. (Duran)

wisdom greater than deeds—These are people who do not carry out what they learn; therefore their knowledge of the Torah will not endure, for through lack of practice they will gradually forget. As we say in the Talmud (Sanhedrin 99a, ARN 23), "Who learns but does not practice is like one who sows but does not reap, like a woman who bears children and buries them." (Vitry)

--- How can we do more—or better—than we know? Scripture tells of Israel's acceptance of the Torah before knowing its details, as it is said (Exodus 24:7), ...and they said: *All that the Eternal One has spoken we will do and we will hear.*

103

Avot 3:10a[38]

הוּא הָיָה אוֹמֵר:

כָּל־שֶׁרוּחַ הַבְּרִיּוֹת נוֹחָה הֵימֶנּוּ,

רוּחַ הַמָּקוֹם נוֹחָה הֵימֶנּוּ.

וְכָל־שֶׁאֵין רוּחַ הַבְּרִיּוֹת נוֹחָה הֵימֶנּוּ,

אֵין רוּחַ הַמָּקוֹם נוֹחָה הֵימֶנּוּ.

HE WOULD say:
If the hearts of others are at ease with you, God's[39] heart will be at ease with you. If the hearts of others are not at ease with you, God's heart will not be at ease with you.

at ease—If you please people you please God. Why? Because you add to the harmony that God intended for the creation. There are people in whose presence we feel a deep sense of ease. They have "presence" of a spiritual nature, or an abiding serenity, a spirit that emanates from within that touches all who encounter them. (CS)

the hearts of others—What matters here is not an outward show of favor, but how other people are made to feel deep within their hearts, where it cannot be seen. (see Meam Loez, Avoth, p. 147.) (CS)

--- This does not say "all other people," for it is impossible to please everyone; no one is acceptable to all others [nor need one be]. So Esther 10:3 says of Mordechai, esteemed by most of his brethren—not by all. (Nachmias)

--- You stand in relations of love and duty toward people and toward God; if then your spirit is tranquil because in these relations you leave nothing unfulfilled, this emanates from you and there is peace, not discord, and your partner in this relationship feels it too; —and vice versa. (TH) See Proverbs 3:3–4: *Let steadfast love and truth not leave you; ...write them on the tablet of your heart, and you will find divine and human grace and favor.*

Where is God?

Behold, I will stand before you there on the rock at Horeb. (Exodus 17:6) The Holy One said to Moses: In every place that you find a trace of human footsteps, there I am before you. (Midrash Mechilta, Vayassa, B'shalach, 6)

Avot 3:10b

רַבִּי דוֹסָא בֶּן הַרְכִּינָס אוֹמֵר:

שֵׁנָה שֶׁל שַׁחֲרִית,

וְיַיִן שֶׁל צָהֳרַיִם,

וְשִׂיחַת הַיְלָדִים,

וִישִׁיבַת בָּתֵּי־כְנֵסִיּוֹת שֶׁל עַמֵּי הָאָרֶץ,

מוֹצִיאִין אֶת־הָאָדָם מִן הָעוֹלָם.

RABBI DOSA ben Harkinas[40] says:
Late morning sleep,
midday wine,
children's chatter,
and attending the assemblies of the unlettered[41]
drive one out of the world.[42]

midday wine—Leading to neglect of Torah. See Ecclesiastes 10:16: *Woe unto the land whose king is a boy, and whose princes feast in the morning.* (ARN)

children's chatter—Prolonged talk with youths who waste their time at idle gatherings. (Vitry) [see Maimonides on 3:12]

assemblies of the unlettered—Do not sit down with those who loiter at street corners in the market place, when you could be learning Torah. (ARN)

The Voice of Jacob

The voice is the voice of Jacob, but the hands are the hands of Esau. (Genesis 27:22)

The nations of the world asked Abnimos[43] the Weaver of Words: "Will we able to defeat this nation Israel?"

In reply he told them:

"Go to their Houses of Study. If you can hear the voices of children chanting, you will know that you cannot overcome them. If there is silence, you will know that you will succeed.

"For it is written that their father said: *The voice is the voice of Jacob.* As long as the voice of Jacob can be heard in the House of Study, this people is safe from the hands of Esau." (Midrash Pesikta de Rav Kahana 121a; Midrash Lamentations Rabbah, Intro., 2)

Avot 3:11[44]

רַבִּי אֶלְעָזָר הַמּוֹדָעִי אוֹמֵר:
הַמְחַלֵּל אֶת־הַקֳּדָשִׁים,
וְהַמְבַזֶּה אֶת־הַמּוֹעֲדוֹת,
וְהַמַּלְבִּין פְּנֵי חֲבֵרוֹ בָּרַבִּים,
וְהַמֵּפֵר בְּרִיתוֹ שֶׁל אַבְרָהָם אָבִינוּ,
וְהַמְגַלֶּה פָנִים בַּתּוֹרָה שֶׁלֹּא כַהֲלָכָה,
אַף עַל פִּי שֶׁיֵּשׁ בְּיָדוֹ תּוֹרָה וּמַעֲשִׂים
טוֹבִים, אֵין לוֹ חֵלֶק לָעוֹלָם הַבָּא.

RABBI ELAZAR[45] the Modite says:
If you treat holy things with disrespect,
despise the festivals,
shame[46] your friend in public,
break the covenant of Abraham our Father,
or [brazenly] distort the meaning of the Torah[47]—
though you know Torah and perform good deeds, you will have no share in the world-to-come.

N.B.: We should hallow the commonplace; instead, we despise the sacred. (CS)

N.B.: The thread that runs through these condemned actions is the contempt one shows for sacred things—e.g., festivals, people in general, one's own people in particular, Torah tradition, etc.—in a specially pointed context: Israel's struggle to survive after the war against Rome. (Neusner)

N.B.: One does not commit the transgressions mentioned in this mishnah because of an overpowering impulse (as in the case, e.g., of eating forbidden foods or committing an unchaste act). The transgressions listed here arise out of a tendency toward heresy. (Meiri)

N.B.: This saying comes near to being a Pharisaic definition of heresy—not wrong thought (as in Christianity) but wrong action, separation of self from community, defiance of the authority that sets the accepted standard; but Pharisaism never persecuted its heretics, and if it affirmed that they had no part in the life hereafter, at least it did not cut short their life here. (TH)

despise the festivals—One who does not prepare festive meals for them, nor honors them by going to special expense, buying new clothes, special delicacies, etc. (Aknin)

shame your friend—"If you shame your friend in public, it is as though you have shed blood." (Talmud Baba Metzia 58b)

--- Better fling yourself into a fiery furnace than shame your friend in public. (Vitry)

break the covenant—a reference to circumcision; so one who "breaks the covenant" is in this context one who disdains circumcision as a sign of the covenant.

distort the meaning—"From the day the Temple was destroyed, nothing has remained for God in the world but the four cubits of Halachah." (Talmud Berachot 8a) From that it follows that to distort the Torah is to drain God's world of meaning.

Knowing and Doing

1. *...and do what is right in God's eyes...* (Exodus 15:26) That is, what is right in business, or in commerce. Thus you learn that one who conducts business and commerce in truth and faithfulness, and who delights the hearts of others[48] is regarded as having fulfilled the whole Torah. (Midrash Mechilta, Vayassa, B'shalach, v. 2, p. 96)

2. Rabbi Elazar said: What blessing did Moses say when he received the Torah? "Praised be...who has chosen the Torah and sanctified it, and who delights in those who fulfill it." He did not say, 'those who labor to learn it,' or, 'those who meditate on it,' but 'those who fulfill it.' You may say: "I have not learned the Torah, what am I to do?" God says: "All wisdom and all Torah is one easy thing: if you revere Me and fulfill the words of the Torah you have all wisdom and all Torah in your heart." (Midrash Deuteronomy Rabbah, B'rachah, 11:6)

Avot 3.12

רַבִּי יִשְׁמָעֵאל אוֹמֵר:
הֱוֵי קַל לָרֹאשׁ,
וְנוֹחַ לַתִּשְׁחֹרֶת,
וֶהֱוֵי מְקַבֵּל אֶת־כָּל־הָאָדָם בְּשִׂמְחָה.

RABBI ISHMAEL[49] says:
Be submissive to the government,
patient under oppression,[50]
and greet everyone with joy.

N.B.: Rabbi Ishmael may have said his words having the Bar Kochba war in mind (he opposed it), or (more narrowly) in view of the conflict within the Sanhedrin that resulted in power being shared by the two leaders, Rabbi Gamaliel and Rabbi Elazar ben Azariah (see Talmud Berachot 28a). (CS)

be submissive—The Hebrew of the first two clauses is vague enough to give rise to diverse interpretations. For example: "Be easy with your betters, affable to your inferiors." And: "Take your superiors lightly [with a grain of salt], and be cool to [the teachings of] the young." (CS)

greet everyone with joy—Do not think that avoidance of familiarity with the young (see 3:10 and commentary) means that you should greet the young with a scowl. On the contrary, you must receive every person—high and low, free or slave—with joy. This is even stronger than Shammai's statement (1:15), "Greet everyone with a cheerful countenance." (Maimonides)

N.B.: 3:9–12 carry the theme of Torah beyond learning to doing (9–10), and beyond knowing to holding on to what is holy in the past and present, refusing to despair of self, cult, people (11), and, finally, insisting that hope be tempered by endurance—surviving an oppressive state (12). (Neusner)

Avot 3:13

רַבִּי עֲקִיבָא אוֹמֵר:

RABBI AKIBA[51] says:

שְׂחוֹק וְקַלּוּת רֹאשׁ מַרְגִּילִין אֶת־הָאָדָם לְעֶרְוָה.

Japery and irreverence[52] lead one to lewdness.

מָסֹרֶת סְיָג לַתּוֹרָה,

Tradition is a fence[53] for the Torah.

מַעְשְׂרוֹת סְיָג לָעֹשֶׁר,

Tithes are a fence for wealth.

נְדָרִים סְיָג לַפְּרִישׁוּת,

Vows are a fence for abstinence.[54]

סְיָג לַחָכְמָה שְׁתִיקָה.

The fence for wisdom is silence.[55]

tradition—Some say this refers to the Oral Torah, which serves as a fence to the Written. (Nachmias)

vows—Make a fence around yourself (with vows) only when your Yetzer is too strong to control otherwise. (Rabbi Jonah ben Abraham)

--- "One who takes a vow is called a sinner even if he fulfills it." (Talmud Nedarim 77b). The Nazirite (Numbers 6) takes a vow, but is not wholly approved. (CS)

abstinence—As it is possible to abuse things that are permitted, so is it possible to sin by abstaining from the right use of these things—such as food, sex, and all else that God made and called "very good." We will be called to account for our abstinence from these permitted things. (Jerusalem Talmud Kiddushin 4:12, Talmud Nedarim 10a)

silence—Do not speak in the presence of those greater than you in wisdom. If you interrupt them, the distraction may keep you from learning what they have to teach. (after Rabbi Jonah ben Abraham)

--- When Mendel of Vorki was a guest in Kotzk, its rebbe asked him, "Where did you learn the art of silence?" His first impulse was to answer; then he thought more deeply and once again he practiced his art. (Buber, Or ha-Ganuz, p. 453)

--- "The wise know what they say, fools say what they know." (J.H. Caro, in Bunim, I, p. 314)

--- "Fools lose everything that's given to them." (Talmud Chagigah 4a) (see 4:1)

Avot 3:14[56]

הוּא הָיָה אוֹמֵר:

חָבִיב אָדָם, שֶׁנִּבְרָא בְצֶלֶם. חִבָּה

יְתֵרָה נוֹדַעַת לוֹ שֶׁנִּבְרָא

בְצֶלֶם, שֶׁנֶּאֱמַר: בְּצֶלֶם אֱלֹהִים עָשָׂה

אֶת־הָאָדָם.

חֲבִיבִין יִשְׂרָאֵל, שֶׁנִּקְרְאוּ בָנִים

לַמָּקוֹם. חִבָּה יְתֵרָה נוֹדַעַת לָהֶם

שֶׁנִּקְרְאוּ בָנִים לַמָּקוֹם, שֶׁנֶּאֱמַר:

בָּנִים אַתֶּם לַיהוה אֱלֹהֵיכֶם.

חֲבִיבִין יִשְׂרָאֵל, שֶׁנִּתַּן לָהֶם כְּלִי

חֶמְדָּה. חִבָּה יְתֵרָה נוֹדַעַת לָהֶם שֶׁנִּתַּן

לָהֶם כְּלִי חֶמְדָּה שֶׁבּוֹ נִבְרָא הָעוֹלָם,

שֶׁנֶּאֱמַר: כִּי לֶקַח טוֹב נָתַתִּי לָכֶם,

תּוֹרָתִי; אַל־תַּעֲזֹבוּ.

HE WOULD say:
Beloved is human kind, for we are created in the divine image.
Even greater was the love that made us aware that we are created in the divine image, as it is said (Genesis 9:6), *God made human kind in the divine image.*
Beloved are Israel, who are called children of the Omnipresent. Even greater was the love that made made them aware that they are called children of the Omnipresent, as it is said (Deuteronomy 14:1), *You are children of the Eternal, your God.*
Beloved are Israel, who have been given a precious instrument. Even greater was the love that made them aware that they had been given that precious instrument with which the world was created,[57] as it is said (Proverbs 4:2), *I have given you a good doctrine, My Torah; do not forsake it.*

the image—Rabbi Isaac ben Reuben said that this comes to teach that one dare not treat the human face disrespectfully. (Aknin)

--- "Image" does not mean physical likeness; it refers to the intelligence and understanding, and it distinguishes human kind from the beasts. (Nachmias)

made us aware—Making it known to us was God's way of showing additional love to humankind. I may do you a favor merely out of pity, without even bothering to let you know about it, because I regard you—the beneficiary—as my inferior. Not so here—God so loves us that God made our nature (and its origin) known to us. (Maimonides)

--- ...but it is an especial mark of God's love to His human children that they have been endowed with the consciousness of these Divine possibilities within them. (Hertz, p. 59)

--- "When the universe has crushed us we will still be nobler than that which kills us, because we know that we are dying, and of its victory the universe will know nothing." (Pascal, Pensées, No. 347)

N.B.: Akiba is saying: The Temple is gone, yet we still matter to God, and what we do continues to matter. (Neusner) (see 4:1, 4:7)

Avot 3:15

הַכֹּל צָפוּי, וְהָרְשׁוּת נְתוּנָה. ALL IS foreseen, yet free choice[58] is given.

וּבְטוֹב הָעוֹלָם נִדּוֹן. The world is judged as good.

וְהַכֹּל לְפִי רֹב הַמַּעֲשֶׂה. And all depends on which deeds are more numerous.

free choice—"Everything is in the hands of Heaven, except the fear of Heaven." (Talmud Berachot 33b)

--- *Therefore choose life* (Deuteronomy 30:19)—It would have been impossible to tell us to choose, had we no freedom of choice. (Vitry)

--- God created the *Yetzer*, and God created its remedy: Torah and repentance. (Meiri)

The world is judged as good—That is, we are given the benefit of the doubt. There is a presumption of innocence in the divine judgment, as there should be in human judgment. See, also, 1:16, and Talmud Avodah Zarah 3a, Midrash to Psalms 149.

--- "The Holy One, ever to be praised, does not search for faults in His creatures."

--- The Holy One, ever to be praised, judges the world with the attribute of mercy, and a person who is neither completely righteous not completely wicked is judged as righteous. That is what is meant by the verse (Exodus 34:6), *abounding in goodness.* (Duran)

And all depends—This continues the thought that the word is judged as good. That judgment, says Akiba, depends on what tips the scales—our good deeds or our transgressions. We may no longer use this imagery, and yet, on the whole, do we not agree? Akiba knew that "tipping the scales" is not a quantitative concept. The "weight" or quality of our deeds is relevant both to divine and human judgment. (CS)

Choice

Three things are under our control: mouth, hands, and feet. Three things are not under our control: eyes, ears, and nose. (Midrash Tanchuma, Tol'dot)

Avot 3:16

הוּא הָיָה אוֹמֵר:
הַכֹּל נָתוּן בָּעֵרָבוֹן, וּמְצוּדָה פְרוּסָה
עַל כָּל־הַחַיִּים.
הַחֲנוּת פְּתוּחָה,
וְהַחֶנְוָנִי מַקִּיף,
וְהַפִּנְקָס פָּתוּחַ,
וְהַיָּד כּוֹתֶבֶת.
וְכָל־הָרוֹצֶה לִלְווֹת, יָבֹא וְיִלְוֶה.
וְהַגַּבָּאִים מַחֲזִירִים תָּדִיר בְּכָל־יוֹם,
וְנִפְרָעִין מִן הָאָדָם, מִדַּעְתּוֹ וְשֶׁלֹּא
מִדַּעְתּוֹ, וְיֵשׁ לָהֶם עַל מַה שֶׁיִּסְמֹכוּ,
וְהַדִּין דִּין אֱמֶת. וְהַכֹּל מְתֻקָּן לַסְּעֻדָה.

HE WOULD say:

Everything is given on loan, and a net is spread over all the living.

The shop is open,

the owner extends credit,

the ledger lies open,

and the hand writes.

Whoever wishes, may come and borrow.

The collectors go around day in, day out, and collect whether one likes it or not. They can defend [the rightness of] what they do. The judgment is fair. And all is made ready for the feast.

N.B.: This passage asserts a trustworthiness in the divine, not a severity. (TH)

Everything is given on loan—We and our children are held responsible for whatever we receive in this world. Therefore, when we inherit from our parents, let us not think, "This wealth is my inheritance to do with as I please." The fact is that we own nothing, we receive it only on loan, and we will have to pay for it. A parable: You enter a city and find no one there. You walk into a house and there is a table set with food and drink. You lay into it with a will, thinking, "This is all mine." Do you suppose the owners will not return and demand payment for everything you eat? Where will you go, in order to avoid paying? (Rabbi Jonah ben Abraham) [see discussions on 5:8–9 about the Year of Release for the land.]

a net is spread—That is, the net of the Angel of Death. None can escape the day of death and the day of judgment. (Vitry)

The collectors—A figure of speech for death and other sufferings that are visited upon us. (Maimonides)

the feast—Just as when you come home you find readied for your feast only what you have taken the trouble to buy—meat, cheese, etc.—so shall souls find a feast prepared for them in the world–to–come, made up of what they have 'purchased' in this world. For some it will be bitter and, for some, sweet. (Meiri)

Avot 3:17

רַבִּי אֶלְעָזָר בֶּן עֲזַרְיָה אוֹמֵר:

אִם אֵין תּוֹרָה, אֵין דֶּרֶךְ אֶרֶץ;

אִם אֵין דֶּרֶךְ אֶרֶץ, אֵין תּוֹרָה.

אִם אֵין חָכְמָה, אֵין יִרְאָה;

אִם אֵין יִרְאָה, אֵין חָכְמָה.

אִם אֵין בִּינָה, אֵין דַּעַת;

אִם אֵין דַּעַת, אֵין בִּינָה.

אִם אֵין קֶמַח, אֵין תּוֹרָה;

אִם אֵין תּוֹרָה, אֵין קֶמַח.

RABBI ELAZAR ben Azariah[59] says:
Where there is no Torah, there is no right conduct;[60]
where there is no right conduct, there is no Torah.
Where there is no wisdom, there is no reverence;
where there is no reverence, there is no wisdom.
Where there is no understanding, there is no knowledge;
where there is no knowledge, there is no understanding.
Where there is no meal,[61] there is no Torah;
where there is no Torah, there is no meal.

N.B.: We have here a series of complementary contrasts—we're not to choose one side, not to deny any part of life or self. We need both. (Neusner)

N.B.: The inner and outer realms need each other. (TH)

Torah/derech eretz—Without the commandments of the Torah it is impossible to reach ethical perfection, even if by nature one is ideally suited for it. Similarly, if one has no natural inclination toward ethical conduct, the commandments of the Torah cannot bring one to such perfection. For the commandments put one on the right path only in a general way, and they are unable to provide for new and subtle problems which constantly require the guidance of ethics and morality. (Meiri)

knowledge/understanding—The knowledge in question is the inborn capability to acquire knowledge; understanding is what comes as a result of study and research. (Meiri)

Torah and the world's work—Some say this passage means that if everyone were studying Torah and no one attended to worldly chores, the world would perish—and vice versa. (Nachmias)

Beyond the Letter of the Law

1. Rabbi Yochanan said: Jerusalem was destroyed because people stood on their rights and would not go beyond the letter[62] of the law. (Talmud Baba Metzia 30b)

2. Mari bar Isak—his brother came from Bei Chozai after a long absence and said to him: "Give me my share of the inheritance." He replied: "I don't know you." They

came before Rav Chisda, who said: "He gave you the right answer, as it is said (Genesis 42:8), *Joseph recognized his brothers, but they did not recognize him.* So we know that he[63] went away without a beard and came back with one. Go bring witnesses that he is your brother." The man said in return: "I have witnesses but they're afraid of him, because he's a powerful man." So Rav Chisda said to Mari: "You will have to bring witnesses that this man is not your brother." "Is this the law?" he complained. "The burden of proof is on the one who makes the claim!" And Rav Chisda retorted: "This is how you and all who are like you are judged!" (Talmud Baba Metzia 39b)

3. You make your judgment, acquit the innocent, obligate the one in the wrong, and, seeing that a poor man owes money, pay it yourself, this is [the meaning of] (II Samuel 8:15), *...administered justice and equity.*[64] Justice to this one and Tzedakah to that one—returning the money due this one, and paying it yourself. (Talmud Sanhedrin 6b)

Avot 3:17

הוּא הָיָה אוֹמֵר:

כָּל־שֶׁחָכְמָתוֹ מְרֻבָּה מִמַּעֲשָׂיו, לְמָה הוּא דוֹמֶה? לְאִילָן שֶׁעֲנָפָיו מְרֻבִּין וְשָׁרָשָׁיו מֻעָטִין, וְהָרוּחַ בָּאָה וְעוֹקַרְתּוֹ וְהוֹפַכְתּוֹ עַל פָּנָיו, שֶׁנֶּאֱמַר: וְהָיָה כְּעַרְעָר בָּעֲרָבָה וְלֹא יִרְאֶה כִּי־יָבוֹא טוֹב, וְשָׁכַן חֲרֵרִים בַּמִּדְבָּר, אֶרֶץ מְלֵחָה וְלֹא תֵשֵׁב.

אֲבָל כָּל־שֶׁמַּעֲשָׂיו מְרֻבִּין מֵחָכְמָתוֹ, לְמָה הוּא דוֹמֶה? לְאִילָן שֶׁעֲנָפָיו מֻעָטִין וְשָׁרָשָׁיו מְרֻבִּין, שֶׁאֲפִילוּ כָּל־הָרוּחוֹת שֶׁבָּעוֹלָם בָּאוֹת וְנוֹשְׁבוֹת בּוֹ, אֵין מְזִיזוֹת אוֹתוֹ מִמְּקוֹמוֹ, שֶׁנֶּאֱמַר: וְהָיָה כְּעֵץ שָׁתוּל עַל־מָיִם, וְעַל־יוּבַל יְשַׁלַּח שָׁרָשָׁיו, וְלֹא יִרְא כִּי־יָבֹא חֹם; וְהָיָה עָלֵהוּ רַעֲנָן; וּבִשְׁנַת בַּצֹּרֶת לֹא יִדְאָג, וְלֹא יָמִישׁ מֵעֲשׂוֹת פֶּרִי.

He would say:[65] When our[66] wisdom is greater than our deeds—what are we like? A tree with many branches but few roots. The wind will blow and uproot it and throw it down, as it is said (Jeremiah 17:6), *He will be like a bush in the desert and not see when good comes, dwelling in the scorched places of the desert, in a barren, unpeopled land.*

But when our deeds are greater than our wisdom—what are we like? A tree with few branches but many roots. Were all the world's winds to come and whip it, they could not budge it, as it is said (Jeremiah 17:8), *He shall be like a tree planted near water, that spreads out its roots near a stream; he shall not be afraid when heat comes; his leaves will be green; in the year of drought he shall have no care, and shall not cease to yield fruit.*

Avot 3:18

רַבִּי אֶלְעָזָר חִסְמָא אוֹמֵר:
קִנִּין וּפִתְחֵי נִדָּה
הֵן הֵן גּוּפֵי הֲלָכוֹת.
תְּקוּפוֹת וְגִמַּטְרִיָאוֹת פַּרְפְּרָאוֹת
לַחָכְמָה.

RABBI ELAZAR[67] of Kisma says:
The laws of bird offerings[68] and the nullification of vows—these are the most central laws.[69]
Astronomical calculations[70] and gematria[71] are the periphery[72] of wisdom.

vows—The laws for the absolution of vows (in tractate Nedarim) rely upon a sage's good judgment. You take a vow referring to one set of conditions, which you think prevails. But you discover that the facts were not at the time as you supposed them to be. So your vow to begin with was never valid, having been based on a false perception of the facts. If, on the other hand, things *later* change and turn out not as you expected, your original vow is unaffected. A sage and only a sage can distinguish the one situation from the other. (Neusner)

gematria—"Satan has no power on Yom Kippur, because the numerical value of the letters השטן, *HaSaTaN*, is only 364." (Hertz, p. 55) His point is that the solar year has 365 days, so the remaining day is Yom Kippur, on which 'Satan has no power.' And see 4:10, commentary. (CS)

117

The following section supplements Pirké Avot, by adding passages from the rabbinic literature that either quote or tell about the sages of Avot.

3:1

Akavia ben Mehalalel

1. Akavia ben Mehalalel testified to four things. They said to him: "Akavia, concede these four things and we will appoint you Prefect[73] for Israel." He replied: "I would rather people called me a fool all my life than to have God see me as a villain for a single hour. Let no one be able to say that I changed my views to gain office." They put him under the ban, and under the ban he died, and the Court stoned his coffin.

Rabbi Judah said: "God forbid that Akavia should have been banned. No man in Israel was greater in wisdom and the fear of sin than Akavia ben Mehalalel." (Mishnah Eduyot 5.6–7)

2. As he was dying he said to his son: "My son, concede those four things that I used to uphold."

"Why didn't you concede them, then?"

"Because I heard them when they were the views of the majority, and they heard them from a majority. I held to my tradition and they held to theirs. But you have heard from an individual and they from a group, and it is better to let go the view of an individual in favor of the larger number."

"Commend me to your colleagues," his son said to him.

"I will not commend you."

"Have you found a fault in me?"

"No, but your deeds will draw you near, just as your deeds will estrange you." (Mishnah Eduyot 5:6-7)

3.2a

Rabbi Chananiah, Prefect of the Priests

1. Rabbi Chananiah, Prefect of the Priests,[74] says: If you place the words of the Torah on your heart, things like the fear of war and famine, the likelihood that you will fall victim to your passions, or become dependent on others will cease to worry you. Thus is it written in the Book of Psalms by David, king of Israel (Psalm 19:9), *God's precepts are just, delighting the mind...* If you do not do this, all these things will burden you. Thus is it written by Moses, our Teacher (Deuteronomy 28:46f.): *These will be signs and proofs against you and your offspring for all time.* (ARN 20; Midrash Seder Eliyahu Zuta 15)

3.2b

Rabbi Chananiah ben T'radion

1. Rabbi Elazar ben Perata and Rabbi Chananiah ben T'radion were imprisoned, and Elazar said to Chananiah: "You are fortunate that you were arrested on only one count. I have been arrested on five." Chananiah answered: "You are fortunate, for you will be set free. You engaged in the study of Torah and did deeds of loving kindness, while I did nothing but study Torah." Chananiah was following the teaching later enunciated by Rabbi Huna. He had said: "One who engages only in the study of Torah is like one who has no God."

Had Chananiah really not done deeds of loving kindness? Did not Rabbi Eliezer ben Jacob say: "Let no one put money in the almsbox unless a scholar like Rabbi Chananiah is its superintendent"?

They had trust in him, for he was trustworthy, but he did not practice charity himself.

But is it not taught that he said: "Since money dedicated as Purim money for the poor has got mixed up with the ordinary tzedakah money, I gave both to the poor, and I replenished the Purim money from my own money."

He did practice tzedakah, but not as much as he should have. (Talmud Avodah Zarah 17b)

3.3

Rabbi Simeon bar Yochai

1. Rabbi Aba said: In the old days everyone would select [which of his disciples would lead the next generation]. For example, Rabbi Yochanan ben Zakkai appointed Rabbi Eliezer and Rabbi Joshua. Then Rabbi Joshua appointed Rabbi Akiba. And Rabbi Akiba appointed Rabbi Meir and Rabbi Simeon [bar Yochai]. He said: "Let Rabbi Meir sit first." Rabbi Simeon turned pale, so Rabbi Akiba said: "Be content that your Creator and I recognize your powers."[75] (Jerusalem Talmud Sanhedrin 1:2)

2. Rabbi Simeon bar Yochai said: "Had I been at Sinai when Israel was given the Torah I would have begged the Holy One that people be created with two mouths, one for the study of Torah and one to take care of other needs."

He reconsidered and said: "The world can hardly bear the trouble that one mouth brings—what would it do if we had two!?" (Jerusalem Talmud Berachot 2:1)

3. Rabbi Judah, Rabbi Yosé, and Rabbi Simeon [bar Yochai] were talking once; Judah "the converts' son" was with them.

Rabbi Judah said: "This nation [Rome] has done many good things! They've built markets, bridges, bathhouses..."

Rabbi Yosé said nothing, but Rabbi Simeon bar Yochai spoke up: "They've done nothing except for their own benefit. They've set up whores in the marketplaces, the bathhouses are for their own recreation, and the bridges are for collecting tolls."

Judah "the converts' son" talked about this and the authorities heard. They decreed: "Judah praised us—let him be rewarded. Yosé kept quiet—let him be exiled to Sepphoris. Simeon spoke against us—let him be killed."

This was the time after the defeat of Bar Kochba, and the Roman rule of the Jews had grown ever more oppressive; Rabbi Simeon bar Yochai and his son were forced to hide to escape the decree of death. First they hid in the House of Study, where Simeon's wife daily brought them food and drink. After a while they realized that this was too dangerous, and took refuge in a cave. There they spent twelve years, sustained by a miracle: a carob tree grew for them, and a spring welled up for them. The hand of God upheld them as they immersed themselves in Torah.

The time came to leave the cave, and they looked about at the world they had not seen so long a time. Bar Yochai was surrounded by disciples. The sun dazzled his eyes. In the distance farmers could be seen tilling the soil, as though nothing had changed in all this time.

Turning to the men around him, Bar Yochai said: "Look. See how those people neglect eternal life for the needs of an hour."

All the scene before them was consumed by flames.

A voice from Heaven came to them:

"Have you come out in order to destroy my world? Go back to your cave!" (based on Talmud Shabbat 33b–34a; Midrash Genesis Rabbah 79)

4. We have learned: Rabbi Simeon bar Yochai says: "When we praise ourselves, we should speak in a low voice and when we dispraise ourselves, we should do it loudly. The former? When one makes the declaration of the tithe.[76] The latter? When one makes the declaration of the First Fruits.[77] (Talmud Sotah 32b)

5. *You are My witnesses, says the Eternal One, and I am God.* (Isaiah 43:12). Rabbi Simeon bar Yochai taught: "When you are My witnesses, I am the Eternal; and when you are not My witnesses, as one might say, I am not the Eternal." (Midrash Pesikta de Rav Kahana 102b)

6. Rabbi Yochanan said in the name of Rabbi Simeon bar Yochai: How do we know that it is a transgression to allow one's dead to go unburied overnight? Scripture says (Deuteronomy 21:23), *the body shall not remain overnight ... but you shall bury it the same day...*

To honor the dead one may delay the burial overnight. What is 'honoring the dead?' Letting people know [so that they can come to the funeral]; bringing eulogists; obtaining a coffin and shroud. (Talmud Sanhedrin 46b–47a)

7. Rabbi Simeon bar Yochai said: The Holy One hates people who enters their house—and needless to say the house of others—abruptly.[78] And I don't love them either.

Rav said: Never enter your town or your house without warning.

When Rabbi Yochanan went to visit Rabbi Chanina he would clear his throat, because of (Exodus 28:35), *So that his sound is heard when he comes.* (Midrash Leviticus Rabbah 21)

8. Rabbi Simeon ben Menasya said in the name of Rabbi Simeon bar Yochai: Beauty, strength, wealth, honor, wisdom, long life, and children are good for the righteous and good for the world.

These seven qualities that the sages attributed to the righteous were all fulfilled in Rabbi[79] and his sons.

3:5

Rabbi N'chunia ben Hakanah

1. Both when he entered and left the House of Study Rabbi N'chunia ben Hakanah would utter a brief prayer. People wondered: what was the reason for this prayer? He explained that he would pray upon entering that no one might go astray on his account, and upon leaving he would give thanks for his lot. (Berachot 28b)

2. His disciples asked Rabbi N'chunia ben Hakana: "What accounts for your longevity?" He answered: "I never accepted honor at another's expense; I never went to bed cursing a friend; I was generous with my money."

"I never accepted honor at another's expense"—like Rav Huna. One day he was carrying a rake when Rav Chana bar Hanilai came along and offered to carry it. He told him: "If at home you habitually carry your own tools, well and good; if not, I don't want to be honored at your expense."

"I never went to bed cursing a friend"—like Mar Zutra, who would say when going to bed: "I forgive anyone who may have done me an injury."

"I was generous with my money"—as Mar once said: "Job was a generous man, always seeing to it that the shopkeeper kept his change." (Talmud Megillah 28a)

3:7

Rabbi Elazar of Bartota

When the charity overseers caught a glimpse of Elazar of Bartota they would hide, for he would give them everything he had. [And, of course, they did not want him to impoverish himself.]

He was in the market one day to shop for his daughter's wedding, and the charity overseers sought to hide from him. He caught up with them and adjured them, saying: "What are you collecting for?" "The wedding of two orphans." "By the

Temple Service, their need is greater than my daughter's!" He took what came to hand and gave it away, leaving himself a single Zuz. He bought wheat with it and stored it. His wife later asked his daughter: "What did your father bring you?" "Whatever it is," she answered, "is stored away." She went to see, and found the barn so full of wheat that the door would not open. Going to the House of Study, his daughter told him: "Come see what the One who loves you has done for you!" "By the Temple Service!" he vowed. "This wheat is set aside [for charity], and your share in it is no more than that of one of the paupers of Israel!" (Talmud Ta'anit 24a)[80]

3:8

Rabbi Dostai bar Yannai

1. Rabbi Dostai son of Rabbi Yannai expounded: Come and see that the way of the Holy One is not like the way of flesh and blood. If I bring an expensive gift to the king, it may or may not be accepted. And if you argue that it will be accepted, I may or may not be received by the king. The Holy One is not like that: one who gives [as little as] a penny to a poor person gains entry to the presence of the Shechinah, as it is said (Psalm 17:15), *As for me, I will behold Your face in righteousness;*[81] *when I awake I shall be satisfied with beholding Your form.*

2. Rabbi Isaac said: "Why don't the fruit of Genissar grow in Jerusalem? So that pilgrims might not say, 'It would have been enough to have gone up for the fruits of Genissar alone'—for then the pilgrimage would not have been made for its own sake."

Rabbi Dostai bar Yannai said a similar thing: "Why are the hot springs of Tiberias not found in Jerusalem? So that pilgrims might not say, 'It would have been enough to have gone up for the hot springs alone'—for then the pilgrimage would not have been made for its own sake." (Talmud Pesachim 8b)

3:8

Rabbi Meir

1. Rabbi Acha bar Chanina said: "God knows that none of his generation equalled Rabbi Meir. Why then did the Halachah not follow his view? Because his colleagues could not follow his reasoning. He would argue persuasively that the unclean was clean, then argue just as persuasively that the clean was unclean."

They taught: His name was not Rabbi Meir, but Rabbi N'horai. Why then was he called Rabbi Meir? Because he enlightened[82] the Sages in the Halachah. (Talmud Eruvin 13b)

2. Rabbi Yochanan said: Rabbi Meir's lectures consisted of Halachah, Agadah, and fables in equal parts. And of his 300 fox fables we have only one:

The parents have eaten sour grapes and the children's teeth are set on edge (Jeremiah 31:28).

A fox once said to a wolf: "Go into the Jewish Quarter on the eve of Shabbat and help them prepare the feast. Then you'll be able to eat with them on Shabbat."

When he tried to enter they fell upon him with sticks. He came to kill the fox, who said: "They only beat you because of your father: once, when he was helping them prepare the meal, he ate all the good parts."

"They beat me because of my father?" asked the wolf.

"Certainly," said the fox. Isn't it said, *"The parents have eaten sour grapes and the children's teeth are set on edge?"* But come with me and I'll show you where you can eat your fill."

So the wolf accompanied the fox to a well. A wooden bar was fixed to its rim, and to it a rope was attached. Tied to each end of the rope was a bucket. The fox got into the upper bucket and it sank down. The lower bucket then rose. The wolf shouted down to the fox: "What are you doing down there?" And the fox replied: "There's meat and cheese aplenty down here!" And, pointing to the moon's reflection in the water, he exclaimed: "Look at this!" It looked like a round of cheese.

The wolf said: "How can I get down there?"

"Get into the upper bucket."

As he got in, it descended, while the fox's bucket went up.

Now their positions were reversed, and the wolf called out: "How do I get up?"

The fox answered (Proverbs 11:8): *"The righteous are delivered from trouble, and the wicked takes their place.* And doesn't it say (Leviticus 19:36), *Just balances, just weights [shall you have]...?"* (Talmud Sanhedrin 38b–39a)

3. And others say the fable went this way...

A lion was about to devour a fox, who said to him: "How can you think you'll be satisfied with the likes of me? Come with me and I'll show you a fat man whom you can tear to pieces and eat your fill of."

There was a covered pit nearby; a man was sitting behind it and praying.

The lion said to the fox: "I fear this man's prayer; it may bring me down."

The fox said to him: "Neither you nor your son have anything to fear; the punishment will hit your grandson. Go sate your hunger. Your grandson's time is far off."

So the lion sprang and leaped—and fell into the pit.

The fox went over to the edge of the pit and gazed down upon the lion. "Didn't you say," cried the lion, "that the punishment would not fall on me but on my grandson?"

"Your grandfather must have sinned," replied the fox.

The lion lamented (Jeremiah 31:28), *"The fathers have eaten sour grapes and the children's teeth are set on edge."*

"You should have thought of that in the first place," said the fox. (T'shuvot Hag'onim, p. 362, Harkaby)

4. Rabbi Meir said this frequently: [God says:] "With all your heart and soul commit yourself to know My ways and show zeal to learn My Torah. Keep My Torah in your heart and the fear of Me before your eyes. Keep your mouth from sin(ful talk) and keep your distance from all iniquity. Then I will be with you wherever you go." (Talmud Berachot 17a)

5. One may not prepare wine and oil on the Sabbath for one who is sick. Rabbi Simeon ben Elazar said in Rabbi Meir's name: One may indeed do so.

Rabbi Meir once fell ill and we were going to prepare a remedy with wine and oil, but he did not permit it. We said to him: "Shall your words be annulled in your own lifetime?" He said to us: "When I take one view and my colleagues another, my heart has never given me leave to act contrary to their views." (Talmud Shabbat 134a)

6. We have learned: Rabbi Meir would say: "Don't invite a friend to dinner whom you know is unable to accept the invitation; never offer gifts knowing they will not be accepted ...; do not, with an empty flagon, say, 'Anoint yourself with oil' [when you know it will be refused]. But if it is done to honor someone in the sight of others, it is permitted." (Talmud Chulin 94a)

7. Rabbi Meir said: "One who consoles a friend after the twelve months of mourning is like a doctor who says to someone whose broken leg has healed of its own accord: 'Come to me and I will break your leg and heal it, so that you can see how well I can do it.'" (Talmud Moed Katan 21b)

8. Our sages taught: After the death of Rabbi Meir, Rabbi Judah said to his disciples: "Rabbi Meir's disciples do nothing but argue. They don't come to learn Torah, but to win debates. Do not allow them to enter."

One day Symmachus knocked and came in and began to debate with Rabbi Judah. Rabbi Judah lost his temper and said: "Didn't I tell you not to let Rabbi Meir's disciples in because they do nothing but argue!"

Rabbi Yosé spoke up: "It will be said, 'Meir died, Rabbi Judah lost his temper, Yosé kept quiet'—and what will become of the Torah!"[83] (Talmud Kiddushin 52b)

9. [When he was quoting teachings of Rabbi Meir] Rabbi [Judah the Prince] taught his son Simeon in the following manner: "Others say ...."

Simeon asked: "Who are these 'others,' whose waters we drink but whose names we never mention?"

He replied: "People who wanted to uproot your honor and the honor of your father's house."

Simeon said (Ecclesiastes 9:6), *"Their love and their hate, and their envy, too, is gone now."*

And his father replied (Psalms 9:7), *"The enemy has ceased to be, but the ruins are everlasting."*

"These words apply," said his son, "only if they really were enemies. It was not so with these sages."

Then Rabbi [relented and] taught: "They said in Rabbi Meir's name…"

Rava said: "Even Rabbi—because he was a humble man—taught, 'They said in Rabbi Meir's name.' But 'Rabbi Meir said' did not pass through his lips."[84] (Talmud Horayot 13b–14a)

11. Rabbah bar Rav Shela happened upon Elijah. He said to him: "What is the Holy One doing?" Elijah told him: "Reciting the Halachah taught by all the sages—but not Rabbi Meir's teaching." "Why not?" he asked him. Elijah explained: "Because he [Meir] learned Torah from Acher."[85] "And what of that?" he argued. "Rabbi Meir found a pomegranate; he ate its fruit and threw out the rind." Elijah then said: "Now God is saying: 'My son Meir says…'" (Talmud Chagigah 15b)

12. They said in Rabbi Meir's name: "We come into the world with clenched fists, as though to say: 'The whole world is mine to acquire.' We leave the world with hands wide open, as though to say: 'I have acquired nothing in this world.'" (Midrash Ecclesiastes Rabbah 5:21)

13. On a Sabbath afternoon, while he was at the house of Study, the two sons of Rabbi Meir died. Their mother laid them on a bed and covered them.

Upon his return home after the evening prayer, Meir asked for his sons. "They have gone to the House of Study," his wife Beruriah told him. "I was just there," said Meir, "but I did not see them." She simply said: "It is time for Havdalah."[86]

Meir took the wine and proclaimed the Havdalah. Then he said: "Where are the boys?" "No doubt," said she, "they will be home soon; meantime, eat your evening meal." He ate and gave thanks.[87]

Afterward, Beruriah began: "Rabbi, I must ask you a question. Some time ago, several jewels were given me for safekeeping. Now their owner has come and wants them back. What should I do?"

Meir was taken aback: "You know the law as well as I. What you hold in trust you must return on demand!"

"In spite of the law," she answered, "I would have kept them, had you not said this."

Beruriah then took Meir by the hand and led him to the room where his boys lay covered by a sheet.

He began to weep. Then he screamed: "My sons! My teachers! They brightened my face with their Torah!"

Beruriah said: "Rabbi, I have returned the jewels to their owner, just as you told me to."

Then Meir said: *The Eternal gives; the Eternal takes; praised be the name of the Eternal.* (Job 1:21) (Midrash Proverbs 31; Yalkut Shimoni 31)

14. *You are children of your Eternal God.* (Deuteronomy 14:1)
Rabbi Judah bar Ilai said: If you behave like children, you are called "children." If you do not behave like children, you are not called God's "children."
Rabbi Meir said: You are called "children," and nothing but '"children." Even though you are called "foolish," "untrustworthy," and "corrupt," (Jeremiah 4:22; Deuteronomy 32:20; Isaiah 1:4), in each instance you are called "children." And even after you have been repudiated (Hosea 1:10), you are yet again called "children." (Talmud Kiddushin 36a)[88]

15. *He has despised the word of the Eternal One.* (Numbers 15:31). Rabbi Meir said: This is the one who studies (Torah) but does not teach it to others. Rabbi Nathan said: This is the one who could study Torah, but does not. (Midrash Sifre Numbers, Shelach, 112)

3:9

Chanina ben Dosa

1. Every day a Divine Voice comes forth to say: The whole wide world is fed by My son Chanina's merit, and yet from one Sabbath eve to the next my son Chanina gets along on one Kav of carobs! (Talmud Ta'anit 24b)

2. Chanina ben Dosa and his wife lived in poverty. It was his way always to pray for others, not for himself.

A day came when Chanina's wife could stand no more: there was nothing in the house, and no money for the Sabbath. She said to her husband: "Must we always suffer?" "What do you want me to do?" he asked. She answered: "Pray on your own behalf for once."

Chanina obeyed her, and prayed that something be given them. His prayer was answered: a hand reached down from heaven and gave him a gold bar in the shape of a cylinder. It looked like a table–leg. Chanina and his wife rejoiced at this answer to their prayer. They would now have enough for many Sabbaths.

That night Chanina dreamed that he and his wife were in Paradise. They could see all the sages sitting at golden tables with three legs. Their table, however, had only two.

That morning Chanina told his wife about his dream. She said to him: "Do you really want all the others to have tables with three legs, while ours has only two?" "What do you want me to do?" he asked. "Pray that the gold table–leg be taken back," was her reply.

Chanina prayed again, and a hand reached down and retrieved the gold bar.

It is said: The second miracle was greater than the first. (Talmud Ta'anit 24b–25a)

3. At twilight one Sabbath eve, Rabbi Chanina ben Dosa found his daughter downcast. She told him: "I mistook a jar of vinegar for a jar of oil, and I kindled the Shabbat light with the vinegar." "What does it matter, daughter? The One who makes oil burn will make vinegar burn." They taught: It burned long enough for them to use it for kindling the Havdalah light.[89] (Ibid. 25a)

4. Rabbi Chanina ben Dosa was walking along the road one day, carrying a basket of salt on his head. It began to rain. He called out: "Ribono shel Olam,[90] all the world is at ease, and Chanina is in distress!" The rain stopped. When he got home he said: "Ribono shel Olam, all the world is in distress and Chanina is at ease!" The rain returned. (Talmud Ta'anit 24b)

5. Our sages taught: A snake was terrorizing people in a certain place, so they came and told it to Rabbi Chanina ben Dosa. "Show me his hole," said he. He put his heel into the hole. The snake bit him and died. He put it on his shoulder and brought it to the House of Study. "See, my children," he explained, "it's not the snake that kills, but sin." From then on they said: "Woe to the one who encounters a snake, and woe to the snake that encounters Rabbi Chanina ben Dosa!" (Talmud Berachot 33a)

6. They said of Rabbi Chanina ben Dosa that he would pray on behalf of the sick; afterward he would say: "This one shall live, that one shall die." "How do you know?" he was asked. He replied: "If the prayer flows, I know it is accepted; if not, I know it has failed." When Rabban Gamaliel's son was ill, he dispatched two sages to Rabbi Chanina ben Dosa to pray for mercy. He saw them coming and went to the upper story and prayed. Coming down, he said to them: "Go, the fever has broken." "Are you a prophet?" they exclaimed. "Neither a prophet nor the son of a prophet. But this is known to me: if my prayer flows, it is accepted; if not, it fails." They recorded the time, and on their return, Rabban Gamaliel said: "By God, you made no mistake. That very moment his fever broke and he asked for a drink of water!"

And once, the story goes, Rabbi Chanina ben Dosa went to learn Torah with Rabban Yochanan ben Zakkai, whose son fell ill. "Chanina, my son, pray for mercy on my behalf, and he will live!" said he. He put his head between his knees, prayed for mercy, and ben Zakkai's son lived. Rabban Yochanan ben Zakkai said: "Had ben Zakkai prayed all day long, it would not have helped." "Is Chanina greater than you, then?" asked his wife. He answered: "No, but he is like a servant before the king, while I am like a prince before the king." (Talmud Berachot 34b)

7. It happened that robbers stole Rabbi Chanina ben Dosa's donkey. They tethered it in a courtyard and left straw, barley, and water, but it would not eat nor drink. So they said: "What's the point of keeping it here to die and pollute the courtyard?" So they opened the door and let it go. The donkey ambled along until it found its way back to Rabbi Chanina. His son heard its braying and said: "Father, it sounds like

our animal!" He replied: "Son, open the door, it's perishing of hunger." He got up, opened the door for her and gave her straw, barley, and water. She ate and drank. That's why they said: "Just as the early tzaddikim were chasidim,[91] so were their animals." (ARN 8)

8. A man once left some chickens at the house of Rabbi Chanina ben Dosa. His wife found them and he told her not to eat their eggs. In time the eggs and chickens multiplied and created problems for them, so he sold them and bought some goats with the proceeds. The man who had left the chickens there once passed by and said to a friend: "Here's where I left my chickens." Rabbi Chanina heard this and said to him: "Have you any proof of this?" The man showed him some proof, whereupon Rabbi Chanina gave him the goats. (Talmud Ta'anit 25a)

9. When Rabbi Chanina ben Dosa died, that was the end of the men of deeds. (Talmud Sota 49a)

10. Our sages taught: The daughter of N'chunia the well-digger for pilgrims [to Jerusalem] fell into a deep pit.

They told Chanina ben Dosa what had happened.

In the first hour he said to them: "She is well."

In the second hour he said: "She is well."

In the third hour he said: "She has come out."

They asked her: "Who pulled you out?"

"An old man came along. He was leading a ram."

The people looked at Chanina and said to him: "Are you a prophet?"

"Neither a prophet nor the son of a prophet," replied Chanina. "I only thought: How can the very thing that this good man works on be the cause of his child's misfortune?"

Rabbi Acha said: "All the same, that well-digger's son died of thirst." (Talmud Baba Kamma 50a)

3:11

Rabbi Elazar the Modite

1. *If you will diligently hearken to the voice of your Eternal God, and do what is right in God's eyes...* (Exodus 15:26).

Rabbi Elazar the Modite said: *If you will diligently hearken*—the whole Torah is contained in this principle.

...and do what is right in God's eyes—in business. People are refreshed in spirit by an honest person, and such a person is regarded as one who fulfills the whole Torah. (Midrash Mechilta to Exodus 15)

2. *... make known to them the way in which they are to walk and the work they are to do.* (Exodus 18:20).

"the way"—that is, the study of Torah;

"the work"—that is, good deeds.

So says Rabbi Joshua.

Rabbi Elazar the Modite says:

"Make known to them"—the house of study;

"the way"—visiting the sick;

"they are to walk"—to bury the dead;

"in which"—deeds of loving kindness;

"and the work"—the letter of the law;

"[and the work] they are to do"—beyond the letter of the law. (Midrash Mechilta, Amalek, Yitro, 4)

3:12

Rabbi Ishmael

1. Our sages taught: *...and take no bribe.* (Exodus 23:8)—even verbal bribes are forbidden, for it does not say *...and take no money.*

What is a verbal bribe? Samuel was once traversing a bridge and a man came along and gave him his hand. "Why are you doing this?" he asked. When the man said: "I have a case coming up," he responded: "I am disqualified from being your judge." (K'tubot 105a)

2. A man brought the required one–sixtieth part of his flock's first shearing to Rabbi Ishmael son of Rabbi Elisha, who asked him where he came from. When the man told him, he asked: "And between there and here you found no priest to give this to?" "I have a case for you," the man said, "so I thought I would save myself trouble and bring the shearing to you." "You have disqualified me," said Rabbi Ishmael. And he refused to take the offering. He then referred the man to two sages who heard his case. When the man had gone he said: "He could have argued this way or that, had he wished." And he added: "Blast all who take bribes! I took nothing; and had I taken, I would have been within my rights, and look at what I'm doing. What then of those who take bribes?!" (Talmud K'tubot 105b)

3. This was Rabbi Ishmael's practice: When two came before him for judgment, one a gentile and the other a Jew, he would apply whichever system of law the gentile preferred—the law of Israel or the secular law. (Midrash Sifre Deuteronomy §10)

4. *You shall keep My statutes: through them a human being shall live.* (Leviticus 18:5) Rabbi Ishmael said: How can one know that [in a time of persecution] a Jew who is ordered, "Serve the idol and your life will be spared," should do it, and not be killed? Because it says: "through them a human being shall live," and not "through them a human being shall die."

If, however, one is told this in public, shall he obey? No, for it says (Leviticus 22.32), *You shall not profane My holy name, but I will be hallowed among the people of Israel.* If you sanctify My name, I will sanctify My name through you, even as Mishael, Chananiah, and Azariah did: for when all the world bowed down to the idol, they stood erect as palm trees. Of them the Tradition[92] says (Songs 7:8), *This, your standing up, is like a palm tree.* This day I am sanctified through them in the eyes of the nations who deny the Torah, this day I will punish their enemies, this day I will revive the dead; I am the Eternal; I punish, and I am faithful to reward. (Tosefta Shabbat 16:17)

5. Rabbi Yochanan said: What does the text mean (Psalm 68:12), *The Eternal utters; the bearers of tidings are a great host?*[93] Every utterance that issues from the Power[94] is divided into seventy languages.[95]

The School of Rabbi Ishmael taught: *My word is like fire...and like a hammer shattering rock* (Jeremiah 23:29). As this hammer creates innumerable sparks, so does every utterance that issues from the Holy One divide into seventy languages.

6. The School of Rabbi Ishmael taught: *My word is like fire...and like a hammer shattering rock* (Jeremiah 23:29). As a hammer creates innumerable sparks, so does a single text yield many meanings. ((Midrash Sanhedrin 34a)

7. Who are the Fathers of the World? Rabbi Ishmael and Rabbi Akiba. (Jerusalem Talmud Rosh Hashanah 1:5)

8. Rabbi Meir said: When I came [to learn Torah] before Rabbi Ishmael, he said to me: "What is your trade, my son?" "I am a scribe," I told him. "My son," he said, "be very careful in your work, for it is a work of Heaven. If you leave one letter out, or put in one letter too many, you find a whole world destroyed!" (Talmud Erubin 13a; Sota 20a)

9. We have found warrant for saying a blessing over food; whence do we derive it for the blessing [recited at the reading] of the Torah? Rabbi Ishmael said: It stands to reason:[96] If a blessing is said for temporal life, how much more should it be said for eternal life! If we say blessings over what is fleeting, should we not over what is eternal?[97] (Talmud Berachot 48b)

3:13

Rabbi Akiba

1. Resh Lakish said: *This is the book of the generations of Adam.* (Genesis 5:1). This teaches that the Holy One showed him each generation and its interpreters,[98] each generation and its sages. When he reached the generation of Rabbi Akiba, he rejoiced in his Torah and was grieved by his death. He said (Psalm 139:17), *How dear to me, O God, are Your friends.* (Talmud Sanhedrin 38b; SA 2.11:18.139)

2. Rabbi Akiba was a shepherd in Kalba Sabua's employ. When Kalba Sabua's daughter Rachel saw that he was modest yet dignified, she said to him: "If I marry you, will you go to the House of Study?" He agreed, and she betrothed herself to

him. Kalba Sabua discovered this, so he threw her out and disinherited her. She went and married Rabbi Akiba. In winter nights they would sleep in a granary, and he would pick the straw out of her hair. He said to her: "Were it within my power I'd give you a 'Jerusalem of Gold.'"[99] Elijah came in the form of a man and called to them from the entrance: "Let me have some straw—my wife is in labor and I have nothing on which she can lie down." Rabbi Akiba said to his wife: "Look at this man—he doesn't even have straw!" She said: "Go and learn in the House of Study." He went and sat there twelve years before Rabbi Eliezer and Rabbi Joshua.

After twelve years he returned with twelve thousand disciples. Everyone came out to greet him. His wife heard and she too went out. The neighbors said to her: "Borrow some clothes and dress yourself up." *"The righteous man knows the soul of his animal"* (Proverbs 12:10), she said in reply. When she got to him she threw herself down and began to kiss his feet. His disciples ran to drive her away. "Leave her be," he told them. "All that we have—you and I—is due to her."

Her father heard that a great man had come to town. He thought: "Let me go to him; perhaps he will annul my vow."[100] Rabbi Akiba said to him: "Had you known her husband would become a great man, would you have made that vow?"[101] He answered: "Even one chapter, even one Halachah!" "I am that man!" He threw himself down and kissed Rabbi Akiba's feet and gave him half his property. (Talmud K'tubot 62b-63a; Nedarim 50a)

3. How did Rabbi Akiba begin? They said: At age forty he had learned nothing. He stood once at the mouth of a well in Lod and said: "Who cut into this stone?" They said to him: "Akiba, have you never read that (Job 14:19) *Water cuts through stones?*—the water that falls on it constantly, day by day [has done it]." Akiba exclaimed: "Is my heart harder than stone? I will go and learn a chapter of Torah." He went to the schoolhouse and with his son began to read from a tablet. They held onto the top of the tablet, the two of them. He wrote out א-ב, *aleph-bet*, and learned it, א-ת, *aleph-tav*, and learned it, *Leviticus*, and learned it. He kept on learning until he had learned the entire Torah.

Then he went and sat before Rabbi Eliezer and Rabbi Joshua. He said to them: "Sages, open up the meaning of the mishnah to me." When they had taught him a single halachah he went away and pondered it, saying: "This Aleph: why was it written? This Bet: why was it written? This word: why was it said?" Then he returned and confounded them with his questions.

All those years Rabbi Akiba labored in Rabbi Eliezer's presence without encouragement. Then the time came when Rabbi Akiba contradicted Rabbi Eliezer, and Rabbi Joshua [with whom Rabbi Akiba had agreed] said to Rabbi Eliezer (Judges 9:38), *This people whom you have despised ... go now and do battle against them!*

They said: Before Rabbi Akiba left this world he owned silver and golden tables and golden steps for getting into his bed. His wife went out adorned with golden ornaments. His disciples reproached him: "Master, you shame us [before our wives] with what you do for her." He replied: "She suffered many afflictions with me for the sake of the Torah." (ARN 6)

4. Rabbi Akiba gave his wife a 'city of gold.'[102] When Rabban Gamaliel's wife saw her she became jealous and complained to her husband. He said to her: "And did you do for me what she did for him? She would go and sell her braids and give him the money so that he could study Torah!" (Jerusalem Talmud Shabbat 6:1)

5. We have learned: Rabbi Akiba said: "When I was an unlettered man,[103] I would say: 'Give me a scholar and I'll bite him like a donkey!'" His disciples said: "Like a dog, Master!" "No," he said, "a donkey breaks bones when it bites, a dog doesn't." (Talmud Pesachim 49b)

6. Rabbi Akiba—a manysided man. He was like a laborer who takes his sack out to the field. He finds wheat and puts it in, barley and puts it in, buckwheat too, beans the same, and greens as well. When he gets back he separates them all—wheat in its place, barley, buckwheat, beans and greens. That's what Rabbi Akiba did, making the Torah clear in all its forms. (ARN 19)

7. Rabbi Tarfon said to Rabbi Akiba: "Who parts from you parts from life." And he also said to him: "Akiba, it is of you that scripture says (Job 28:11), *the thing that is hid he brings forth to light.*" Rabbi Akiba brought to light things hidden from others. (Talmud Kiddushin 66b; ARN 6)

8. Once it happened that the Precentor[104] called on Rabbi Akiba to stand up and read the Torah, but he did not stand up. When they had left the synagogue he calmed his disciples, saying: "I assure you that it was not out of arrogance that I declined to stand up and read the Torah! Why, then? Because I had not prepared myself." His words astounded them. (Midrash Tanchuma, Yitro)

9. We have learned: Rabbi Judah said: "This was Rabbi Akiba's way: When he led the congregation in prayer, he would be brief, in order not to burden them; when he prayed by himself...one left him in this corner and returned to find him in that one. And why? Because of his bowings and prostrations." (Talmud Berachot 31a)

10. Our sages taught: Four entered the Pardes,[105] and these are they: Ben Azzai and Ben Zoma, Acher [Elisha ben Abuyah], and Rabbi Akiba. Rabbi Akiba said to them: "When you get to the pure crystal stones, do not say, Water! Water! For it is written (Psalm 101:7), *One who utters lies will not abide in My sight.*" Ben Azzai gazed and died. Concerning him Scripture says (Psalm 116:15), *Precious in the sight of the Eternal is the death of the righteous.* Ben Zoma gazed and went mad. Concerning him Scripture says (Proverbs 25:16), *If you have found honey, eat only what you need,*

lest you be sated with it and vomit. Acher hacked at the roots.[106] [Only] Rabbi Akiba went out in peace.

Rabbi Akiba went up in peace and came down in peace. Concerning him Scripture says (Songs 1:4), *Draw me, we will run together.* The ministering angels wanted to strike at Rabbi Akiba, too, but the Holy One said to them: "Let that man be; he is worthy of partaking in My glory." (Talmud Chagigah 14b, 15b)

11. Rabbi Yochanan Hasandlar pretended to be a peddler and kept passing the prison in which Rabbi Akiba was confined,[107] shouting: "Who wants needles? Who wants pins? Chalitzah without witnesses, what is the ruling?" Rabbi Akiba heard him through the window and said: "Have you any spindles? Have you...valid!" (Jerusalem Talmud Yebamot 2:5)

12. Rabbi Akiba would say: If your spirit is at peace with your deeds, that is a good sign for you; if not, it is a bad sign.[108] (Tosefta Berachot 3)

13. Two men are in the desert and one of them has a jug of water. If they share it, both will die; if only one of them drinks it, he will survive until he reaches a habitation. Ben Petura holds: Better they share it and die than that one should look upon the death of his companion. Rabbi Akiba came and taught: *That your brother may live with you* (Leviticus 25:36)—your life precedes that of your companion. (Talmud Baba Metzia 62a)

14. Akiba said: Rather make your Sabbath a weekday than need the help of your fellows. (Talmud Pesachim 112a)

15. One day, as Rabbi Akiba was walking through a graveyard, he came across a man bent low, carrying a load of wood like a beast of burden. Akiba said: "Why such heavy labor, my son? If you are a slave and suffering from abuse on that account, let me redeem you and set you free. And if you are free, but poor, let me help you."

To this the man replied: "Sir, you cannot help me. I am of the dead, not the living. It has been decreed that day after day I must gather wood, and this wood is then used to burn me."

"What could you have done to earn such a fate?"

The man replied: "In life I was a tax-collector. I favored the rich and was a scourge to the poor. And I seduced a betrothed virgin on the Day of Atonement."

"Even so," said Akiba, "is there nothing that can be done for you?"

"I know of nothing," said the man. But after a while he added: "I did hear that my punishment would be reduced if I had a son who could stand up in the congregation and praise God. And although I had no son at the time of my death, my wife was with child. I do not know whether she bore a boy or a girl, or whether the child lived. And if I did bear a son, who would teach him?"

Akiba asked his name and that of his wife, and left the suffering wretch. He then travelled from town to town asking for her. One day he came to a village where the wife was known. The villagers remembered her husband with horror. He had had a son, and the boy was still living there, in degradation. He had not been circumcised, and he had been taught nothing.

For forty days Akiba fasted, provoking a voice from Heaven to call out: "For this boy you fast?" Akiba answered: "Yes." First he taught the boy the alphabet, then Torah. And he taught him to stand up in the congregation to recite the praise of the Holy One: "Hallowed be the name of God..."[109]

Then the charcoal burner appeared to Akiba in a dream and said: "I have been redeemed from Gehenna." Akiba cried out in joy. He, too, sang God's praise (Psalm 135:13): *Your name is everlasting, Your remembrance for all generations.* (Midrash Seder Eliyahu Zuta, p. 22)

16. In the bitter time after the defeat of Bar Kochba, Hadrian emperor of Rome determined to make an end to the House of Israel. He issued decrees forbidding the practice of the essentials of faith, including the study of Torah.

Rabbi Akiba ben Joseph defied Hadrian's will and continued to teach in public.

One day Pappas ben Judah came to him and said: "How can you sit here teaching Torah? Have you no fear of death?"

Rabbi Akiba affirmed his intention to teach.

"There are times," Pappas insisted, "when one must bend with the wind."

Akiba was calm. "The people who call you wise, Pappas, don't know you. It is written (Deuteronomy 6): *Love your Eternal God with all your heart, with all your mind, with all your being.* It is not written that when enemies come to destroy us, we should help them.

"Hear this fable.

"A fox came to a riverbank and in the water he saw the fish swimming back and forth in great alarm. The fox asked: 'Friends, what is wrong? Why this agitation?' They answered: 'We are trying to escape our enemies, and the nets and traps they have set for us.' The fox put on his friendliest smile and said: 'Friends, have no fear. I will save you. Come onto the dry ground and stay with me. I will keep you safe, and together we will live a peaceful and happy life.'

"'Fox,' answered the fish, 'The people who call you wise don't know you. Do we look like fools? We're having enough trouble staying alive even in water, our natural element; how do you expect us to live on dry ground, where we cannot breathe? We will take our chances in the water.'

"We, too, Pappas, will do better taking our chances in our own element." (Talmud Berachot 61b)

17. Rabbi Judah said in the name of Rav:

When Moses climbed the mountain to receive the Torah, he found the Holy One sitting and fashioning little crowns for the Torah's letters.

Moses said: "Ribbono shel olam, for whose sake are you doing this?"

God replied: "Some day a man named Akiba ben Joseph will enter the world; he will discover heaps and heaps of teachings from every one of these little hooks."

Moses said: "Ruler of the world, let me see him."

"Turn around."

Moses turned around and found himself sitting in the eighth row of the House of Study where Akiba was teaching. He listened eagerly to the discussion; to his amazement and dismay, he did not understand it! Then a student asked Akiba how he knew a particular thing, and he answered: "This is a teaching given to Moses on Sinai."

And Moses was comforted.

Turning back, he said to the Holy One: "Ruler of the world, You have such a man as this, yet You give the Torah through me!"

God replied: "Be still; that is how I have ordained it."

Moses then said: "Ruler of the world, You have shown me his Torah; show me his reward."

"Turn around."

Moses turned around and saw Akiba's flayed flesh hanging in a butcher's shop. He turned back and said before God: "Ruler of the world, this is Torah and this its reward!?"

The Holy One said: "Be still; that is how I have ordained it." (Talmud Menachot 29b)

3.17

Rabbi Elazar ben Azariah

1. *The grasshopper rose up and covered the land of Egypt* (Exodus 8:2).

Rabbi Akiba says: "It was a single grasshopper that filled the land of Egypt."[110]

Rabbi Eliezer ben Azariah said to him: "Akiba! What are you doing here? Stop expounding midrash and stick to Nega'im and Oholot.[111] It was a single grasshopper, and it called the others and they came." (Midrash Sanhedrin 16b)

2. They came and said to him:[112] "Is our rabbi willing to become head of the Academy?"[113] In reply he said: "Let me consult my household." He went and consulted his wife, who said: "What if they depose you?" "People say," he answered, "You use a crystal cup today, and tomorrow it breaks." She went on to say: "You have no grey hairs." He was eighteen years old that day, and—wonder of wonders—his hair turned streaky grey! [That's why Elazar ben Azariah later said, "I am like a man of seventy."] (Talmud Berachot 27a-28b)

3. Rabbi Elazar ben Azariah said: "Lo, I am like a man of seventy." Though he had achieved power[114] he prolonged his days. Thus you learn that [ordinarily] power shortens one's days. (Jerusalem Talmud Berachot 1:6)

4. Rabbi Elazar ben Azariah said: Never say, "I can't eat pig, I can't wear kilayim."[115] Say, "I can, but my Divine Parent has decreed otherwise."

5. Who says, "I will sin and return [to God], sin and return," will not be given the opportunity to return; who says, "I will sin and the Day of Atonement will atone," [will find that] the Day of Atonement does not atone. For transgressions against God[116] the Day of Atonement atones; for transgressions against other human beings, the Day of Atonement does not atone, until one has made peace with the other.[117]

Thus did Rabbi Elazar ben Azariah expound: *You will be cleansed of all your sins before the Eternal* (Leviticus 16:30)—For transgressions against God the Day of Atonement atones; for transgressions against other human beings, the Day of Atonement does not atone, until one has made peace with the other. (Talmud Yoma 85b)

6. Rav Sheshet said in the name of Rabbi Elazar ben Azariah: One who desecrates the festivals is like an idolater, for it is said (Exodus 34:17), *You shall not make for yourself a molten god.* Just afterward it is said (ibid. 34:18), *Observe the Festival of Unleavened Bread.* (Talmud Pesachim 118a)

7. Rabbi Yochanan said: Earning one's daily bread is twice as hard as childbirth, for in connection with childbirth it is said (Genesis 3:16), *In pain shall you bear children,* while regarding food it is said, *By toil shall you eat of it.* [118]

And Rabbi Yochanan said: Getting sustenance is harder than being redeemed, for in connection with redemption it is written (Ibid. 38:16), *The angel who redeems me from all harm*—an angel only—while regarding sustenance it is written (Ibid. 38:15), *The God who watches over me.*

Rav Sheizvi said in the name of Rabbi Elazar ben Azariah: Sustenance is harder to get than the splitting of the Red Sea, for it is said (Psalms 136:25), *God gives bread to all the living*, and, alongside it (ibid.), *God cuts the Red Sea into pieces.* (Talmud Pesachim 118a)

3:18

Elazar of Kisma

Rabbi Yochanan ben Beroka and Rabbi Elazar of Kisma went one day to Peki'in, to greet the Elder, Rabbi Joshua.

He said to them: "What new thing did you learn in the House of Study today?"

In reply they said: "Master, we are your disciples and drink [only] of your waters."

"All very well! Yet one cannot attend the House of Study without hearing some new thing! Whose Shabbat was it?"

"That of Rabbi Elazar ben Azariah."

"And on what did he preach?"

"From the Section Hakhel."

"And what did he say?"

"*Gather the people, the men, the women, and the little ones* (Deuteronomy 31.12). If the men came to learn and the women to listen, what did the 'little ones' come for? So that those who brought them might be rewarded."

"You had this gem and were going to keep it from me!?" (Talmud Chagigah 3a; ARN 18)

•••••••

In Sum

In the time between the destruction of the Temple and the Bar Kochba defeat, the Sages affirm both our human insignificance and our grandeur, our misery and our hope, the uselessness of individual aspiration and the necessity of individual choice. They reflect on wisdom, on community, on ultimate questions, and they insist that we must and can make sense of our life. (CS)

You have to make sense of things. That means you must rely on your ability to determine matters which, in the end, can never be wholly and finally settled. The essentials of the Torah sometimes present us with doubts and confusion. Everything then depends on our own judgment. That is the ultimate irony. Akavia (see 3:1) would have been amazed. (Neusner)

•••••••

Notes

1 Dates Uncertain

2 See, also, 2:1, where Rabbi uses an almost identical sentence.

3 This Mishnah is divided in two parts here for the sake of clarity.

4 Ca. 20–70 CE.

5 That is, Deputy to the High Priest.

6 This Mishnah has been divided into two parts for the sake of clarity.

7 ?–135 CE. He was the father of Beruriah, wife of R. Meir.

8 On the passage as a whole, see also 3:3, 3:6, and see, also, Matthew 18:20, where Jesus is quoted as saying: "Where two or three are gathered in my name, there am I in the midst of them."

9 Literally, the Eternal (One), and so throughout this verse.

10 That is, God has laid his reward aside for him.

11 Neusner errs here: this is the second such passage; 1:18 is the first.

12 Simeon bar Yochai, 100–160 CE.

13 literally, at one table

14 The use of the quotation from Isaiah depends on a play of words on the Hebrew word מקום, makom—'a place'—since in rabbinic literature it is a name for God, who is 'The Place,' 'The Omnipresent.'

15 The Hebrew of this mishnah is in the singular.

16 Ca. 80–135 CE.

17 Or, minds. לב, lev, means heart, but [especially in biblical Hebrew] tends to be used for thought rather than feeling.

18 Or, "who turn their hearts to what is useless;" see Deuteronomy 6:7.

19 Literally, "...are liable for their own lives."; "...are guilty against themselves."

20 End of 1st C. CE. Dates uncertain.

21 דרך ארץ, derech eretz. See Note at 2:2.

22 Possibly, free of prejudices.

23 See, also, 3:2b, 3:3.

24 1st half of 2nd C. CE.

25 See, also, 2:4.

26 1st–2nd C. CE.

27 2nd half of 2nd C. CE.

28 The Hebrew of this passage is in the 3rd person.

29 Or, 'forfeited your life', 'are guilty against yourself.' See 3:4.

30 This passage continues the thought of its predecessor. The Hebrew is in the 3rd person singular.

31 Late 2nd C. CE.

32 Mid–2nd C. CE. (C.110-165/180 C.E. See 4:10)

33 See 3:7.

[34]The Hebrew of this passage is in the 3rd person singular.

[35]1st C. CE.

[36]See, also, 2:5, 3:17.

[37] This comment depends on a translating the text literally as "When your fear of sin comes before your wisdom."

[38]The Hebrew of this passage is in the 3rd person singular.

[39]מקום, makom, the Omnipresent.

[40]10–90 CE.

[41]Or, "synagogues of the ammei ha-aretz." See Note on am ha–aretz at 2:5.

[42]That is, These distractions drive one out of the world of Torah, the world of the spiritual life.

[99]Oinamaos of Gadara, a 2nd–C. CE philosopher.

[44]The Hebrew of this passage is in the 3rd person singular.

[45]65–135 CE.

[46]Literally, 'whiten the face of' (by causing the blood to drain).

[47]The law, from the Hebrew הלך, halach, 'to go.' Thus: The Way to Go.

[48]For this phrase, see Avot 3:10.

[49]Ca. 60–140 CE.

[50]Or, "Be quick to serve a superior." See 3:2a and relevant Note.

[51]Ca. 50–135 CE.

[52]Literally, 'lightheadedness.' We need safeguards to protect us against failure to live lives that serve God. (TH)

[53]See, also, 1:1.

[54]See, also, 4:18.

[55]See, also, 1:17.

[56]The 1st 2 Hebrew sentences of this passage are in the 3rd person singular.

[57]The Midrash (Genesis Rabbah 1:1) pictures God as consulting the Torah (the 'precious instrument') and using it as the blueprint for the Creation.

[58]Or, 'free will.'

[59]Ca. 70–130 CE.

[60]Or, 'worldly labor.' דרך ארץ, derech eretz, is also translated as good manners, civility, etc. See Note at 2:2.

[61]Or, 'food,' 'sustenance.' See, also, 2:2, 2:5, 4:10.

[62]Or, line.

[63]That is, Joseph.

[64]צדקה, Tzedakah, righteousness.

[65]See, also, 2:5, 3:9.

[66]Some of the Hebrew of this passage is in the 3rd person singular.

[67]Late 2nd C. CE.

[68]This refers to the purification offerings brought by women to the Temple (which at the time of the writing of this passage was no longer standing), and the complications arising therefrom (see Neusner).

[69]Hebrew הלכות, *Halachot*, plural of הלכה, *Halachah*. See Note at 3:11.

[70]That is, the calculation of the equinox.

[71]Use of the numerical value of the Hebrew letters to interpret text, and the like; also, 'geometry.'

[72]From Greek 'peripheria,' meaning, 'Periphery.' Or, 'desserts,' 'savories,' 'adornments.' The Hebrew פרפר, *Parpar* means 'butterfly,' which suggests 'evanescence,' hence, also: 'ephemera.'

[73]That is, Vice–President of the Sanhedrin.

[74]Deputy to the High Priest.

[75]but Rabbi Meir is older and therefore has priority.

[76]Deuteronomy 26:13.

[77]Ibid., 26:8.

[78]Without warning or invitation.

[79]Judah the Prince. See 2:1

[80] Most of us would think of the cobbler's children who go without shoes, and our admiration for Elazar's generosity is tempered by our wish that he had been a little better balanced.

[81]צדק, *tzedek* = righteousness; צדקה, *Tzedakah* = charity.

[82]מאיר, *me'ir* = he enlightens.

[83] That is, Torah is advanced by argument. José may have disagreed with Judah on whether Meir's disciples were sincere.

[84]The Talmud (ibid.) records a dispute between Rabban Simeon ben Gamaliel, Rabbi Meir, and Rabbi Natan over their prerogatives as leaders.

[85] Elisha ben Abuyah, who became an apostate and turncoat, See, further, 4:20 and the section on Elisha ben Abuyah.

[86]הבדלה, the ritual that distinguishes the holy time—Sabbath or Festival—that has come to an end, from the secular time that is beginning. See *On the Doorposts of Your House*, p.50 (CCAR Press, 1995, Chaim Stern, editor).

[87] That is, he recited the Thanksgiving after Meals. See *On the Doorposts of Your House*, p.9 (CCAR Press, 1995, Chaim Stern, editor).

[88] That is, God—your Divine Parent—continues to cherish you.

[89] See Note 54, above.

[90]רבונו של עולם, Master (Ruler) of the World.

[91]חסיד, *chasid* = loyal, pious, saintly; צדיק, *tzaddik* =a saint, a righteous person.

[92]That is, כתובים, *K'tuvim*, 'Writings,' the third section of the Hebrew Bible.

[93]bearers of tidings = the women who bring tidings, news.

[94]One of the many names for God in rabbinic literature.

⁹⁵70 is the rabbinic convention for all the human languages and nations.

⁹⁶It is an inference from minor to major.

⁹⁷ Literally, "over what gives eternal life."

⁹⁸In the Hebrew, a play on words: דור דור ודורשיו, *dor dor v'dor–shav.*

⁹⁹An ornament, called also "City of Gold."

¹⁰⁰Wherein he had disinherited his daughter.

¹⁰¹ See Avot 3:18 and Comment.

¹⁰²See No. 2, above.

¹⁰³עם הארץ, *am ha–aretz,* literally, [one of] the people of the land, the masses, the folk, the peasantry.

¹⁰⁴the leader or arranger of the worship service.

¹⁰⁵the Grove of mystical experience [פרדס, *pardes,·*Paradise]

¹⁰⁶ of the faith: he became an apostate.

¹⁰⁷By the Romans, after the Bar Kochba uprising, 135 CE.

¹⁰⁸See Avot 3:10.

¹⁰⁹*Yitgadal v'yitkadash,* the first words of the Kaddish, the prayer for the dead.

¹¹⁰The Hebrew for grasshopper is in the singular.

¹¹¹That is, "Akiba, you are a master of Halachah, not of Agadah."

¹¹²Rabbi Elazar ben Azariah.

¹¹³To replace Rabban Simeon ben Gamaliel, after his long dispute with Rabbi Joshua, in which he had conducted himself with arrogance.

¹¹⁴Or, authority, eminence, greatness.

¹¹⁵Clothes made of two materials, such as flax and wool. See Leviticus 19:19.

¹¹⁶Hebrew מקום, *makom,* [the] 'Place,' one of the many rabbinic names for God.

¹¹⁷That is, until there is a reconciliation based on restitution or making right the wrong done the other.

¹¹⁸The Hebrew has, for the first, בעצב, *b'etzev,* and, for the second, בעצבון, *b'itzavon.* The second is taken as more intensive.

Avot 4

A Note

This chapter follows the Bar Kochba war—a tremendous defeat, involving the disappointment of messianic hopes, the loss of Jerusalem, enormous loss of life, chaos, despair. The rabbis had to reconstruct their world, maintaining their ties with the past while creating a structure for the future (hence the redaction of the Mishnah). Their most important achievement was to survive while refusing to give up hope and faith, despite the death of millions. In the aftermath of their holocaust, they kept going. The sages cited in chapter 4 date from ca. 150–250 CE, the time of the compilation of Avot, a time when Babylonian Jewry had begun its rise, and the Mishnah was already in existence. (Neusner)

●●●●●●

Additional readings on the sages whose sayings are featured in this chapter begin on page 181.

Avot 4:1

בֶּן זוֹמָא אוֹמֵר:

אֵיזֶהוּ חָכָם? הַלּוֹמֵד מִכָּל־אָדָם,

שֶׁנֶּאֱמַר: מִכָּל־מְלַמְּדַי הִשְׂכַּלְתִּי.

אֵיזֶהוּ גִבּוֹר? הַכּוֹבֵשׁ אֶת־יִצְרוֹ,

שֶׁנֶּאֱמַר: טוֹב אֶרֶךְ אַפַּיִם מִגִּבּוֹר,

וּמֹשֵׁל בְּרוּחוֹ מִלֹּכֵד עִיר.

אֵיזֶהוּ עָשִׁיר? הַשָּׂמֵחַ בְּחֶלְקוֹ,

שֶׁנֶּאֱמַר: יְגִיעַ כַּפֶּיךָ כִּי תֹאכֵל,

אַשְׁרֶיךָ וְטוֹב לָךְ.

אֵיזֶהוּ מְכֻבָּד? הַמְכַבֵּד אֶת־הַבְּרִיּוֹת,

שֶׁנֶּאֱמַר: כִּי־מְכַבְּדַי אֲכַבֵּד, וּבֹזַי יֵקָלּוּ.

BEN ZOMA[1] says:
Who is wise? One who learns from every person, as it is said (Psalm 119:99), *From all my teachers I have gained understanding.*[2]
Who is strong? One who shows self-control,[3] as it is said (Proverbs 16:32), *One slow to anger is better than a hero,*[4] *and one who shows self-control than one who takes a city.*
Who is rich? One who is contented with life's portion, as it is said (Psalm 128:2), *When you eat what you have worked for, happy are you, fortunate your lot.* (*Happy are you*—in this world; *fortunate your lot*—in the world–to–come.)
Who is respected? One who respects others,[5] as it is said (I Samuel 2:30), *For those who respect Me I will respect, and those who despise Me will be held in contempt.*

wise—If you knew a great deal but disdained to increase your knowledge, you would be a fool. If you were ignorant but yearned to increase your wisdom, you would deserve to be called wise. (Rabbi Jonah ben Abraham)
--- "Who is wise? One who foresees the consequences of things." (Talmud Tamid 32a)
--- "Fortunate the generation in which the elder listens to the younger." (Talmud Rosh Hashanah 25b)
--- One day the rebbe of Zanz invited three men into his house. To each he put the same question: "Tell me what you would do if you found a purse full of coins." "If I knew the owner," replied the first, "I would return it without a moment's delay." The rebbe dismissed him, saying, "You are a fool." The second said, "I'm not fool enough to give up a purse full of money if it comes my way." The rebbe dismissed him, saying, "You are a scoundrel." And to the same question, the third man answered, "Rebbe, how can I know until I find it? If my Yetzer gets the better of me, God forbid, I will keep it. If, as I hope, I will be strong enough to overcome it, I will try to

return it to its rightful owner." "Your words are good!" the rebbe exclaimed. "You are truly wise!" (See Buber, *Or ha-Ganuz*, p. 386)

who learns from everyone—Including inferiors. (Vitry)

strong—And some say, strong is the one who turns an enemy into a friend. (ARN)

--- The wise know themselves to be unknowing.

The strong know themselves to be weak.

The rich know themselves to be poor in days.

The respected fear they will be unmasked. (CS)

Avot 4:2

בֶּן עַזַּאי אוֹמֵר:

הֱוֵי רָץ לְמִצְוָה קַלָּה כְּבַחֲמוּרָה;

שֶׁמִּצְוָה גוֹרֶרֶת מִצְוָה, וַעֲבֵרָה

גוֹרֶרֶת עֲבֵרָה, שֶׁשְּׂכַר מִצְוָה

מִצְוָה, וּשְׂכַר עֲבֵרָה עֲבֵרָה.

BEN AZZAI[6] says:
Run to do a minor Mitzvah as [though it were] a major,[7] and flee from transgression. For one good deed[8] leads to another, and one transgression leads to another; and the reward of one good deed is another, while the punishment of one transgression is another.

run to do—If you have fulfilled one commandment and do not regret it, you will in the end be led to fulfill many; and if you commit one transgression and do not regret it, it will lead in the end to many. (ARN)

--- *I will run on the path of Your commandments, for You broaden my heart.* (Psalm 119:32)

--- If you commit a transgression, do not be distressed by that one, but by the one coming after it; if you have done a good deed, do not rejoice in that one, but in the one coming after it. (ARNB)

a minor mitzvah—One that seems minor to you. (Vitry)

one good deed leads to another—When I have done one thing I naturally find it easier to do the next, though that one, in comparison with the first, may actually be more difficult. One grows accustomed to carrying out the commandments, and develops the habit of doing them. (Rabbi Jonah ben Abraham)

--- The reward for doing a minor Mitzvah is the opportunity of doing an even greater one. (Vitry)

--- Some interpret this as follows: The reward for doing a good deed (Mitzvah) is in having done it. (Nachmias)

"Minor: and "major" Mitzvah—See the discussion at 2:1.

Avot 4:3

הוּא הָיָה אוֹמֵר:
אַל תְּהִי בָז לְכָל־אָדָם,
וְאַל תְּהִי מַפְלִיג לְכָל־דָּבָר,
שֶׁאֵין לְךָ אָדָם שֶׁאֵין לוֹ שָׁעָה,
וְאֵין לְךָ דָּבָר שֶׁאֵין לוֹ מָקוֹם.

HE WOULD say:
Despise no one,
and regard nothing as impossible,
for you will find no one whose hour does not come,
and not a thing that does not have its place.

Despise no one—4:3 follows logically from 4:2. In God's world no one is nothing, and no thing is useless. What we do matters. In a time of reconstruction, wise words. (Neusner)

--- It was the favorite saying of the sages of Yavneh: I am a creature of God and you are a creature of God. My work may be in the city, yours is perhaps in the field. As you rise early to your work, so I rise early to my work. As you do not claim that your work is superior to mine, so do I not claim that my work is superior to yours. And should one say, 'I do more important work and the other does less important work,' we have already learned: "More or less, it does not matter, so long as the heart is inclined toward Heaven." (Talmud Berachot 17a, quoting 5a)

--- "Just as I need the trees that bear fruit, so do I need the barren trees." (Midrash Exodus Rabbah 7:4)

All the World We Have

The Holy One created Adam, took him on a tour of the Garden of Eden, and said to him: "See how pleasant are My works, how praiseworthy! And all this is for you. Take care, then, not to misbehave and ruin My world, for if you do, no one will come after you to mend it. (Midrash Kohelet Rabbah 9)

Half a Loaf

Rabbi Chanina was a stern opponent of every form of superstition, from astrology to sorcery, and so he taught his disciples.
Two of them happened to go to the woods one day to chop firewood.
While they were engaged on their task an astrologer came along and engaged them in conversation. When he was satisfied that he had learned enough about them to practice his craft, he cast their horoscopes and told them: "You will not leave this forest alive."
They continued their work. When they were done, they tied the wood into two bundles and set off on their way home.

146

After walking some distance they met an old man who, seeing them, said: "Do you have any food to give a hungry man?" They had only a single loaf of bread between them, but this they willingly cut, giving the man half their bread.

They came out of the forest and returned home, and later told people about their encounter with the astrologer. In turn, some of these people taunted the astrologer about the failure of his prediction, so he went to Chanina's disciples and said: "Open your bundles of wood." They did, and found half a snake in each bundle.

The astrologer wondered: "How did you merit your escape from certain death? What did you do to deserve it?"

"We did nothing at all," they replied. "All that happened is that while we were walking in the woods we met an old man with whom we shared a loaf of bread."

"What is a sentence of death," exclaimed the astrologer, "when the God of the Jews will nullify it for half a loaf of bread!" (Jerusalem Talmud Shabbat 6:9)

Avot 4:4

רַבִּי לְבִיטַס, אִישׁ יַבְנֶה, אוֹמֵר:
מְאֹד מְאֹד הֱוֵי שְׁפַל רוּחַ,
שֶׁתִּקְוַת אֱנוֹשׁ רִמָּה.

רַבִּי יוֹחָנָן בֶּן בְּרוֹקָא אוֹמֵר:
כָּל־הַמְחַלֵּל שֵׁם שָׁמַיִם בַּסֵּתֶר,
נִפְרָעִין מִמֶּנּוּ בַּגָּלוּי. אֶחָד שׁוֹגֵג
וְאֶחָד מֵזִיד בְּחִלּוּל הַשֵּׁם.

RABBI LEVITAS[9] of Yavneh says:
Be very, very humble, "for the hope of human kind is the worm."[10]

RABBI YOCHANAN ben Beroka[11] says:
Whoever profanes the name of Heaven in secret, will pay the price in public. This is true whether one profanes the name of Heaven inadvertently or deliberately.

humble—Note well that you are commanded to be humble and not to speak to others with arrogance and contempt, but you are most certainly not commanded to humiliate yourself before others. (Duran)

--- Note that despite the many qualities of Moses, greatest of the prophets, the quality for which he is specially praised is his humility. (Nachalat Avot) [see Numbers 12:3]

hope...worm—All that we crave ends up as food for the worms. (TH)

--- We die, but our hope, not our doom, lies in that fact. (Neusner)

profanes the name of Heaven—Does anything that offends against the majesty of God; this speaks of one outwardly pious, inwardly unclean. (TH)

[In this connection, Midrash Genesis Rabbah 65:1, says, "The pig stretches out, displaying its hooves, saying: 'I too am kosher.'"]

--- As he lay dying, Rabban Yochanan ben Zakkai gave his disciples this blessing: "May your fear of Heaven be as great as your fear of flesh and blood." "No more than that, Rabbi?" "Would that it were that much! When we transgress we say, 'If only no one sees me!'" (Talmud Berachot 28b) [for a fuller text and context, see chapter 2, "Rabban Yochanan ben Zakkai," No. 3.]

--- What is it? Raba said: "When I take meat from the butcher and do not pay him immediately." (Talmud Yoma 86a)

inadvertently or deliberately—That is, both inadvertent and deliberate sinners face ultimate public discovery: in the case of inadvertance, however, that publicity itself is the only retribution. Thus, both inadvertent and deliberate sinners are punished, but not to the same degree. (Maimonides)

Avot 4:5[12]

רַבִּי יִשְׁמָעֵאל בְּנוֹ אוֹמֵר:
הַלּוֹמֵד עַל מְנָת לְלַמֵּד, מַסְפִּיקִין
בְּיָדוֹ לִלְמֹד וּלְלַמֵּד.
וְהַלּוֹמֵד עַל מְנָת לַעֲשׂוֹת, מַסְפִּיקִין
בְּיָדוֹ לִלְמֹד וּלְלַמֵּד, לִשְׁמֹר וְלַעֲשׂוֹת.
רַבִּי צָדוֹק אוֹמֵר:
אַל תַּעֲשֵׂם עֲטָרָה לְהִתְגַּדֵּל בָּהֶם, וְלֹא
קַרְדֹּם לַחְפֹּר בָּהֶם. וְכָךְ הָיָה הִלֵּל
אוֹמֵר: וּדְאִשְׁתַּמֵּשׁ בְּתָגָא חֲלַף.
הָא לָמַדְתָּ, כָּל הַנֶּהֱנֶה מִדִּבְרֵי תוֹרָה
נוֹטֵל חַיָּיו מִן הָעוֹלָם.

RABBI ISHMAEL[13] his son says:
Learn in order to teach, and it is given you to learn and to teach.
Learn in order to do, and it is given you to learn and teach, to keep and do.[14]

RABBI ZADOK[15] says:
Do not make [your Torah learning] a crown with which to glorify yourself, nor a spade to dig with. This is what Hillel used to say: "Who uses the crown passes away."[16] Thus you have learned [that] those who derive worldly benefit from the Torah's words make themselves lifeless.[17]

learning—"In learning the Torah, always choose the particular topic to which your heart is drawn." (Talmud Avodah Zarah 19a)

learning and doing—"Better not to be born, than to learn without intending to put into practice what one has learned." (Talmud Berachot 17a, Jerusalem Talmud Shabbat 1:5, Midrash Sifre Bechukotai [and see 1:17, 3:9, 3:17, 5:14])

--- The disciples of the Baal Shem Tov heard that a certain man was a sage. Some of them were anxious to see and hear his 'Torah.' The master gave them permission to go, but first they asked him, "How will we know that he is a true tzaddik?" The Baal Shem replied: "Ask him for advice on how to pray and learn without distraction. If he answers, you will know there is nothing to him." (see Buber, *Or ha-Ganuz*, p. 84).

N.B.: 4b–5 expresses an ideal, not a reality—namely, that everything fits: the punishment to the crime, the reward to the good deed; that Torah will be studied for its own sake, that all depends on motivation. (Neusner)

Learning and doing Torah

1. Rabbi Jeremiah said: If you have neither learned Torah nor taught it, if you have neither kept Torah nor done it, but if, being able to encourage and help others, you have done that, you are blessed. (Jerusalem Talmud Sotah 7:4)

2. You may think: "I will learn Torah so that I may be called wise, or gain admission to the Academy, or gain long days in the world-to-come;" therefore it says

(Deuteronomy 6, etc.), *You shall love the Eternal your God.*[18] (Midrash Sifre Deuteronomy, Ekev, 48)

3. Rabbi Benai'ah would say: Torah studied for its own sake becomes an elixir of life; Torah not studied for its own sake becomes a deadly poison. (Talmud Ta'anit 7a)

4. Who makes use of the crown of Torah is uprooted from the world. Do the words of the Torah for their own sake .... Do not make them a crown with which to exalt yourself, or a tool for weeding your garden. (Talmud Nedarim 62a) [See, also, 1:13, etc. We often find the phrase "the crown of Torah" in rabbinic literature.]

5. *You shall diligently keep these commandments to do them.* (Deuteronomy 6:17; 11:22). Lest one suppose it enough to keep the words of the Torah in mind and sit in quiet and not do them, it says: *to do them.* One who has learned the words of the Torah has fulfilled one Mitzvah; one who has learned and kept them has fulfilled two; one who has learned and kept and done them surpasses all. (Midrash Sifre Deuteronomy, Ekev, 48)

14. Rabbah bar Rav Huna said: One who knows Torah but who has no fear of Heaven is like a keeper of the treasury who has the inner keys but not the outer. (Talmud Sanhedrin 31b)

6. You may learn Halachot, Midrashim, Haggadot,[19] but if you have no fear of sin you have nothing. I say to my neighbor: "I have a thousand measures of wheat, wine, and oil." My neighbor responds: "Have you storehouses in which to put them? If yes, you have all; if no, you have nothing." So with you: you may have learned everything; only if you have the fear of sin is it yours. (Midrash Exodus Rabbah, Mishpatim, 30:14)

7. First do good deeds and then ask Heaven for knowledge of Torah; first emulate the righteous and upright, and then ask Heaven for wisdom; first take hold of the way of humility, and then ask Heaven for understanding. (Midrash Tanna de be Eliyahu, p. 3)

8. Rabbi Chiyah said: Better not to have been born than to learn Torah without intending to fulfill it.

Rabbi Yochanan said: Better never to have seen the light than to learn Torah without intending to fulfill it. (Sanhedrin 37b)

Rabbi Acha said: [Only one] who learns in order to do is worthy of receiving the Holy Spirit. (Midrash Leviticus Rabbah, B'chukotai, 35:7)

9. One learns in order to do; one does not learn in order not to do. Better not to have been born than not to learn to do. (Midrash Sifra 110c)

Avot 4:6[20]

רַבִּי יוֹסֵי אוֹמֵר:

כָּל־הַמְכַבֵּד אֶת־הַתּוֹרָה גּוּפוֹ

מְכֻבָּד עַל הַבְּרִיּוֹת;

וְכָל־הַמְחַלֵּל אֶת־הַתּוֹרָה גּוּפוֹ

מְחֻלָּל עַל הַבְּרִיּוֹת.

RABBI YOSÉ[21] says:

All who honor the Torah[22] are themselves honored.[23]

All who dishonor the Torah are themselves dishonored.[24]

How to dishonor the Torah—When a learned Jew cheats someone, it disgraces the Torah which that person is supposed to know. When someone asserts things he or she does not believe merely because 'the Torah' seems to teach them, it disgraces the Torah, because the Torah stands for truth, and a single standard of truth, at that. When (in order to be liked) one pretends that people who do not know what they are talking about when they speak of Torah really do know. Tolerating ignorance of Torah dishonors the Torah. (after Neusner)

All who honor the Torah—By teaching it to the right kind of pupil... (Vitry)

--- Who honor its commandments by their eagerness to do them, who honor sages—for they are pillars of the Torah—and the books they compose. (Maimonides)

themselves—That is: when you are honored because you honor the Torah, you can be sure that you are being honored for yourself—for your own sake—and not for something extraneous, such as wealth or position.

Honoring Torah

1. Rava said: "How foolish people are, who rise in honor of a Torah scroll, but not of a sage." (Talmud Makkot 22b; and see Talmud Kiddushin 32b)

2. Bar Kappara expounded: What small passage contains in principle the whole Torah? *In all your ways affirm God, who will make straight your path(s).* (Proverbs 3:6) (Talmud Berachot 63a)

3. [God says:] Had you not accepted My Torah, I should not recognize you, I should not regard you more than any of the idolatrous nations of the world. (Midrash Exodus Rabbah, Ki Tissa, 47.3)

4. Even exile among the nations is not exile for Israel, when it immerses itself in Torah. (Midrash Tanna de be Eliyahu, p. 148)

Two Students

When Ilfa and Rabbi Yochanan were young, they studied Torah together. So poor were they that they talked the matter over and decided to give up their studies.

"We will go into business," they said. "That way we shall at least fulfill the Torah's commandment (Deuteronomy 15:4), *There shall be no poor among you.*"

The day they spoke of this, they were walking in the countryside and had gone a considerable distance. Coming to a wall, they sat down to rest on it, not noticing that is was crumbling and near collapse. They had taken along some food and began to eat it. As they were eating, Rabbi Yochanan heard two angels talking.

One said: "These two are giving up eternal life for the life of an hour.[25] Let us knock this wall down and make an end to them."

"Leave them alone," said the other. "One of them is destined for greatness."

"Did you hear anything just now?" said Yochanan. Ilfa had heard nothing.

Yochanan concluded that the words were meant for him. He therefore said to Ilfa: "I am going to return to my studies."

"And what of the verse that says *'There shall be no poor among you'?*"

"I have thought of another one I can fulfill (Deuteronomy 15:11): *The poor shall never cease out of the land.*"

Avot 4:7

רַבִּי יִשְׁמָעֵאל בְּנוֹ אוֹמֵר:

הַחוֹשֵׂךְ עַצְמוֹ מִן הַדִּין פּוֹרֵק מִמֶּנּוּ

אֵיבָה וְגָזֵל וּשְׁבוּעַת שָׁוְא.

וְהַגַּס לִבּוֹ בַּהוֹרָאָה שׁוֹטֶה, רָשָׁע וְגַס

רוּחַ.

RABBI ISHMAEL[26] his son says:
One who avoids serving as a judge[27] is shielded from enmity, robbery, and perjury.
And one arrogant in pronouncing judgment[28] is a fool, is wicked, and [additionally, is] haughty.

N.B.: This counsel of prudence points out the dangers inherent in acting as a judge; it does not, however, teach that one should or even may excuse himself from the office. If that is your duty, you must fulfill it with an awareness of its pitfalls and temptations: so with other professions. (TH)

arrogant in ... judgment—One who rushes to render decision, one, e.g., who declares, "I am the expert." (Vitry)

--- This involves two things: first, rushing to decide without any sense of caution; second, having made a wrong decision, mulishly arguing to justify that decision in order to prevail. (Meiri)

--- "The entire community will fall into ruins if its people insist on the letter of the law in every matter, however small, and show no inclination to temper justice with mercy." (Talmud Baba Metzia 30b)

arrogant in teaching—The Great Maggid once said to his disciples, "Let me tell you the best way to teach Torah: forget yourselves, stop thinking of yourselves; become nothing but an ear hearing what the Torah itself is saying within you. And the minute you start hearing yourself talking—stop." (see Buber, *Or ha–Ganuz*, p. 114)

--- "The Holy One says of one who is arrogant, 'There is not room enough in the world for both of us.'" (Talmud)

Judges and Judging

1. *You shall not take a bribe* (Deuteronomy 16:9). Not merely not to acquit the guilty or condemn the innocent, but not even to acquit the innocent or condemn the guilty. (Midrash Sifre Deuteronomy, Shof'tim, 144)

2. Rabbi Samuel bar Nachmani said in the name of Rabbi Jonathan: A judge who dispenses true justice brings the Shechinah to Israel, as it is said (Psalm 82.1), *God stands in the council of God; God judges in the midst of the judges.*[29] A judge who does not dispense true justice causes the Shechinah to depart from Israel, as it is said (Psalm 12:6), *Because the poor are despoiled, because the needy groan, I will now arise [and depart], says the Eternal One.*[30] (Talmud Sanhedrin 7a)

3. *Do not curse the judge*[31] (Exodus 22.27). Our sages said: A man once had a lawsuit, so he came to court with his friend and the judge held in his favor. He said: "This judge is the wisest man in the world! He's an angel!" Another time he had a lawsuit and came to court. The same judge ruled against him. When he went out he said: "This man is the world's greatest fool!" They said to him: "Yesterday's angel, today's fool!" (Midrash Exodus Rabbah 31)

4. Those who are wise, humble, patient,[32] sin–fearing, of good repute [when young], and pleasing to people[33]—they make them judges in their city. (Tosefta Sanhedrin 7)

5. Rav Judah said in the name of Samuel: Who has had a quarter log[34] of wine must not sit as a judge. (Erubin 64a)

6. A judge who is sued may not remain a judge.

If so, anyone can come along and get a judge off the bench by means of a lawsuit? No: Only a judge who is sued and fined does not remain a judge. (Talmud Baba Batra 58b)

7. When three sit and judge, the Shechinah is in their midst. (Talmud Berachot 6a)

8. If you have something to testify in your neighbor's favor, you may not remain silent. (Midrash Sifra 89a)

Avot 4:8

אַל תְּהִי דָן יְחִידִי,

שֶׁאֵין דָן יְחִידִי אֶלָּא אֶחָד.

וְאַל תֹּאמַר: קַבְּלוּ דַעְתִּי,

שֶׁהֵן רַשָּׁאִין, וְלֹא אַתָּה.

HE WOULD say:
Do not serve as the sole judge, for there is only One who judges all alone.
And do not say,[35] "You must adopt my view," for the choice is theirs, not yours.[36]

all alone—Strictly speaking, the Torah permits it [see Talmud Sanhedrin 5a with regard to disputes concerning property]. This is not a legal but a moral warning. [Not everything that's permitted is wise.] (Maimonides) [And see 3:6]

"adopt my view"—Even if something seems to you self-evident, do not say to your colleagues, "Adopt my view and abandon your own." Offer proofs and refutations of theirs. If you have not done this, or if you and they have, and the arguments are evenly balanced, do not say, "Adopt my view, because I am greater than you." You are not permitted to speak this way. (Aknin)

--- "One who judges a case in absolute truth for even one instant is regarded by Scripture as a partner with the Holy One in the work of creation." (Talmud Shabbat 10a)

Compromise

1. We have learned (Deuteronomy 16:20), *Justice, justice shall you pursue.* One for judgment and one for compromise.[37] How so? Two boats sailing in a river meet: if they continue on their courses they will collide and sink; if one waits both can get through. Two camels meet in a narrow mountain–pass: if both keep going they both will fall; if one waits while the other moves on, they can both make it. How to do it? A loaded one precedes an unburdened one; one nearer its destination defers to the one further away. if they are equally near, let them negotiate a compromise that will benefit them both. (Talmud Sanhedrin 32b)

2. Rabbi Eliezer son of Rabbi Yosé the Galilean says: Compromise is forbidden, and a compromiser is a sinner; rather, let the judgment split the mountain, as it is said (Deuteronomy 1:17), *For the judgment is God's.* And this is what Moses would say: "Let the judgment split the mountain." But Aaron loved peace and pursued peace, and made peace between people, as it is said (Malachi 2:6), *The law of truth was in his mouth...he walked with Me in peace and uprightness.*

Rabbi Joshua ben Korcha says: It is a Mitzvah to compromise, as it is said (Zechariah 8:16), *Render in your cities*[38] *judgments that are true and make for peace.* When can there be judgment that includes peace? You must say: in compromise.

And so it says about David (II Samuel 8:15), *And David administered judgment and equity.* Where are the two found together? In compromise. (Talmud Sanhedrin 6b)

3. Rabbi Simeon ben Menasya says: There are times when one should compromise, and times when one should not. When two come before you for judgment, it is appropriate to tell them go to out and compromise before you have heard them or before you know the likely result. Once you have heard them out and you know how you will decide, you cannot tell them to compromise, as it is said (Proverbs 17:14), *The beginning of strife is like letting out water.* Quit, then, before the quarrel breaks out. (Talmud Sanhedrin 6b; Tosefta Sanhedrin 1)

Avot 4:9

רַבִּי יוֹנָתָן אוֹמֵר:

כָּל־הַמְקַיֵּם אֶת־הַתּוֹרָה מֵעֹנִי

סוֹפוֹ לְקַיְּמָהּ מֵעֹשֶׁר.

וְכָל־הַמְבַטֵּל אֶת־הַתּוֹרָה מֵעֹשֶׁר

סוֹפוֹ לְבַטְּלָהּ מֵעֹנִי.

RABBI JONATHAN[39] says:

Whoever keeps the Torah in affliction[40] will in the end keep it in well-being.

And whoever neglects the Torah in well-being will in the end neglect it in affliction.

beginnings and endings—What is begun in youth will likely be continued in age. (TH)

--- If you start 'poor' in knowledge of Torah, and labor in it, you will end up with 'riches;' and if you are 'rich' in knowledge of Torah, and you neglect it, you will end up 'poor.'

--- This passage speaks of the way things should be, not as they are. (Neusner)

Keeping Torah

1. Rabbi Yochanan was traveling from Tiber'as to Sepphoris, and Rabbi Chiyah was supporting him. They came to a field, and Rabbi Yochanan said: "This field was mine, and I sold it to enable me to acquire the Torah." They came to a vineyard and an olive grove, and Rabbi Yochanan said the same. Rabbi Chiyah began to weep. "Why are you crying?" asked Rabbi Yochanan. Rabbi Chiyah said: "Because you have left nothing for your old age." Then Rabbi Yochanan said: "Is it a light thing in your eyes what I have done? I have sold what was created in six days,[41] and acquired what was given in forty days, as it is said (Exodus 34.28), *Moses was there with the Eternal forty days and forty nights.* (Leviticus Rabbah, Emor, 30.1)

2. The words of the Torah endure only with one who is prepared to suffer death on their behalf. (Talmud Berachot 63)

3. *On this day Israel came to Mount Sinai.* (Exodus 19:1). Why on this day? When you learn Torah, do not let its commands seem old to you. Regard them as though the Torah were given this day. Hence it says, 'on this day,' and not, 'on that day.' (Midrash Tanchuma B, Yitro, 38b)

4. *You shall meditate on it day and night* (Joshua 1:8). Rabbi Yochanan said: This is no command or obligation, but a blessing. Because Joshua loved the words of the Torah he was blessed: they shall never depart from your mouth. They taught in the school of Rabbi Ishmael: The words of the Torah should not seem an [onerous] obligation to you; on the other hand, you are not free to release yourself from them. (Talmud Menachot 99b)

Suffering and its Gifts

The Holy One gave Israel three gifts, all through suffering: Torah, the land of Israel, the world–to–come. (Talmud Berachot 8a)

Avot 4:10

רַבִּי מֵאִיר אוֹמֵר:
הֱוֵי מְמַעֵט בָּעֵסֶק וַעֲסֹק בַּתּוֹרָה.
וֶהֱוֵי שְׁפַל רוּחַ בִּפְנֵי כָל־אָדָם.
וְאִם בִּטַּלְתָּ מִן הַתּוֹרָה, יֶשׁ לָךְ
בְּטֵלִים הַרְבֵּה כְּנֶגְדָּךְ. וְאִם עָמַלְתָּ
בַּתּוֹרָה, יֶשׁ לוֹ שָׂכָר הַרְבֵּה לִתֶּן לָךְ.

RABBI MEIR[42] says:
Do as little business as you can, and
make Torah your [real] business.[43]
Be humble in spirit before every person.
If you neglect Torah, you will find many
to help you. And if you labor in Torah, it
has good wages for you.[44]

Be humble—Not only in the presence of your superiors. (Maimonides)
--- "As water flows from the high ground and settles in the low, so are the words of
Torah alive only in the humble." (Talmud Ta'anit 7a)
good wages—And in the world–to–come as well, namely, the 310 worlds that God
has set aside for every righteous person, as it is said (Proverbs 8:21), *To give
substance* ('Yesh') *to those who love Me.* The numerical value of יש, *Yesh*, is 310. Our
mishnah uses the same word in reference to the Torah's 'good wages'—an allusion to
the 310 worlds. (Nachalat Avot)
If you neglect Torah—Or, "If you neglect Torah, many occasions of neglect will arise
for you." That is, the less you do, the harder is becomes to recover lost ground. (CS)

Consulting on Creation

Rabbi Samuel bar Nachman said in the name of Rabbi Jonathan: When Moses was
writing the story of creation, he reached this sentence (Genesis 1:26): *And God said:
Let us make a being in our image, in our likeness...* He said: "Ruler of the world, why
do you give heretics a talking point? I don't understand!" God answered: "Son of
Amram, write—and let those who choose go astray!"
The Holy One added: "Do not both great and humble descend from Adam, My
creation? Therefore, when people of high station have occasion to consult with one
of lesser rank, let them not say, "Why bother seeking the views of one beneath me?"
Rather, let them learn from their Maker, the Creator of the heights and the depths.
Though supreme over all, God consulted the ministering angels before the creation of
humankind. (Midrash Genesis Rabbah 8)

Avot 4:11

רַבִּי אֱלִיעֶזֶר בֶּן יַעֲקֹב אוֹמֵר:
הָעוֹשֶׂה מִצְוָה אַחַת,
קוֹנֶה לּוֹ פְּרַקְלִיט אֶחָד.
וְהָעוֹבֵר עֲבֵרָה אַחַת,
קוֹנֶה לּוֹ קַטֵּגוֹר אֶחָד.
תְּשׁוּבָה וּמַעֲשִׂים טוֹבִים כִּתְרִיס
בִּפְנֵי הַפֻּרְעָנוּת.
רַבִּי יוֹחָנָן הַסַּנְדְּלָר אוֹמֵר:
כָּל־כְּנֵסִיָּה שֶׁהִיא לְשֵׁם שָׁמַיִם
סוֹפָהּ לְהִתְקַיֵּם. וְשֶׁאֵינָהּ לְשֵׁם שָׁמַיִם
אֵין סוֹפָהּ לְהִתְקַיֵּם.

RABBI ELIEZER ben Jacob[45] says:

Do one good deed,[46] gain one advocate.

Commit one transgression, gain one accuser.

Repentance[47] and good deeds are a shield against punishment.

RABBI YOCHANAN Hasandlar[48] says:

Every assembly for the sake of Heaven[49] will in the end have permanent value.[50] But one not for the sake of Heaven will in the end not have permanent value.

one advocate...one accuser—Every human action, small though it may seem, may have a high significance; what we do matters. (CS)

Repentance and good deeds—Repentance is mentioned first because "In the place where the penitent stand, the wholly righteous cannot stand." (Talmud Berachot 34b, Talmud Sanhedrin 99a) (Nachmias)

Every assembly for the sake of Heaven—This is perhaps a reflection on the aftermath of the Bar Kochba defeat (135 CE). The very survival of the people was in doubt, and the task of reconstruction was daunting. Nonetheless, this "coming together" for the sake of Heaven, however difficult, would in the end succeed. God would not allow it to fail. (Neusner)

--- Common experience would seem to contradict this maxim; but it is a deeper truth that God does not allow wholly to fail what is done for His sake; and the whole history of the Jewish people in their dispersion confirms that truth. (TH)

Avot 4:12

רַבִּי אֶלְעָזָר בֶּן שַׁמּוּעַ אוֹמֵר:

יְהִי כְבוֹד תַּלְמִידְךָ חָבִיב עָלֶיךָ

כְּשֶׁלָּךְ,

וּכְבוֹד חֲבֵרְךָ כְּמוֹרָא רַבָּךְ,

וּמוֹרָא רַבָּךְ כְּמוֹרָא שָׁמַיִם.

RABBI ELAZAR ben Shamua[51] says:
Let your disciple's honor be as dear to
you as your own,[52]
and your colleague's honor [as great as]
your reverence of your teacher,
and your reverence of your teacher as
your reverence of Heaven.

your disciple's honor—"We compete with all but two—our children and our disciples." (Talmud Sanhedrin 105b)

your colleague's honor—"The competition of scholars increases wisdom." (Talmud Baba Batra 21a)

reverence of your teacher—Reverence is due the teacher of Torah, because Torah is sacred, and reverence is due God the giver of Torah; to pay that reverence is an equal obligation in each case, though the objects of reverence need not be equal. (TH)

--- God has put the honor of scholars on the same plane as the honor due to God, because by teaching people Torah and good works the scholar brings them to the life of the world–to–come. (Aknin)

--- Our masters taught: A sage is given precedence over a king. For when a sage dies [he is irreplaceable:] we have none like him; when a king dies, anyone is eligible to replace him.

N.B.: 4:11b–12 are connected, saying that people come together for good purposes and evil. When we advance God's purposes, our comings–together succeed. And only when we avoid selfish purposes can we advance our own purposes. (Neusner)

The Bandit and the Sage

I

In his youth Simeon ben Lakish was a bandit renowned for his strength and daring. One day, seeing a beautiful young woman swimming in the river Jordan, he leaped in after her. When he came up to her, he found—a man!

It was Rabbi Yochanan.

Rabbi Yochanan said: "Strength like yours would be better used by sages learning Torah."

Simeon replied: "Beauty like yours would be better used by young women."

And Rabbi Yochanan said: "I have a sister even more beautiful than I. Turn to God, and you may win her as your wife."

This appealed to him, and Simeon agreed. He became Rabbi Yochanan's disciple. He learned Bible and Mishnah, and in due course was a notable scholar and sage. And Rabbi Yochanan's sister agreed to become his wife. (Baba Metsia 84a)

II

Once it happened at the House of Study, that they were discussing the question, 'What is the last stage in the manufacture of metal implements such as swords, knives, daggers, saws and scythes?'

Rabbi Yochanan held: "When they have been hardened in the furnace." Rabbi Simeon ben Lakish (Resh Lakish) disagreed: "You are wrong. When they have been tempered in water."

"Well," remarked Rabbi Yochanan, "a bandit should know his trade." Infuriated, Resh Lakish shouted: "You call me a bandit? Then what did I gain by giving up that trade?" "What did you gain?" his brother-in-law retorted. "Is it nothing to you that you were brought under the wings of the Shechinah?"

Nevertheless, Resh Lakish was unable to recover from the hurt that Yochanan's remark had inflicted on him. He grew more and more despondent. After a time, he sickened and died.

And Rabbi Yochanan was deeply stricken over the death of his brother-in-law. This came to public notice and the sages sent Rabbi Elazar ben Pedat, a most subtle thinker, to console him.

Whenever Rabbi Yochanan would express an opinion, Elazar would say: "I have seen a baraita[53] that supports you." Far from being comforted, Rabbi Yochanan was enraged: "How different it was with Resh Lakish!" he cried. "I would say something, he would raise two dozen objections, and I would be forced to come up with as many answers. So it came about that out of our debates the Torah grew and flourished. But you—you keep saying you have seen a baraita that supports me! Do I need you constantly to tell me how right I am? Leave me alone!"

So it was: none could console him for the loss of Rabbi Simeon ben Lakish, and in the end his mind gave way.

The sages prayed for him, and he died. (Ibid.; J. Megillah 1.1)

Avot 4:13

רַבִּי יְהוּדָה אוֹמֵר:

הֱוֵי זָהִיר בַּתַּלְמוּד, שֶׁשִּׁגְגַת

תַּלְמוּד עוֹלָה זָדוֹן.

רַבִּי שִׁמְעוֹן אוֹמֵר:

שְׁלֹשָׁה כְתָרִים הֵם:

כֶּתֶר תּוֹרָה,

וְכֶתֶר כְּהֻנָּה,

וְכֶתֶר מַלְכוּת,

וְכֶתֶר שֵׁם טוֹב עוֹלֶה עַל גַּבֵּיהֶן.

RABBI JUDAH[54] says:
Be careful in teaching,[55] for an error may amount to deliberate sin.[56]
RABBI SIMEON[57] says:
There are three crowns:
the crown of Torah,
the crown of priesthood,
and the crown of royalty,
but the crown of a good name is best of all.[58]

Be careful—Look deeply into what you study, so as not to mislead others when you teach or render a decision. (after Vitry)

--- Where Torah and Mitzvot are concerned, error is a common thing. Failure to keep this in mind is negligence, not innocence. (Rabbi Jonah ben Abraham)

The crown of Torah—Two of the crowns are already taken. The crown of Aaron belonged to Aaron and is reserved for his descendants. The crown of royalty belonged to David and is reserved for his descendants. The crown of Torah, however, belongs to all who choose it, and whoever wishes may come and take it. (Talmud Yoma 72b)

the crown of a good name—comes from personal worth and upright character, and is thus more important than what may be no more than an appearance of dignity or position whose acquisition depends on other things than worth. (CS)

is best of all—Or, more literally, "rises above them." That is, each of the three crowns alludes to an attainable virtue: Torah, worship, deeds of loving kindness (see 1:2). When we attain these three, we ascend to the crown of a good name.

Three names

Each of us has three names: what our parents call us, what others call us, and what we call ourselves.[59] (Midrash Kohelet Rabbah 7)

Avot 4:14

רַבִּי נְהוֹרַאי אוֹמֵר:

הֱוֵי גוֹלֶה לִמְקוֹם תּוֹרָה, וְאַל תֹּאמַר

שֶׁהִיא תָבוֹא אַחֲרֶיךָ, שֶׁחֲבֵרֶיךָ

יְקַיְּמוּהָ בְּיָדֶךָ. וְאֶל בִּינָתְךָ אַל תִּשָּׁעֵן.

RABBI NEHORAI[60] says:
Go into exile to a place of Torah, and do
not imagine that it will come to you, that
your friends will help you to grasp it.[61]
*And do not rely [only] on your own
understanding* (Proverbs 3:5).

N.B.: It has been suggested that this mishnah is a reflection on Rabbi Elazar ben Arach, who went to live "in a place of no Torah," and whose early promise never came to fruition. See 2:8–9. (CS)

Go ... to a place of Torah—The Torah that one studies with others is more firmly mastered than the Torah one studies by oneself. Colleagues question one another, each tries to answer the questions of others, there is a give and take until the subject is clarified. (Aknin)

--- If you wait for a teacher to come along, or for your friends to return from where they have gone to learn, the opportunity may never present itself, and meanwhile time keeps escaping from you. (Meiri)

--- Do not say that your friends will return and teach you. There is no comparing what one learns directly from a teacher to what one learns from a disciple's report. (Vitry)

--- Learning too is social—we must go after it and gain it by converse with teachers and students. (Neusner)

Avot 4:15

רַבִּי יַנַּאי[62] אוֹמֵר:

אֵין בְּיָדֵינוּ לֹא מִשַּׁלְוַת הָרְשָׁעִים

וְאַף לֹא מִיִּסּוּרֵי הַצַּדִּיקִים.

רַבִּי מַתְיָא בֶּן חָרָשׁ אוֹמֵר:

הֱוֵי מַקְדִּים בִּשְׁלוֹם כָּל־אָדָם, וֶהֱוֵי

זָנָב לָאֲרָיוֹת וְאַל תְּהִי רֹאשׁ לַשּׁוּעָלִים.

RABBI YANNAI[62] says:
We have in our hands neither the prosperity of the wicked nor the suffering of the righteous.

RABBI MATYA ben Charash[63] says:
Be first in greeting any person, and be a tail to lions rather than a head to foxes.

We have in our hands—The most straightforward interpretation of this saying, often inserted into the translation itself, is that we cannot explain the way things are. Another interpretation: We cannot determine the way things are or will be. Another: Our lot is not like that of the wholly wicked or wholly righteous; we are neither the one nor the other, and their suffering and reward alike are beyond us. (CS)

--- "At the tranquillity of the wicked we have not arrived; the sufferings of the righteous we have not approached." (ARNB)

Be first in greeting—Taken literally, the Hebrew can mean, 'Give priority to the welfare of every person you meet.' (Bunim, II, p. 142)

lions and foxes—Better by far to be the disciple of your superior than the master of your inferior. The former leads to your improvement, the latter to your deterioration. (Maimonides)

--- The tail of a lion is still a lion and the head of a jackal is still only a jackal.

--- The proverb says: Be a head to foxes rather than a tail to lions. Rabbi Matya ben Charash says: Be a tail to lions rather than a head to foxes. (Jerusalem Talmud Sanhedrin 4:5)

--- Greatness is found by choosing your company well. Such greatness is not self-aggrandisement, but willingness to make room for others, and to take second place. (Neusner)

Affliction

1. One is obliged to give thanks for evil as one gives thanks for good, as it is said (Deuteronomy 6:5), *You shall love your Eternal God...with all your being* [64]—for each and every measure that God metes out to you, give God thanks.

Rabbi Meir says: How do we know that as one gives thanks for good one must give thanks for evil? Scripture says (Deuteronomy 8:10), *And you shall praise your Eternal God.* —praise your Judge[65] for every judgment, whether it be a reward or a punishment.

What does it mean to say, 'One is obliged to give thanks for evil as one gives thanks for good?' Do you mean that just as we say the blessing 'The Good and Beneficent One,' when good befalls us, so do we say that blessing when evil befalls us? Yet we have learned: "For good tidings one says 'Praised be the Good and Beneficent One;' for evil tidings one says 'Praised be the True Judge.'"

Rava said: This comes to urge us only that we should accept whatever happens with joy. Rabbi Acha said in the name of Rabbi Levi: How do we know this? *I will sing of loving kindness and of judgment* (Psalm 101:1).—whichever is given me, I will sing.

Rabbi Samuel bar Nachmani derives it from this verse (Psalm 56:11): *In God, whose word I praise, in the Eternal, whose word I praise.* 'In the Eternal, whose word I praise' refers to the good that is meted out to us; 'in God, whose word I praise' refers to the punishment we receive.

Rabbi Tanchum said: We know it from this (Psalm 116:13; 116:3,4): *I will lift up the cup of salvation and call upon the name of the Eternal ...I find distress and anguish and call upon the name of the Eternal.*

And the Sages say: From this (Job 1:21): *The Eternal gives, the the Eternal takes, praised be the name of the Eternal.* (Talmud Berachot 54a, 48b, 60a)

2. Rabbi Akiba says: ...when God brings you good, give thanks; and when God makes you suffer, give thanks. (Midrash Mechilta, Yitro, Bachodesh 10)

3. Rav Huna said: *and it was good.* (Genesis 1:31)—when we experience good; *and it was very good.* (ibid., 1:31)—when we experience affliction. How can affliction be called "very good?!" It is, for through its agency people come to the life of the world–to–come. Thus did Solomon say (Proverbs 6:23), *The reproofs of discipline are the path of life.* What then is the path that leads humankind to the life of the world–to–come? You must say: affliction. (Midrash Genesis Rabbah 9)

4. *Your rod and Your staff, they comfort me* (Psalm 23:4). 'Your rod'—these are the afflictions. 'Your staff'—this is Torah. (Midrash Songs Rabbah 2)

5. Rabbi Yochanan fell ill and Rabbi Chanina came to see him. He said: "Do you love afflictions?" "Neither them nor their reward." He said: "Give me your hand," and he lifted him up. (Talmud Berachot 5a)

6. *When an ox or sheep or goat is born.* (Leviticus 22:27). The Holy One said: An ox is pursued by a lion, a bull by a leopard, a goat by a wolf. Offer Me one of the pursued, not the pursuers. (Midrash Leviticus Rabbah 27)

7. *And the Eternal One said to Satan*[66] *"Behold he is in your power; only spare his life."* (Job 2:6). Rabbi Isaac said: Satan's distress was greater than that of Job. It is as though you told a servant: 'Break this bottle without spilling the wine in it.' (Talmud Baba Batra 16a)

8. Rava said: We are not held accountable for what we say in our time of anguish. (Talmud Baba Batra 16b)

9. Sufficient is the trouble in its time. (Talmud Berachot 9b)

10. Troubles dim the eyes. (Midrash Lekach Tov, Bereishit 48)

11. Later troubles make one forget the earlier. (Talmud Berachot 13a)

12. Rabbi Levi said: No trouble befalls one that doesn't benefit another. (Midrash Genesis Rabbah 38)

Avot 4:16

רַבִּי יַעֲקֹב אוֹמֵר:
הָעוֹלָם הַזֶּה דּוֹמֶה לַפְּרוֹזְדוֹר בִּפְנֵי
הָעוֹלָם הַבָּא. הַתְקֵן עַצְמְךָ בַּפְּרוֹזְדוֹר,
כְּדֵי שֶׁתִּכָּנֵס לַטְּרַקְלִין.

RABBI JACOB[67] says:
This world is like an anteroom to the
world-to-come. Prepare yourself in the
anteroom, so that you may enter the
palace.[68]

N.B.: When we hear the sages speak as they do, we have to remember that they knew what we know: a life of tragedy, a world of evil, an age of mass destruction, a time of chaos and disorder. If then they could frame the issues of life as they did, so too can we hear their message: a life of goodness in a world of evil; a life of reconciliation in a world of destruction; a life to affirm the abiding value of decency in a world contemptuous of reason and of love. The survivors then have this to say to the survivors now: for a Jew, it is a sin to despair. (Neusner)

the world-to-come—Rav would say: In the world-to-come there is neither eating, nor drinking, nor procreating, nor business dealings, nor envy, nor hatred, nor competition. Instead, the righteous sit with crowns on their heads and enjoy the splendor of the Shechinah. (Talmud Berachot 17a) [Other passages (e.g., Talmud Berachot 64a) picture this 'sitting' as the sitting of scholars discussing and debating Halachic questions, that is, Torah (see 2:7 and note on 'Yeshivah')]. (CS)

Prepare yourself—One prepares oneself before arriving. This world is like the shore, the other like the sea; this world is like Sabbath Eve, the other like the Sabbath. If you prepare food on shore you will eat when at sea; if you make ready on Sabbath Eve, you will be able to celebrate on the Sabbath. (After Midrash Ruth Rabbah III.3)
--- Live a life of preparation. What we do is important—even unto the next world. Speaking to a people in crisis, the founders spoke to individuals. And they spoke not of survival but of the good life, of obligation. (Neusner)

Death & Mourning

1. We have learned: In the old days the arrangements for the funeral were worse for the family than the death itself.[69] It came to the point that they would leave the dead and flee. Then Rabban Gamaliel decreed for himself an inexpensive funeral and they buried him in a flaxen garment. Thus it came about that everyone emulated him.
Rav Papa said: Nowadays people use even the cheapest of materials. (Talmud K'tubot 8b)
2. Our sages taught: In the old days the mourners would stand still and all the people would pass them [after the burial, to say words of consolation]. Then two [prominent] Jerusalem families quarreled at a funeral, each wanting to go first, so

they decreed that all the people should stand still and the mourners should pass between them. (Talmud Sanhedrin 19a)

3. Our sages taught: In the old days, they would bring the meal of consolation to the homes of the rich in gold and silver vessels, while to the homes of the poor they would bring it in rough straw baskets. This shamed the poor, so they decreed that for the honor of the poor straw baskets be used for everyone.

In the old days they would give rich mourners drinks in crystal vessels and the poor in ordinary glass. This shamed the poor, so they decreed that ordinary glass be used for all. (Talmud Moed Katan 27a)

4. They taught: The Sages decreed ten cups for the house of mourning: three before eating, to increase the appetite; three during the meal, to settle the stomach; and four after the meal, to correspond with the four blessings in the Thanksgiving after Meals. They added four more, in honor of the town chazzanim,[70] the town officials, the Temple,[71] and Rabban Gamaliel.[72] People began to get drunk, so they went back to the original custom. (Talmud K'tubot 8b; Semachot 4)

5. They said in the name of Bar Kappara: When one sheds tears for a decent[73] person, the Holy One inscribes them[74] in Heaven's archives. (Talmud Shabbat 108b)

6. Rav Judah said in the name of Rav: Anyone who mourns excessively for someone who has died is weeping for someone else.

A woman in Rav Huna's neighborhood had seven sons and one of them died. She wept excessively. Rav Huna sent her a message not to do this and she ignored him. He sent her another message: "It will be well with you if you listen, and if not—prepare shrouds for the rest of your sons." They all died. In the end he sent her another message: "Prepare a shroud for yourself"—and she died. (Talmud Mo'ed Katan 27b)

7. Rav said: Our dead are not forgotten until twelve months have passed. (Talmud Berachot 58b)

What Death Can Touch

When Rabbi Yochanan heard that Rabbi Eliezer was mortally, ill, he went to see him for the last time.

Eliezer lay in his bed; the room was dark. Some words passed between them, and then, as Yochanan lifted his arm in a gesture, a shaft of light caught it, and his bare skin illuminated the room. Eliezer began to weep, and Yochanan said to him: "Why are you weeping, Eliezer? Do you regret your life? Or do you think that even such as you failed to learn enough Torah in his lifetime?"

"True enough, old friend. While I had strength and time I should have learned more."

"Do not let yourself grieve, Eliezer. We have learned: 'A little more, a little less—no matter, so long as the heart is turned to Heaven.'" Eliezer was not comforted; he continued to weep.

Yochanan went on: "Do you weep because of the years you were poor? If so, what need had you for two tables?"

Into the silence broken only by the soft sound of tears, Yochanan ventured yet again: "Do you perhaps mourn the sons you never had? If that: I mourn the sons I did have. Look now: here is the bone[75] of my tenth!"

Now Eliezer raised himself up and gave answer: "Let me tell you the reason for my tears: I weep for your beauty, that must fade into dust!"

"Old friend," cried Yochanan, "oh, my dear old friend, for that you well may weep." And the two old men shed tears together. (Baba Metsia 84a)

Avot 4:17

הוּא הָיָה אוֹמֵר:
יָפָה שָׁעָה אַחַת בִּתְשׁוּבָה וּמַעֲשִׂים
טוֹבִים בָּעוֹלָם הַזֶּה מִכָּל־חַיֵּי הָעוֹלָם
הַבָּא, וְיָפָה שָׁעָה אַחַת שֶׁל קוֹרַת רוּחַ
בָּעוֹלָם הַבָּא מִכָּל־חַיֵּי הָעוֹלָם הַזֶּה.

HE WOULD say:
Better one hour of repentance[76] and good deeds in this world than all the life of the world–to–come,
and better one hour of bliss in the world–to–come than all the life of this world.

Better...and better—The world of change and a changeless one: in the former, the highest form of change may be expressed as teshuvah and good deeds, whereby one turns to and serves God; in the latter, the highest form of existence is the perfect peace of beholding God. (TH)

--- Each world has the virtue for which it is particularly suited. Only in this world can one do good deeds; only in the other world can one experience perfect bliss. (after Vitry)

--- One cannot explain a comparison of what cannot be compared. (Midrash Shemuel)

Repentance—"In the place where the penitent stand, the wholly righteous cannot stand." (Talmud Berachot 34b, Talmud Sanhedrin 99a) [A mended limb may be stronger than one never broken.]

good deeds in this world—"There is no reward for a good deed in this world." (Talmud Kiddushin 39b)

--- *Therefore observe faithfully the Mitzvah, the laws, and the rules of justice that I command you this day.* (Deuteronomy 7:11) "'This day' you are to do them, but not 'this day' are you to receive their reward." (Talmud Avodah Zarah 3a). "Do them 'this day;' receive their reward the next day." (Talmud Erubin 22a). [and see 2:16, 4:11]

ON PARADOX: The first message of the survivors of the catastrophe of the destruction of Jerusalem and the end of the Temple cult was a message of Torah. The first message of the survivors of the last hope, when the Temple mountain was plowed over by the Romans and the doors of Jerusalem locked against the Jews, is before us: So take up the work. What a paradox! For what work was left to do, when the old ways in which Israel served God no longer lay open? The paradoxical mode of thought that turns taking into giving, opposites into one another, led our sages to look for the opposite in the things they saw: Despair? Then hope! Destruction? Then build! The end of all things? Then renew them! No further means of working for God? Then take up the task! (Neusner)

A foretaste

Three are a foretaste of paradise:[77] Sabbath, sun, and sex. (Talmud Berachot 57a)
One eats the fruit of six things in this world, but their true reward is in the world-to-come: hospitality, visiting the sick, sincerity in prayer, going early to the House of Study, bringing up children learned in Torah, giving others the benefit of the doubt. (Talmud Shabbat 127a)

Avot 4:18

רַבִּי שִׁמְעוֹן בֶּן אֶלְעָזָר אוֹמֵר:

אַל תְּרַצֶּה אֶת־חֲבֵרְךָ בְּשָׁעַת כַּעְסוֹ,

וְאַל תְּנַחֲמֶנּוּ בְּשָׁעָה שֶׁמֵּתוֹ מֻטָּל לְפָנָיו,

וְאַל תִּשְׁאַל לוֹ בִּשְׁעַת נִדְרוֹ,

וְאַל תִּשְׁתַּדֵּל לִרְאוֹתוֹ בִּשְׁעַת קִלְקָלָתוֹ.

RABBI SIMEON ben Elazar[78] says:
Never try to pacify[79] a neighbor who is in the grip of rage,
nor try to console one who has only just been bereaved,
nor question the wisdom of a vow[80] newly made,
nor rush to see your neighbor who has just been disgraced.

Never try to pacify—"Even as we are commanded to speak up when our words will be listened to, so are we commanded to hold our peace when our words will not be listened to." (Talmud Yebamot 65b)

vow—People make vows and sometimes have cause to regret them. In certain circumstances the court can annul a vow, provided that the one who made it did not intend to be bound by those (unforeseen) circumstances. Thus, in the passage above, we are advised not to push the maker of a vow into a corner, wherein he will bind himself so tightly that later on he will be unable to escape the terms of his vow, despite his discovery of its folly.

Avot 4:19

שְׁמוּאֵל הַקָּטָן אוֹמֵר:
בִּנְפֹל אוֹיִבְךָ אַל־תִּשְׂמָח וּבִכָּשְׁלוֹ
אַל־יָגֵל לִבֶּךָ. פֶּן־יִרְאֶה יהוה וְרַע
בְּעֵינָיו וְהֵשִׁיב מֵעָלָיו אַפּוֹ.

SAMUEL THE Younger[81] says:
Do not be glad when your enemies fall, do not rejoice when they stumble, lest the Eternal see it and be displeased, and turn away the divine wrath from them.
(Proverbs 24:17–18)

He makes the Biblical passage his own saying.

Avot 4:20

אֱלִישָׁע בֶּן אֲבוּיָה אוֹמֵר:
הַלּוֹמֵד יֶלֶד, לְמָה הוּא דוֹמֶה? לִדְיוֹ
כְּתוּבָה עַל נְיָר חָדָשׁ. וְהַלּוֹמֵד זָקֵן,
לְמָה הוּא דוֹמֶה? לִדְיוֹ כְּתוּבָה עַל
נְיָר מָחוּק.
רַבִּי יוֹסֵי בַּר יְהוּדָה, אִישׁ כְּפַר
הַבַּבְלִי, אוֹמֵר:
הַלּוֹמֵד מִן הַקְּטַנִּים: לְמָה הוּא דוֹמֶה?
לְאוֹכֵל עֲנָבִים קֵהוֹת וְשׁוֹתֶה יַיִן מִגִּתּוֹ.
וְהַלּוֹמֵד מִן הַזְּקֵנִים: לְמָה הוּא דוֹמֶה?
לְאוֹכֵל עֲנָבִים בְּשׁוּלוֹת וְשׁוֹתֶה יַיִן יָשָׁן.
רַבִּי אוֹמֵר:
אַל תִּסְתַּכֵּל בַּקַּנְקַן אֶלָּא בַּמֶּה שֶׁיֶּשׁ
בּוֹ. יֵשׁ קַנְקַן חָדָשׁ מָלֵא יָשָׁן,
וְיָשָׁן שֶׁאֲפִילוּ חָדָשׁ אֵין בּוֹ.

ELISHA BEN Abuyah[82] says:
Learning as a child: what is that like? Ink inscribed on new paper. Learning in old age: what is that like? Ink inscribed on blotted paper.

RABBI YOSÉ bar Judah[83] of Kefar Habavli says:
Who learns from the young is like one who eats unripe grapes and drinks wine straight from the vat. Who learns from elders is like one who eats ripe grapes and drinks vintage wine.

RABBI[84] SAYS:
Don't look at the flask but at what's in it. There are new flasks full of old wine, and old ones that don't even contain new wine.

Learning—The Mivchar Ha-p'ninim has an epigram: "Learning Torah when young: what is that like? Engraving on stone. Learning Torah in old age: what is that like? Engraving on sand." (Rabbi Jonah ben Abraham)

--- Learning when young has two advantages: it is easier to impress knowledge on the mind, and one has time left in which to teach others; learning when old has the correlative disadvantages: it is harder to absorb learning, and there is little time left for teaching others. (Midrash Shemuel)

--- "As elders would feel no shame to ask a younger for water, so should they feel no shame to ask a younger to teach them a chapter, verse, or even a letter of Torah." (Midrash Songs Rabbah 1:1)

Teaching Torah

1. Rabbi Judah said: "As a small piece of kindling can set aflame a great tree, so young disciples can sharpen the wits of great scholars. Rabbi Chanina therefore said: 'Much Torah have I learned from my teachers, more from my colleagues, but from my students most of all.'" (Talmud Ta'anit 7a)

2. The Holy One does not do as people do. Human beings do not fill a full vessel, they fill one that is empty; the Holy One fills the full. If you have heard, you will

hear; if you have not heard, you will not hear. If you have heard the old, you will hear the new; if you have turned your heart away, you will not hear. (Talmud Berachot 40a)

3. Rabbi Ishmael's nephew Ben Dima asked him: "As I have learned all the Torah, what of Greek wisdom?" Ishmael quoted this verse (Joshua 1:8), "This Torah shall not depart from your mouth; meditate on it day and night. Go find an hour that belongs neither to day nor to night, then learn Greek wisdom."

Rabbi Samuel bar Nachman said in the name of Rabbi Jonathan: This verse is actually neither a Mitzvah nor a [moral] obligation, but a blessing. The Holy One saw that the words of Torah were exceedingly precious to Joshua, as it is said (Exodus 33:11), *And his attendant, Joshua son of Nun, a youth, would not stir out of the Tent.*[85] Therefore the Holy One said to him: Joshua, since the words of Torah are so precious to you—*This Torah shall not depart from your mouth.* (Talmud Menachot 99b)

4. Rabbi Samuel bar Nachman said in the name of Rabbi Jonathan: Who teaches his friend's son Torah is reckoned by Scripture as though he had begotten him, for it is said (Numbers 3:1), These are the offspring of Aaron and Moses, and it is said (ibid. 3:2), These are the names of Aaron's sons. To teach you: Aaron begot and Moses taught; therefore they are called by his name. (Talmud Sanhedrin 19b)

5. Rabbi Samuel bar Nachman said in the name of Rabbi Jonathan: It says (Proverbs 17:16), *What good is money in the hands of fools to buy wisdom, when they have no mind?*[86]—Woe to those disciples of the wise[87] who engage in the Torah but who have in them no fear of Heaven! (Talmud Yoma 72b)

Avot 4:21[88]

רַבִּי אֶלְעָזָר הַקַּפָּר אוֹמֵר:
הַקִּנְאָה וְהַתַּאֲוָה וְהַכָּבוֹד
מוֹצִיאִין אֶת־הָאָדָם מִן הָעוֹלָם.

RABBI ELAZAR Hakappar[89] says:
Envy, desire, and [the pursuit of] honor[90]
make one unfit for human society.[91]

Envy...—A parable: (From Mivchar Ha-p'ninim): Two men—one envious, one a glutton—were met by Satan, who said to them, "If one of you will ask for something, it will be given to him, but the other will get a double portion of it." The envious one did not want to ask first, because he did not want his companion to receive a double portion. The glutton wanted both portions, his own and the other's, so he pressed his companion to ask first. Whereupon the envious one asked that they gouge out one of his eyes... (Duran)

Avot 4:22

הוּא הָיָה אוֹמֵר:

הַיְלוֹדִים לָמוּת; וְהַמֵּתִים לִהְיוֹת;

וְהַחַיִּים לִדּוֹן: לֵידַע לְהוֹדִיעַ וּלְהִוָּדַע

שֶׁהוּא אֵל. הוּא הַיּוֹצֵר, הוּא הַבּוֹרֵא,

הוּא הַמֵּבִין, הוּא הַדַּיָּן, הוּא עֵד,

הוּא בַּעַל דִּין, וְהוּא עָתִיד לָדוּן.

בָּרוּךְ הוּא שֶׁאֵין לְפָנָיו לֹא עַוְלָה,

וְלֹא שִׁכְחָה, וְלֹא מַשּׂוֹא פָנִים,

וְלֹא מִקַּח שֹׁחַד, שֶׁהַכֹּל שֶׁלּוֹ.

וְדַע שֶׁהַכֹּל לְפִי הַחֶשְׁבּוֹן.

וְאַל יַבְטִיחֲךָ יִצְרְךָ שֶׁהַשְּׁאוֹל בֵּית

מָנוֹס לָךְ:

שֶׁעַל כָּרְחֲךָ אַתָּה נוֹצָר,

וְעַל כָּרְחֲךָ אַתָּה נוֹלָד,

וְעַל כָּרְחֲךָ אַתָּה חַי,

וְעַל כָּרְחֲךָ אַתָּה מֵת,

וְעַל כָּרְחֲךָ אַתָּה עָתִיד לִתֵּן דִּין

וְחֶשְׁבּוֹן לִפְנֵי מֶלֶךְ מַלְכֵי הַמְּלָכִים,

הַקָּדוֹשׁ בָּרוּךְ הוּא.

HE WOULD say:

Those who are born are to die; those who die are to live again; those who live (again) are to be judged—

to know, to make known, to be made aware that God is God.

God is the Designer, God is the Creator.

God is the Discerner, God is the Judge, God is the Witness, God is the Plaintiff, and

God is the One who will decide.

Before the Blessed One there is neither deception nor forgetfulness nor respect for persons nor taking of bribes, for all things are God's.

And know that all depends on the account.[92]

Nor let your Yetzer[93] persuade you that the grave[94] is a refuge:

For like it or not you were conceived,

like it or not you were born,

like it or not you are alive,

like it or not you will die,

and like it or not you will render a full account before the Sovereign who is supreme over all, the Holy One, ever to be praised.[95]

like it or not—Take careful note of this statement: it mentions things that come to pass in the natural course, over which we have no choice. The mishnah does not say, however, that like it or not you will sin, or transgress, or walk, or stand still, etc. These things are within our power and we are coerced into none of them. (Maimonides)

like it or not you will die—As the Baal Shem Tov lay dying, the townspeople came to him as they always did at this time of the year, and he spoke words of Torah to them. After this he said to the disciples standing around him, "I am not concerned for myself. I am well aware that I am going out through one door and going in through another." And he added, "Now I know what I was created for." (see Buber, *Or ha–Ganuz*, p. 97)

In Sum

Although we find in chapter 4 messages relevant to the time of rebuilding the life of a shattered people, what is striking about this chapter is its timelessness. In the main the Sages cited here are terse. They speak to the individual about the age–old themes: wisdom, enthusiasm, Mitzvah, humility, Torah, Teshuvah, eternal life. The tone has changed, however, and the subtle variations on the old themes are themselves a message of renewal. Thus they connect with the past, affirm the present, and assure the future. (after Neusner)

•••••••

The following section supplements Pirké Avot, by adding passages from the rabbinic literature that either quote or tell about the sages of Avot.

4:1

Simeon ben Zoma

1. Ben Zoma would say: A good guest says: "How much they exerted themselves for me! How much meat, how much wine, how many cakes—and all on my account!" Whereas an ungrateful guest says: "In what way did they trouble themselves? [I ate one loaf, one slice of meat, had one cup]—whatever they did they did for themselves!" (Talmud Berachot 58a)
2. Who sees a group of people in Israel should say: Blessed is the One who discerns secrets[96]. No two are of the same mind or appearance.
Ben Zoma saw a group on the Temple Mount and said: "Blessed is the One who discerns secrets and Blessed the One who created all these to serve me." For he would say: How hard Adam the First Man had to labor before he had a loaf to eat: he had to plow, sow, reap, bind sheaves, pound, winnow, clean, grind, sift, knead, bake—only then could he eat. And I wake up and find all this done for me! And the same is true for the clothes I find waiting for me when I wake up. Every trade and craft is here at the door of my house waiting for me to partake. (Talmud Berachot 58a)
3. When Ben Zoma died, that was the last of the [great] interpreters [of Torah].

Avot 4:2

Simeon ben Azzai

1. Ben Azzai said: You will be called by your [own] name, you will be set in your [own] place, and you will be given of your own; no one touches what is prepared for another, and no nation encroaches on its neighbor even as much as a hairsbreadth. (Talmud Yoma 38a)
2. He (Simeon ben Azzai) would say: Move down two or three steps and stay there. Much better to be told: Go up! rather than: Go down! As it is said (Proverbs 25:7), *for it is better that it be said to you "Come up here" than to be lowered in the presence of a noble whom your eyes have seen.* (ARN 25:4)
3. Ben Azzai would say: It's easier to rule the world than to sit and learn before people who are dressed in linen.[97] (ARN 25:5)
4. Ben Azzai said: Those who waste away for the sake of Torah, eat dried-out dates, wear soiled clothing, and sit faithfully at the doors of the wise—passersby may take them for fools, but in the end you will find that all the Torah is theirs. (ARN 11:2)
5. *Love your neighbor as yourself.* (Leviticus 19:18). Rabbi Akiba says: This is the great principle of the Torah. Ben Azzai says: *This is the book of the generations of Adam...God made them in the divine image.* (Genesis 5:1). This is an even greater

principle, for then you cannot say, 'Since I despise myself I can despise my fellow as well; since I curse myself, let my fellow be accursed as well.' Rabbi Tanchuma said: [Ben Azzai is right, for] if you do thus, know whom you are despising—*God made them in the divine image.* (Jerusalem Talmud Nedarim 9:4; Midrash Genesis Rabbah 24)

7. Ben Azzai says: A man is required to teach his daughter Torah. (Talmud Sotah 20a)

8. They said to Ben Azzai: Some preach well and act well, others act well but do not preach well; you. however, preach well but do not act well! Ben 'Azzai replied: But what shall I do, seeing that my soul is in love with the Torah; the world can be carried on by others. (Talmud Yebamot 63b) [This is the conclusion of a discussion on the duty to marry and have children. Ben Azzai, who did not marry, had participated in the discussion and spoken of that duty.]

4:5

Rabbi Zadok

1. Rabbi Zadok fasted 40 years to avert the destruction of Jerusalem. One could see the food he had eaten, so lean had he become. For his health they brought him figs, from which he would extract the juice, leaving the fruit uneaten.

During Vespasian's siege of Jerusalem Rabbi Yochanan ben Zakkai came before him. Vespasian said: "If a relative or anyone you love is in the city, get them out before my troops enter." So he sent Rabbi Eliezer and Rabbi Joshua to get Rabbi Zadok. They found him at the entrance to the Gate. When he came Rabbi Yochanan stood up [to honor him]. Vespasian said: "Before this feeble old man you stand up?" He replied: "By your life, if there had been one more like him in the city, you could not have vanquished it, had you had twice as many troops!" "What is his virtue?" "He eats one bean and teaches a hundred chapters." "How come he's so lean?" "Because of his fasting and abstinence." [Vespasian] sent physicians who measured out his food and drink a little at a time until he was restored. (Talmud Gittin 56a; Midrash Lamentations Rabbah 1:32)

4:6

Rabbi Yosé

1. Rabbi Yosé said: May my lot be among those who are suspected of wrongdoing yet are innocent.[98] (Talmud Mo'ed Katan 18b)

2. Rabbi Yosé ben Chalafta said: I once was walking and I entered one of the ruins of Jerusalem to pray.

Elijah (may he be remembered for good!) came along and kept guard over me until I concluded. Then he said to me:

"Shalom to you, my Master!" And I said:

"Shalom to you, my Master and Teacher!"

"What were you doing in this ruin?" he asked, and I answered:

"I was praying."

"You should have prayed on the road," said he, and I explained:

"I was afraid a passer-by might interrupt me."

"My son, what did you hear in this ruin?" he asked, and I answered:

"I heard a divine echo moaning like a dove, saying:

'I destroyed My house,

burned My temple,

scattered My children—

among the nations...

Woe!!'"

"By your life! my son, she never lets an hour pass without saying this. What's more, she says it three times a day [at the times fixed for prayer]. Moreover, whenever Israel enters the synagogues and houses of study and intones,

יהא שמה רבא, *Y'hei sh'mei rabbah*—Let God's great name be praised, the Holy One, as it were, nods and says:

'Happy the Sovereign who is thus praised in his palace!

'What remains to parents who exile their children?

'Woe to the children driven from their parents' table!'"[99] (Talmud Berachot 3a)

3. Rabbi Yosé ben Chalafta had praised Rabbi Meir to the citizens of Sepphoris: "A great man, a holy man, a modest man."

Rabbi Meir once saw some mourners on Shabbat and he greeted them. People said to Rabbi Yosé: "Master, this is the man you praised!? "What's wrong?" he asked them. They replied: "He saw some mourners on Shabbat and greeted them."

"He was letting us know that there is no mourning on Shabbat. It is said (Proverbs 10:22), *It is the blessing of the Eternal that enriches.* —that is the blessing of Shabbat. *And there is no increase of sadness.*[100] (ibid.) —that is mourning.

4. Rabbi Yosé taught in Sepphoris:

"Father Elijah was hot-tempered."

Elijah had been accustomed to visit him frequently; now three days passed without a visit.

When at last he did come, Rabbi Yosé asked:

"Why didn't the Master come?"

"You called me a hot-head."

"So the Master lost his temper!" (Talmud Sanhedrin 113a)

5. Rabbi Yosé said:

"Never have I called my wife 'my wife' and my ox 'my ox.' No, I called my wife 'my home' and my ox 'my field.'

"I never contradicted my colleagues; so, well aware though I am that I am no priest, if my colleagues said: 'Go up to the platform,'[101] I would go up."

"I never said anything that I had to retract."

"May my lot fall among those who pray at first light."

"May my lot fall among those who die in the way of Mitzvah."[102]

"May my lot fall among those who begin Shabbat in Tiberias and end it in Sepphoris.[103]

"May my lot fall among those who are suspected [of sin] yet are innocent." (Talmud Shabbat 118b)

6. A Roman matron queried Rabbi Yosé ben Chalafta about the verse (Daniel 2:21), *God gives wisdom to the wise.*[104] "Should it not rather have said, God gives wisdom to the foolish?" "Have you any jewelry?" said he. "Of course." "And if two people came to borrow your jewels—one rich and the other poor—which one of them would you lend them to?" "The rich one," she replied. "Why?" said he. "If he loses them he can repay," said she. "Then," said he, let your ears hear what your mouth has said— why should the Holy One waste wisdom on fools?" (Midrash Tanchuma B, Mekeits)

7. A Roman Matron said to Rabbi Yosé ben Chalafta: "In how many days did the Holy One create the world?" "In six days," was his answer. "And since that time?" she asked. "Since that time the Holy One has been sitting and arranging marriages, deciding who should marry whom."

She laughed: "Anyone can do that! I own many slaves; I could put them together in no time."

"It may be easy for you," remarked Rabbi Yosé, "yet for God this is as difficult as splitting the Red Sea."

Later on the woman brought a thousand male slaves and a thousand female slaves together, arranging them in two facing rows. "Each one is to marry the one opposite him," she commanded. That very night was to be their marriage–night.

The next morning the couples appeared before her—this one had a concussion, that one a missing eye, another a broken leg, and so on. One said: "I cannot stand this woman!" The other: "This man displeases me!"

The matron sent for Rabbi Yosé ben Chalafta and said to him: "Your Torah is entirely correct! You were absolutely right!"

Rabbi Berechiah said: This is what Rabbi Yosé ben Chalafta said to her:

"The Holy One sits and makes ladders, lowering and raising this one, raising and lowering that one."[105] (Midrash Pesikta de Rav Kahana 2, 11b–12a; Midrash Genesis Rabbah 68)

8. Rabbi Yosé ben Chalafta said: *As for me, let my prayer to You be at an acceptable time* (Psalm 69:14). There are particular times for prayer.[106] David was saying to the Holy One: May the hour of my prayer to You be 'an acceptable time.'

9. A woman who have grown very old came before Rabbi Yosé ben Chalafta and said to him: "Master, I have grown too old; hereafter I will live a miserable existence. I've lost the taste for food and drink, and I want to leave this world." He said: "How did you get to live this long?" And she replied: "It's my habit, every day, even when I have something else of importance, to go early to the synagogue." "Leave off going three days in a row," he advised her. This she did, and on the third day she sickened and died. (Midrash Yelamdenu; Yalkut Shimoni, Proverbs, 8)

10. Rabbi Yosé ben Chalafta said to his son Rabbi Ishmael: "If you want to see the face of the Shechinah in this world, immerse yourself in Torah in the land of Israel." (Midrash Socher Tov 105)

11. When Rabbi Yosé died, insight ceased. (Jerusalem Talmud Sota, end)

4:7

Rabbi Ishmael ben Yosé

1. When Rabbi [Judah the Prince] would take issue with Rabbi Yosé, he would say: "We worthless ones contradict Rabbi Yosé! His generation is to ours as the holy of holies to the most profane."
Rabbi Ishmael his [Rabbi Yosé's] son said: "Our generation compared to father's is as dust to gold." (Jerusalem Talmud Gittin 26:7)

2. One day Rabbi Ishmael encountered a man carrying a bundle of wood. The man put them down and stood resting. Then he said: "Help me lift them." "How much are they worth?" asked Rabbi Ishmael. "Half a Zuz." He gave the man a half Zuz and declared them free for all.[107] The man then took possession of them, so he paid him another half Zuz and declared them in the public domain. He saw the man about to go and take them yet again, so he added: "It is free to all—but you!" (Talmud Baba Metzia 30b)

3. Rabbi Ishmael ben Yosé was invited to the home of Rabbi Simeon ben Yosé ben Lekonaya. They gave him a cup, whose contents he swallowed in a single gulp. His host said: "Does the Master not know that 'One who drinks his cup in a single gulp is a glutton'?"[108] "That was not said about a cup as small as yours, wine as sweet as yours, and a body as large as mine." (Talmud Pesachim 86b)

4:9

Rabbi Jonathan

1. What is the proof that danger to human life suspends the laws of Sabbath? R. Jonathan ben Joseph cited, *For it is holy unto you* (Exod. 31:14). The Sabbath is committed to your keeping, not you to its keeping. (Talmud Yoma 85b)

4:11

Rabbi Eliezer ben Jacob

1. We have learned: Rabbi Eliezer ben Jacob says: Someone who steals a measure of wheat, grinds it, kneads it, bakes it, and separates 'Challah' from it—what blessing does he say? What he says is a curse, not a blessing. Concerning him it is said (Psalm 10:3), *And the one greedy for gain curses and renounces the Eternal.*[109] (Talmud Baba Kama 94a; SA 5.3:6.135)[110]

2. In the aftermath of the Roman persecution our sages went to Usha. They were Rabbi Judah, Rabbi Nehemiah, Rabbi Yosé, Rabbi Simeon ben Yochai, Rabbi Eliezer ben Rabbi Yosé the Galilean, and Rabbi Eliezer ben Jacob.

They sent this message to the elders of the Galilee: Whoever has learned, let him come and teach; whoever has not learned, let him come and learn. Thus did they complete all their tasks.

When the time came to leave, they said: We cannot leave a place that welcomed us without giving them a parting gift. So they honored Rabbi Judah by inviting him to be the first to speak, because he had come from that town. It was not that he was the greatest of them in Torah, but the place where a man comes from honors him. They all spoke; now it was the turn of Rabbi Eliezer ben Jacob, who expounded: *Moses and the levitical priests spoke to all Israel, saying: Be silent and hear, O Israel! This day you have become the people of your Eternal God* (Deuteronomy 27:9). Was it that day that they received the Torah? Hadn't they received it forty years earlier— and you say, 'This day!' So it teaches that since Moses had taught them the Torah and they had accepted it with good grace,[111] Scripture regards it as though they had that very day received it from Mt. Sinai.[112] Thus it says, *This day you have become the people of your Eternal God.* And you—our brethren of Usha—who have received our sages with such good grace—all the more! (Midrash Songs Rabbah 2; Leviticus Rabbah 36)

3. Rabbi Eliezer ben Jacob says: *The Eternal One is the hope of Israel* (Jeremiah 17:13). As the Mikveh[113] makes pure the impure, so the Holy One purifies Israel. The Holy One says to Israel: I bade you pray in the synagogue of your city, but if you cannot pray there, pray in your field, and if you cannot pray there, pray on your bed, and if you cannot pray there, then meditate in your heart, as it is said (Psalm

4:5), *Speak within your hearts in your beds and be still.* (Midrash Pesikta de Rav Kahana 158a)

4. *An angel of the Eternal called to him from Heaven, saying, "Abraham, Abraham"* (Genesis 22.11).

Rabbi Eliezer ben Jacob said: [The promise was made] to him, and to [all] the generations.[114]

There is no generation without its 'Abraham,' its 'Jacob,' its 'Moses,' its 'Samuel.'

5. Rabbi Eliezer ben Jacob said: When a dignified and respected person says something base, it's like going into a palace and finding an open sewer. (Midrash Derech Eretz 3)

4:11

Rabbi Yochanan Hasandlar

1. Rabbi Elazar ben Shamua and Rabbi Yochanan Hasandlar were going to Netzivim to learn Torah from Rabbi Judah ben Beteira. As they arrived at Sidon they thought of the land of Israel, and their eyes began to stream with tears. They tore their clothes and recited this verse (Deuteronomy 11:31f.), *When you take possession and settle there, be careful to do all the statutes...* Returning home, they said: The Mitzvah of dwelling in the land of Israel is equal in weight to all the Mitzvot in the Torah. (Midrash Sifre, R'ei)

4:12

Rabbi Elazar ben Shamua

1. Rav called Rabbi Elazar ben Shamua: "Most fortunate of the Sages." (Talmud K'tubot 40a)

2. Rabbi Elazar ben Shamua was walking along the seashore one day, when he saw a ship founder and sink with all aboard. One man was hanging on to a plank, and the waves carried him ashore.

He was naked, and he cried out to some Jews who were passing by on their way to Jerusalem: "I am a descendant of your brother Esau: give me some clothes to cover my flesh with, I've lost all I own in the sea."

"Would that this happened to all your compatriots," they said.

He looked up and saw Rabbi Elazar ben Shamua among them. "I can see that you are an honored elder: surely you honor others. Do me the kindness of giving me something to cover myself with."

Rabbi Elazar was wearing seven fine garments. He took one of them and gave it to the man. He then took him to his house, gave him food and drink and two hundred dinarii, and gave him a ride to his home, with much show of honor, a distance of fourteen parasangs.

Some time later the wicked Caesar died and this man was elevated to the throne. He issued a decree: All the men to death, the women to shame. They pleaded with Rabbi Elazar ben Shamua: "Intercede for us."

He answered: "In this kingdom nothing is done without payment."

"Here are four thousand dinarii. Take them and intercede for us."

He took them and went to the royal gate. "Go and say to the king," he said to the guards, "that a Jew is at the gate who wishes to inquire into the king's health."

"Bring him in," ordered the king.

When the king saw him he leaped up from his throne and bowed low to him. "What are you doing here, my lord? What brings you here?"

"I have come," he answered, "to beg that your decree concerning that province be annulled."

"Does your Torah contain anything false?" asked the king.

"No."

It is written there (Deuteronomy 23:4f., 8), *No Ammonite or Moabite shall enter the congregation of the Eternal. Why? Because they did not meet you with bread and water on the way.* And it is written, *You shall not despise the Edomites, for they are your kin.* Am I not a descendant of your brother Esau? They did not treat me with kindness, and one who transgresses the Torah deserves to die."

Rabbi Elazar ben Shamua said to him: "Nevertheless, forgive them and show them mercy."

"In this kingdom nothing is done without payment."

"I have four thousand dinarii—take them and have pity."

"Keep the four thousand dinarii as payment for the two hundred you gave me. The whole province can live on your account, because you gave me food and drink. In my storehouse you will find seventy garments in return for the one you gave me. Go now in peace to your people."

They said of him (Ecclesiastes 11:1), *Cast your bread upon the waters...* (Midrash Kohelet Rabbah 11)

3. Rabbi Judah and Rabbi Elazar ben Shamua said: "Beautiful is a Mitzvah fulfilled at its proper time." (Midrash Sifra 25a)

4. The world rests on twelve pillars, as it is said (Deuteronomy 32:8), *God fixed the boundaries of the peoples according to Israel's numbers.*[115] Others say: On seven pillars, as it is said (Proverbs 9:1), *Wisdom has built her house, she has hewn seven pillars.*[116] Rabbi Elazar ben Shamua says: On one pillar, and its name is Tzaddik,[117] as it is said (ibid., 10:25), *The righteous is the foundation of the world.* (Chagigah 12b)

5. It was said: Rabbi Akiba had twelve thousand pairs of disciples filling the land, and they all died in his lifetime and at the same time, between Pesach and Atzeret,[118] because they did not treat each other decently, with respect. The world was desolate

until Rabbi Akiba came to our sages in the South and taught Torah to Rabbi Meir, Rabbi Judah, Rabbi Yosé, Rabbi Simeon, and Rabbi Elazar ben Shamua. He said to them: "The first ones died because they begrudged each other their Torah–learning: make sure you don't imitate them."

They arose and filled the whole land of Israel with Torah. (Talmud Yebamot 62b; Midrash Genesis Rabbah 61)

4:13

Rabbi Judah ben Illai

1. They said of Rabbi Judah bar Illai that he would interrupt his study of Torah to join a funeral procession or to help a bride.

They said of Rabbi Judah bar Illai that he would take a sprig of myrtle and dance before the bride and sing: "Lovely bride! Full of grace!" (Talmud K'tubot 17a)

2. Rabbi Judah ben Rabbi Illai said: "See how the later generations are not like the former. The former gave the study of Torah priority over work, and both flourished; the later gave first place to work and second to Torah, and neither flourished."[119] (Talmud Berachot 35b)

3. Rav Judah said in the name of Rav: This was the practice of Rabbi Judah ben Rabbi Illai: At the eve of Shabbat they would bring him a tub with hot water. He would wash his face, his hands, and his feet, and he would sit in a fringed tunic looking like an angel of the Eternal, the God of heaven's hosts. (Talmud Shabbat 25b)

4. *The voice is the voice of Jacob, but the hands are the hands of Esau.* (Genesis 27:32) Rabbi Judah ben Rabbi Illai said: Rabbi[120] would interpret: Jacob cries out over what Esau's hands are doing to him. (Midrash Genesis Rabbah 65)

5. Rabbi Judah ben Rabbi Illai expounded: In the time to come the Holy One will bring the Yetzer Hara and slaughter it in the presence of the righteous and the wicked. It will appear to the righteous as a tall mountain; to the wicked it will look like a thread. Both will weep. The righteous will say: "How could we have conquered so mighty a mountain?" The wicked will say: "How could we have failed to overcome this thin thread?" The Holy One, too, will be astonished, as it is said (Zechariah 8:6): *Thus said the Eternal, God of heaven's hosts: If it will seem a wonder to the remnant of this people...so will it seem a wonder to Me.* (Talmud Sukkah 52a)

4:14

Rabbi Nehorai

1. Rabbi Nehorai says: "Whoever shames a friend will end up shamed. Not only that, but the fiends[121] will torment him, driving him out of the world and showing his disgrace to all." (Talmud Kallah)

2. *And the people of Israel went into the sea on dry ground* (Exodus 14:22).
If they went "into the sea" why does it say: "on dry ground?" And if they went "on dry ground" why does it say "into the sea?" So that you may learn that the sea was not split for them until they had gone in as high as their noses: only then did it become for them "dry ground."

Rabbi Nehorai expounded: The Israelite women were walking through the sea holding their children by the hand. When the children cried, they would reach out and pluck apples and pomegranates for them, which they would find in the sea, as it is said (Psalm 106:9), *God led them through the deep as through a wilderness.* Just as they lacked for nothing in the wilderness, so they lacked for nothing in the deep. (Midrash Exodus Rabbah 2:10)

3. Rabbi Nehorai says: I let all the world's trades go and teach my son nothing but Torah, for one is paid for it in this world, and yet its main reward is in the world–to–come.[122] That is not true of other trades.

Moreover, when you become sick, or old, or afflicted, and can no longer work, you'll die of hunger. Not so with Torah: it stands by you and keeps you from harm in youth and gives you hope in old age. In youth, as it says (Isaiah 40:31), *But they who trust in the Eternal renew their strength as eagles renew their plumes.* In age, as it says (Psalm 92:15), *They still bring forth fruit in old age; they are ever fresh and green.* (Talmud Kiddushin 82a)

4. Rabbi Nehorai would say: One who learns Torah when young is like a cake baked with flour that has been properly mixed (with warm water); one who learns Torah in old age is like a cake kneaded with cold water.[123] (ARN 23)

4:15

Rabbi Yannai

1. Once, as Rabbi Yannai was walking, he noticed a man with the appearance of great dignity. "Sir," said he, "will you honor us by being our guest?" The man assented. Yannai brought him in and gave him food and drink. He engaged him in conversation about Scripture, Mishnah, Agadah, and Talmud,[124] but the man knew nothing. He then said: "Come, lead the thanksgiving [after meals]." "Let Yannai give thanks in his own house," the man said. Rabbi Yannai said to him: "Can you repeat what I say?" "Yes," was his response. "Then say, 'A dog has eaten Yannai's food.'" The guest arose and seized Rabbi Yannai and said: "You have my inheritance and are withholding it from me!" "What inheritance of yours have I got?" asked Yannai. "I was walking past a schoolhouse," the man recounted, "and I heard the voices of little children reciting (Deuteronomy 33:4), *The Torah commanded us by Moses is the heritage of the congregation of Jacob.* It does not say the congregation of **Yannai**, but the congregation of **Jacob**." "All the same," Yannai argued, "what makes you

worthy to eat at my table?" "I will tell you," said his guest. "I have yet to hear an insult to which I have responded in kind; and I have yet to see two people quarreling without getting them to make peace." Rabbi Yannai exclaimed: "You are a man of such quality,[125] and I called you a dog!!" (Midrash Leviticus Rabbah 9)

2. Rabbi Yannai had a tree in his field whose branches had spread to the public domain; there was another man with a tree whose branches were in the public domain. The authorities complained of him, and he came before Rabbi Yannai. "Come back tomorrow," Rabbi Yannai told him. That night Rabbi Yannai sent his workers to cut down his own offending branches. The man returned the next day and Rabbi Yannai told him to cut the branches down. "What of your own tree?" expostulated the man. "Go see, and do as I have done, no more, no less."

Why did Rabbi Yannai not cut the branches off before this?

Till then he had thought he was pleasing the public, because of the shade his branches provided. When he saw that they were complaining, he had them cut down. (Talmud Baba Batra 60a; Midrash Tanchuma, Shof'tim)

3. Rabbi Yannai said: If the Torah had been given complete,[126] there would have been no firm ground on which to stand. What does this mean? The Eternal One spoke to Moses, who said: Ruler of the World, tell me the Halachah. He answered: *To side with the majority* (Exodus 23:2). If the majority permit, it is permitted; if a majority prohibit, it is prohibited, so that the Torah may be interpreted as saying Yes in forty–nine ways and No in forty–nine ways.[127] (Jerusalem Talmud Sanhedrin 4:2)

4. Rabah bar Rav Hunah said: One who has Torah but no fear of Heaven is like a keeper of the treasury who has the inner keys but not the outer.

Rabbi Yannai proclaimed: Woe to the one who has no courtyard and builds a gate for it! (Talmud Sanhedrin 31b)

5. Rabbi Yannai saw a man publicly giving a Zuz to a pauper. He said: "Better to have given him nothing than to have given and humiliated him!" (Talmud Chagigah 5a; Midrash Kohelet Rabbah 12)

4:15

Rabbi Matya ben Charash

1. Matya ben Charash was a man of wealth and God–fearing; He spent all his time in the House of Study toiling in Torah like his Master, Rabbi Meir. His face was radiant as the sun and beautiful as one of the ministering angels, and it was said of him that he never looked at a woman.

One time the satan[128] passed by and and was upset by what he saw. He thought: "Can there be a flawless man?" Instantly he ascended to the heights and said to the Holy One: "Ruler of the World, how does Matya ben Charash stand in Your reckoning?" "A complete saint." "Give me leave to test him." "You will not defeat him." "Nevertheless!" God agreed.

Instantly he went and found him sitting engaged in Torah. The satan took on the appearance of a beautiful woman, whose like has not been seen since Na'amah, Cain's sister, whom the ministering angels themselves could not resist. Seeing her, he averted his face. The satan walked around and stood before him. Seeing himself thus beleagured—for turn as he might she would be standing before him—he thought: "I fear that my Yetzer will overcome me and make me sin." What did that saint do? He called one of his disciples, who attended him, and said: "Son, bring me fire and some spikes." When he had them he passed the spikes through the flames and then drove them into his eyes. Seeing this, the satan was shaken: he fell back and fled. That moment the Holy One called to Raphael, Prince of Healing, and said to him: "Go heal the eyes of Matya ben Charash." When Raphael stood before him, Matya ben Charash said to him: "Who are you?" "I am the angel Raphael, whom the Holy One has sent to heal your eyes." "Let me be," said Matya. "What has been, has been." Raphael returned and said to the Holy One: "Ribbono shel olam, this is what Matya ben Charash said to me." The Holy One replied: "Go tell him not to be afraid. I Myself will guarantee that his Yetzer will never hold sway over him." When Matya ben Charash heard this from the angel's lips he allowed himself to be healed. (Midrash Tanchuma B, Chukat; Yalkut Shimoni, Vayechi)

4:16

Rabbi Jacob

1. When Rabbi Jacob died, stars appeared in broad daylight. (Moed Katan 25b)
2. There is no reward for a Mitzvah in this world.

We have learned: Rabbi Jacob says: There is no Mitzvah in the Torah whose reward is mentioned, which does not involve the resurrection of the dead. In regard to honoring one's father and mother is it said, *that your days may be prolonged and that it may go well with you.* And in regard to the bird's nest it is said (Deuteronomy 22:7): *that it may go well with you and that your days may be prolonged.* A father told his son: "Go up this tower and bring me the chicks. He went up, chased the mother and took the chicks. Going down, he fell to his death: Was this 'long life?' How did it 'go well' with him? The text means: *that your days may be prolonged*—in the world that is all length; that *it may go well with you*—in the world that is all good.

Do you suppose this never happened? Rabbi Jacob saw it.

Rabbi Joseph said: Had 'Acher'[129] understood this text as did his nephew Rabbi Jacob, he would not have gone astray.

And what was Acher's experience? Some say he saw what was described above. And others say: He saw the tongue of Chutzpit the Interpreter lying in the dust and he thought: "The mouth that uttered gems of wisdom licks dust!" So he went astray. And he did not know of Rabbi Jacob's interpretation. (Talmud Kiddushin 39a; Chullin 142a)

4:18

Rabbi Simeon ben Elazar

1. They taught in the name of Rabbi Simeon ben Elazar: Love makes one disregard one's self-regard.[130] Didn't Abraham, for example, have many servants? Yet when it came to doing God's will, it says (Genesis 22:3), *Abraham rose early in the morning and [he himself] saddled his ass.*[131] Hatred has the same effect. Did not Balaam have many servants? Yet when it came to cursing Israel, it says, *Balaam rose in the morning and [he himself] saddled his ass.*[132] (Talmud Sanhedrin 105b; Midrash Genesis Rabbah 55)

2. Rabbi Simeon ben Elazar says: "If the young say to you: 'Build the Temple.'— don't listen to them. But if the elders say to you: 'destroy the Temple.'—listen to them. For the construction of the young is destruction and the destruction of the old is construction. And Reheboam son of Solomon is an example." [see I Kings 12] (Tosefta Avodah Zarah 1; Talmud Nedarim 40a)

3. Rabbi Samuel bar Rabbi Isaac taught in the name of Rabbi Simeon ben Elazar: Kohelet[133] says "Vanity" seven times in correspondence with the seven worlds a person sees:[134]

At the age of one year the child is a potentate, sitting in its carriage, hugged and kissed by all.

At two and three he is like a pig with hands full of dirt: whatever he finds he puts into his mouth.

At ten he leaps like a kid.

At twenty he is like a whinnying horse; he adorns himself and looks for a wife.

Married, he is saddled and becomes a donkey.

He begets children, and becomes shameless as a dog to get a living for himself and his children.

He grows old, and is like a monkey (Kohelet Rabbah 1; Yalkut Shimoni, Ecclesiastes 1)

4. Rabbi Simeon ben Elazar says: If your deeds exceed your wisdom, what are you like? Like one who rides a horse with a bridle: you go as you please. If your wisdom exceeds your deeds, what are you like? Like one who rides a horse without a bridle: You ride, you fall off, you break your neck.[135] (ARNB, 34)

5. We have learned: Rabbi Simeon ben Elazar says: Every Mitzvah to which Israel held fast even at risk of death during the time of Roman persecution, such as [rejecting] idolatry and [affirming] circumcision, is now held even more strongly. And

every Mitzvah for which Israel was not prepared to die in those days, such as Tefillin,[136] is now less strongly held.

The Romans once decreed that anyone who wore Tefillin on his head be beheaded. Elijah went out to the marketplace wearing Tefillin. An informer saw him and ran after him. But by the time the man had caught up with him, he had taken them off his head and had them in his hand. "What do you have in your hand?" asked the man. "The wings of a dove," he answered. He opened his hand and showed him the dove's wings. And that's why they used to call him 'Elijah Dove–Wing.'

And why a dove, of all birds? Because Congregation Israel is compared to a dove, as it is said (Psalm 68:14), ...*wings of a dove sheathed in silver, its pinions in fine gold.* As its wings shield the dove, so do the Mitzvot shield Israel. (Talmud Shabbat 130a; Midrash Yalkut Shimoni, Psalms, 68)

6. We have learned: Rabbi Simeon ben Elazar says: Better to do because of love than out of fear.[137] (Talmud Sotah 31a)

7. Rabbi Simeon ben Elazar says: The Yetzer is like iron. Only when iron is in the furnace can you shape it as you please. Only through the words of Torah can the Yetzer be conformed to your will, for they are like fire. (ARN 16)

8. Rabbi Simeon ben Elazar says: The Yetzer: push it away with one hand, embrace it with the other. (Talmud Sotah 47a)

9. We have learned: Rabbi Simeon ben Elazar says: Act while your hands still have the strength for it. So in his wisdom does Solomon advise (Ecclesiastes 12:1), *Remember your Creator in the days of your youth, before the bad days come, and the years arrive when you will say, 'I have no desire in them.'*

...*before the bad days come*—the days of old age;

...*the years...when you will say, 'I have no desire in them*—the days of the Messiah, when there is neither praise nor blame, neither Yes nor No. (Talmud Shabbat 151a)

10. Rabbi Simeon ben Elazar said: *And, behold, it was very good* (Genesis 1:31). "very good"—that refers to sleep.

Can sleep be very good? Strange! Have we not learned otherwise, that wine and sleep are fitting for the wicked and [therefore] good for the world?[138] Why then does he call sleep very good? Because after a little sleep one can get up and do a lot of work in Torah. (Midrash Genesis Rabbah 9)

11. Rabbi Samuel bar Rabbi Isaac taught in the name of Rabbi Simeon ben Elazar: In dreams we are shown only what is in our own thoughts, as it is said (Daniel 2:29), *O king, the thoughts that came to your mind in your bed...* And, if you like, you can derive it from this (ibid. 2:30): ...*and that you may know the thoughts of your mind.*[139]

Rava said: Know, that in dreams we are not shown palm–trees made of gold or elephants going through the eye of a needle. (Talmud Berachot 55b)

12. The emperor said to Rabbi Joshua ben Chananiah: "You claim to be great sages; tell me what I will dream about."

He replied: "You will see the Persians coming. They will subjugate and despoil you; strangers will tend your flocks with golden rods."

He pondered this all that day; at night he saw. (Talmud Berachot 56a)

13. Rabbi Simeon ben Elazar says: Adam, the first man, tasted nothing until he had done work, as it is said (Genesis 2:15), *God placed him in the Garden of Eden to work it and keep it.* Only after this does it say (ibid. 2:16), *You may eat of any tree of the Garden.*

Rabbi Tarfon says: The Holy One did not let the Shechinah rest on Israel until they had done work, as it is said (Exodus 25:8), *Let them make Me a sanctuary, that I may dwell*[140] *among them.* (ARN 11)

14. *Love your neighbor as yourself* (Leviticus 19:18). Rabbi Akiba says: This is a great principle of the Torah.

Rabbi Simeon ben Elazar says: This word—*Love your neighbor as yourself; I am the Eternal*—was said with a fearful oath: "I the Eternal created them; if you love them, you can depend on Me to reward you well; if not, I am the Judge who will punish." (Midrash Sifra, Kedoshim; ARN 16)

4:19

Samuel the Younger

1. Why was Samuel the Younger called 'The Little?'[141] Because he would humble himself (that is, make himself small). And some say: he was a little less great than [the prophet] Samuel of Ramah. (Talmud Sanhedrin 11a)

2. When Samuel the Younger died, they put his notebook and ledger in his coffin, since he had no son. Rabban Gamaliel the Elder and Rabbi Eliezer eulogized him: "It is right to weep for a man like that; it is right to mourn him. Kings die and pass their crowns to their children, the rich pass their wealth to their children, but Samuel the Younger took all that was desireable and went his way. Thus it says (Proverbs 5:17), *Let it be for yourself alone, and not for strangers with you.*" (Ibid.)

3. Rabban Simeon ben Gamaliel said once: "Call seven people to appear in the Upper Chamber at daybreak." The next morning he found eight there. He said: "The one who came up uninvited must leave." Samuel the Younger got up and said: "I'm the one who came without permission. I didn't come to take part in the intercalation of the year, but only to observe what has to be done." The Patriarch then said: "Sit, my son, sit! It would be right were every year to be intercalated by you, only the Sages said: 'The year may be intercalated only by people specifically invited for that purpose.'"

And Samuel the Younger had not really come uninvited—it was someone else, but he did it to spare the other the embarrassment. (Ibid.)

4:20

Elisha ben Abuyah

1. Elisha ben Abuyah said: Scripture considers one who causes another to do a Mitzvah as though he had done it himself. (ARN 24, 39b)

2. One Sabbath day, as Rabbi Meir sat expounding [Torah] in the House of Study in Tiberias, his Master Elisha was seen in the marketplace riding his horse. When they told this to Rabbi Meir, he broke off and went out. [This took place after Elisha's apostasy and betrayal, and his subsequent excommunication.]

Elisha said to him: "What were you expounding today?" He answered: "*And the Eternal One blessed Job's end more than his beginning.*" (Job 42¹²). "And what did you say about it?" "I said (ibid. 42:10): *And the Eternal gave Job twice as much*—for he doubled all his wealth." "Alas for those who are lost and not found! Your teacher Akiba did not teach this. Instead: *And the Eternal blessed Job's end more than his beginning*—on account of the Mitzvot and good deeds that he had in hand from the beginning.

"What else did you expound?" Meir said (Kohelet 7:8): "*The end of a matter is better than its beginning.*" "And what did you say about it?" "One may do business in one's youth at a loss, and do the same thing in age and gain." [Another version: "One may learn Torah in youth and forget it, and learn it in age and fulfill it."] Elisha said: "Alas for those who are lost and not found! Your teacher Akiba did not teach this. Instead: *The end of a matter is better than its beginning*—a matter is good at its ending when its beginning is good. And he was talking about me.

"My father Abuyah was one of Jerusalem's leading citizens. For the feast of my circumcision he invited all the city's leaders, Rabbi Eliezer and Rabbi Joshua among them. As they were eating and drinking, people began to clap and dance. Some were singing and others were reciting [Greek] acrostics. Rabbi Eliezer said to Rabbi Joshua: 'They are doing theirs, and we are not!' So they sat and went on expounding from Torah to Prophets to Writings, and a divine flame descended and surrounded them. Abuyah said to them: 'Sages, have you come here to burn down my house?' 'God forbid,' they replied. 'We were just sitting and going over the Torah, and its words began to rejoice as when they were given at Sinai, so the flames licked them as they had done at Sinai—for at Sinai they came down as fire (Deuteronomy 4:11)—*And the mountain was burning up to the heart of heaven.*" My father Abuyah said to them: 'Since the power of Torah is so great, I dedicate this son of mine—if he lives—to the Torah.' And because he did not intend this for the sake of Heaven, my Torah did not endure."

"And what else did you expound?" continued Elisha.

"God has made the one as well as the other." (Ibid. 7:14)

"What did you say about it?"

"God has made a counterpart for everything in creation; hills and valleys, seas and rivers, for example."

"Your teacher Akiba did not give such examples; rather: righteous and wicked, Eden and Gehenna.[142] In fact, each person has two [potential] destinations: Eden and Gehenna. Judged righteous, you get two shares of Eden; condemned as wicked, you get two shares of Gehenna... And what else did you expound?"

"Gold and crystal cannot equal it, nor can it be exchanged for vessels of fine gold." (Job 28:17)

"What did you say about it?"

"These are the words of Torah: they're as hard to acquire as gold or fine gold and as easy to lose as crystal."

"Oh, God! As clay pots! But your teacher Akiva did not teach this; rather: as gold and crystal vessels can be repaired even if they are broken, so can a sage who sins be cured."

Rabbi Meir then said to him: "If so, turn back—you too."

"No, not I. I cannot."

"Why not?"

"One day, it was on a Yom Kippur that fell on Shabbat, I was riding my horse behind the House of Study, and I heard a divine voice call out saying (Jeremiah 3:14, Malachi 3:7), 'Return, turncoat children; return to Me and I will return to you—all but Acher,[143] who knew My power and rebelled against Me!'"

When they had reached the Sabbath Boundary[144] he said: "Go back, Meir. My horse's hooves have already crossed the Sabbath Line."

"And you...you turn back, too ..."

"Haven't I already told you? I heard this from behind the Veil[145]—'Return, turncoat children: all but Acher!'"

And what made Acher go bad?

They said: He was sitting and learning in the Valley of Genessar when he saw a man climb a palm tree on Shabbat[146] and take dam and chicks together [from their nest] and go down unharmed. At the close of Shabbat he saw a man go up a palm and take the chicks and leave the dam. When he went down he was mortally wounded by a snake. He thought: "It is said (Deuteronomy 22:7), *You shall surely leave the dam, but you may take the chicks; that it may go well with you and that you may prolong your days.* How did it go well with this man? How did he prolong his days?" [He did not know that Rabbi Akiva had interpreted it as follows: *that it may go well with you*—in the world that is all good; *that you may prolong your days*—in the world that is everlasting.] Others say: He saw the tongue of Chutzpit the Interpreter clutched in a hog's mouth and thought: "The mouth that sent forth pearls rolls in the dust!" So he went astray. [See, also, p. 240, on 4:16, No. 2, on Rabbi Jacob]

3. When Elisha ben Abuyah grew ill, they told Rabbi Meir. He paid him a visit and said: "Come back." The other said: "Is one acceptable even now?" "Doesn't it say," Meir pointed out (Psalms 30:3), *You (re)turn mortals to daka,*[147] meaning, as far as the soul suffers?"

Just then Elisha ben Abuyah wept and died. Rabbi Meir rejoiced, saying: "It seems that my teacher departed in the act of turning." When they buried him a flame went forth from heaven to burn his grave. They told Rabbi Meir. He went and spread his Tallit over him, saying (Ruth 3:13, Psalms 145:9), *"Rest the night*—in this world that is like night, *and it will come to pass in the morning*—in the world–to–come, which is forever morning, *if your redeemer is good he will redeem*—that is the Holy One who is good, of whom it is written, *The Eternal is good to all.* And if he does not want to redeem you, I will redeem you, *as the Eternal lives*; stay over till morning." The flame died down.

They said to Rabbi Meir: "If in the world–to–come they ask you, 'To whom do you want to be near, your father or your teacher?' what will you say?" He answered: "My father, then my teacher." "And will they listen to you?" He said: "Have we not learned, [if there is a fire on Shabbat] 'they save the case of [Torah] scroll along with the scroll'? They will save Elisha for the sake of his Torah." (Talmud Chagigah 15a; Jerusalem Talmud Chagigah 2:1; Midrash Kohelet Rabbah 7)

4. Acher's daughter presented herself to Rabbi [Judah the Prince] and said: "Rabbi, give me sustenance."

"Whose daughter are you?"

"I am the daughter of Acher."

"He still has living descendants? Is it not said (Job 18:19), *He has no offspring, no descendant among his people?*"

"Rabbi, remember his Torah, not his deeds." Just then a flame from heaven came down and scorched Rabbi's footstool.

Weeping, Rabbi exclaimed: "If this is for those who degrade the Torah, how much the more for those who exalt it!" (Talmud Chagigah 15b)

4:21

Rabbi Eliezer Hakappar

1. *Honor the Eternal One with your substance.* (Proverbs 3:9) With what God has graciously given you. Whatever talent you possess, praise God with it; if you have a pleasant voice and are in the synagogue, stand and honor the Eternal with your voice.

Rabbi Eliezer Hakappar's nephew had a pleasing voice, and Rabbi Eliezer Hakappar would say to him: "Chiyah, my boy, stand and honor the Eternal with what [the Eternal] has graciously given you." (Midrash Pesikta Rabbati 5)

2. We have learned: Rabbi Eliezer Hakappar says: *He shall make expiation for the guilt that he incurred through the body.* (Numbers 6:11)[148] How did he incur guilt? He afflicted himself by abstaining from wine. And we go from minor to major: If someone who merely abstains [by vow] from wine is called a sinner, all the more is one a sinner who abstains from other [permitted] things. Hence we see that the ascetic is called a sinner. (Talmud Nedarim 10a)

3. Rabbi Eliezer Hakappar says: Great is peace, for even if Israel were to worship idols they would be exempt from punishment, so long as they remained united. As it is written (Hosea 4:17): *Ephraim is attached to images—let him be.* But once they were divided, it says (ibid. 10:2), *Their heart is now divided—they are guilty.* (Talmud Yebamot 65b)

•••••••

Notes

[1] Simeon ben Zoma, 2nd C. CE.

[2] See at 2:9, commentary, and Jeremiah 9:22.

[3] On 'Yetzer (Hara),' see at 2:11.

[4] Or, 'mighty.' In its biblical context the word might be translated as 'warrior.'

[5] See, also, 2.10, 2.12, 4.12.

[6] ?–135 CE.

[7] See, also, 1:3, 2:1.

[8] Hebrew מצוה, *Mitzvah.*

[9] Dates unknown.

[10] The grave. See Ben Sira 7:17 and Avot 3:1. Note that it says 'hope,' not 'fate' or 'destiny.'

[11] Mid–2nd C. CE.

[12] The Hebrew of this passage is in the 3rd person singular.

[13] 2nd half of 2nd C. CE.

[14] See, also, 1:17, 3:9, 3:17, 5:14.

[15] ??1st C. CE??

[16] See 1:13, where this teaching comes from.

[17] Literally, 'take themselves out of the world'.

[18] That is, do it for unselfish reasons.

[19] That is, the totality of Jewish law and lore.

[20] The Hebrew of this passage is in the 3rd person singular.

[21] Ca. 95–180 CE.

[22] and thus the revelation and the Revealer.

[23] Or, "...are honored above all others."

[24] Or, "...are dishonored above all others."

[25] *chayei sha'ah,* 'the life of an hour.' That is, for some comfort in this fleeting life, they give up Torah, which ensures them eternal life.

[26] Ca. 145–210 CE.

[27] Or, "One who avoids litigation"

[28] Or, "...in teaching."

[29] This seems to be his understanding of this verse.

[30] This is how he must read this verse.

[31] Elohim; usually, 'God.' See Note 65.

[32] Or, composed.

[33] See Avot 3:10.

[34] A liquid measure: about fifth of a pint; this amount bars one from sitting as a judge.

[35] to your fellow–judges.

[36] Or, "...for they may say it, but not you."

[37]That is, there is a reason for the repetition of the word צדק, *tzedek*, 'justice,' in our text.

[38]Or, gates, courts.

[39]Probably Jonathan ben Joseph, mid–2nd C. CE.

[40]Or, 'in poverty.'

[41]This world.

[42]Mid–2nd C. CE (Ca. 110-165/180). See 3:8.

[43]See, also, 2:2, 2:5, 3:17.

[44]See, also, 2:14, 2:16.

[45]Mid–2nd C. CE.

[46]Hebrew, מצוה, *Mitzvah*.

[47]תשובה, *Teshuvah*, (Re)turning [to God], Repentance, Response. See 2:10.

[48]Mid–2nd C. CE.

[49]See, also, 3:2b.

[50]Or, 'will have a lasting result.'

[51]2nd C. CE.

[52]See, also, 2:10.

[53]A source from the period of the Mishnah, and therefore authoritative.

[54]ben Illai, ?–ca. 180 CE.

[55]Or, 'learning.'

[56]That is, violation of the Torah that is here being taught and/or learned.

[57]bar Yochai. See 3:3.

[58]See, also, 2:7.

[59]By our deeds.

[60]2nd C. CE. One source in the Talmud (Erubin 13b) identifies him as Rabbi Meir (See 3:8).

[61]Literally, "will help set up in your hands." Another translation: "Leave home to go to a place of Torah, instead of supposing that it will come to you, for [there] your friends will help you to grasp it."

[62]2nd–3rd C. CE.

[63]2nd C. CE.

[64]The commentator plays on the following words: מודה, מדד, מדה, מאדך (*m'odecha, midah, moded, modeh*).

[65]In rabbinic thought אלהים, *Elohim*, 'God,' stands for God in the modality of strict justice, as יהוה, *Adonai*, 'Eternal [One],' stands for mercy. Additionally, *Elohim* occasionally means 'judge.'

[66]Or, the satan. השטן, *ha-satan*, the accuser or prosecuting attorney. One of God's minions [though perhaps not pleased with his role], he has no independent power, but serves as a foil to illustrate the divine justice.

[67]2nd C. CE.

[68]Or, 'banquet-hall.' See, also, 2:10.

[69]Because of the expense.

[70]Who helped prepare the dead for burial.

[71]Which had been destroyed.

[72]See above.

[73]כשר, *kasher*, fitting.

[74]That is, the tears.

[75]That is, tooth.

[76]See, also, 4.11, 2:10.

[77]עולם הבא, the world-to-come.

[78]140–220 CE.

[79]Or, 'make amends with.'

[80]Or, 'try to persuade him to annul a vow.' See, also, 3:13.

[81]Ca. 10–80 CE.

[82]80–ca. 145 CE. He is included despite the fact that he was a notorious apostate.

[83]2nd C. CE.

[84]See 2:1.

[85]Where he was learning Torah from Moses, whose attendant he was.

[86]Or, heart.

[87]Or, scholars, sages.

[88]See, also, 2:11, 4:6, 4:12, 5:19.

[89]2nd–3rd C. CE.

[90]Or, 'fame.' See, also, 1:13.

[91] Or, 'will ruin a person's life.'

[92]That is, whether on balance one's deeds add up to plus or minus. See, also, 3:15, 3:16.

[93]Hebrew יצר הרע, *Yetzer Hara*. See at 2:11.

[94]Hebrew שאול, Sheol.

[95]See, also, 3:1.

[96]Or, mysteries.

[97]A loose translation might be "wrapped in the vestments of piety, or "adorned in sumptious clothing."

[98]That is, rather than the other way around, or than those who wrongly suspect others.

[99] The original has 'father' where we have 'parents'.

[100]That is the sense in which the text must be taken here, to bear Meir's—Yosé's—interpretation.

[101]That is, to the platform from which the priests blessed the people. More generally, he may mean: I accepted any appointment of theirs to any responsible position.

[102]That is, in the course of doing good deeds or fulfilling a commandment.

[103]Shabbat begins earlier in Tiberias, and in Sepphoris ends later, because of its higher elevation.

[104]The verse could be translated: He gives the wise their wisdom, but the point of the question and answer would then be lost.

[105]Or, He raises them and lowers them for this one, He lowers them and raises them for that one. Tanchuma, Vayishlach, has a slightly different answer: "He raises this one and lowers that one, He enriches this one and impoverishes that one."

[106]That is, when they are listened to.

[107]He made them ownerless, by declaration—הפקר, hefker, in the public domain.

[108]Or, drunkard.

[109]ברך, berech, 'blesses,' is here understood as 'curses.'

[110] A person who follows the prescribed rituals but comes to them with morally dirty hands pollutes the whole process.

[111]Literally, with a cheerful countenance.

[112]That is, as a direct revelation.

[113]מקוה, mikveh, means 'hope.' Its root קוה, kavah, has a second meaning, 'gather, collect,' as, e.g., waters (Genesis 1:9). Hence, mikveh, gathering of waters = ritual bath for purification.

[114]The first time he says 'Abraham,' he means Abraham; the repetition of the name is meant for the 'Abrahams' of the future. Similarly, when the others named here are called, their names are repeated.

[115]That is, the number of Israel's tribes.

[116]Understanding 'Wisdom' to be God or Torah [the vehicle through which God created the world].

[117]צדיק, tzaddik, righteous [person].

[118]That is, in the less than seven weeks between Passover and Shavuot.

[119]Compare Avot 2:2.

[120]Judah the Prince.

[121]Angels of destruction.

[122]That is, the capital invested remains for the world-to-come, while the interest, as it were, is payment—and payment enough—in this world. The image is found elsewhere as well in rabbinic literature, and from there has found its way into the morning service of the prayerbook.

[123]Literally, a cake baked with flour prepared in warm water, as against flour prepared in cold water; the former is preferred. On learning Torah when young or old, see Avot 4:20.

[124]That is, every kind of Torah-learning, from law to lore.

[125]דרך ארץ, derech eretz, literally, 'the way of the land,' but actually given a wide range of applications, including good manners, a craft or trade, etc.

[126]That is, closed, without need of interpretation and exposition, and without room for it.

[127]Literally, the Torah may be interpreted in 49 facets as saying 'Pure,' and 49 'Impure.'

[128]השטן, the accuser or prosecuting attorney. One of God's minions [though perhaps not pleased with his role], he has no independent power, but serves as a foil to illustrate the divine justice.

[129]After his apostasy, Elisha ben Abuyah was called אחר, acher, 'The Other One.' And see 4:20.

[130]Greatness (lit.), dignity, standing.

[131]himself.

[132]himself.

[133]Ecclesiastes

[134]Compare Avot 5:21.

[135]Compare Avot 3:9.

[136]Phylacteries: two boxes containing biblical texts affixed to the head and arm by leather straps and worn during the weekday morning service. They may be said to represent the attachment of head, arm, and heart to the divine.

[137]The reference is to the Mitzvot. Another translation: Greater is one who does [God's will] out of love than one who does it out of fear.

[138] The more they sleep the less time they have for mischief.

[139]In both verses Daniel is interpreting King Nebuchadnezzar's dream.

[140]This comment is particulary neat because of its play on the single root for 'Shechinah' [שכינה] and 'that I may dwell' [ושכנתי], That is, שכן, shachen, 'dwell.' The Shechinah is the Divine Presence, the aspect under which God dwells in this world.

[141]הקטן, ha-katan, can be translated either as 'the younger,' or as 'the little.'

[142]Heaven and Hell.

[143]After his apostasy, the sages preferred to avoid his name and called Elisha ben Abuyah 'Acher,' the Other One.

[144]2000 cubits from the edge of town. That was as far as one was permitted to walk on the Sabbath.

[145]that separates the Shechinah from the ministering angels.

[146]He was committing a transgression with impunity.

[147]That is, as far as contrition, to the end of the suffering caused by sin.

[148]This refers to the oath taken by a Nazirite to abstain from certain otherwise permitted things, including wine. Yet the Nazirite does this as part of a self-dedication to God!

A Note

Chapter 5 differs in several respects from its predecessors. It is mostly anonymous, and many of its passages play with numbers. As Neusner points out, this serves to order a shattered reality. Thus the broken is mended, and the world makes sense after all.

•••••••

Additional readings on the sages whose sayings are featured in this chapter begin on page 243.

Avot 5:1

בַּעֲשָׂרָה מַאֲמָרוֹת נִבְרָא הָעוֹלָם.

וּמַה תַּלְמוּד לוֹמַר? וַהֲלֹא בְּמַאֲמָר אֶחָד

יָכוֹל לְהִבָּרְאוֹת? אֶלָּא לְהִפָּרַע מִן

הָרְשָׁעִים, שֶׁמְּאַבְּדִין אֶת־הָעוֹלָם

שֶׁנִּבְרָא בַּעֲשָׂרָה מַאֲמָרוֹת. וְלִתֵּן

שָׂכָר טוֹב לַצַּדִּיקִים, שֶׁמְּקַיְּמִין

אֶת־הָעוֹלָם שֶׁנִּבְרָא בַּעֲשָׂרָה מַאֲמָרוֹת.

THE WORLD was created by means of ten sayings.[1] And what was that meant to teach us? Could it not have been created with one saying?

[It was done] to exact [additional] payment from the wicked, who [thus] ruin a world created by ten sayings. And to give a greater reward to the righteous, who sustain a world created by ten sayings.

ten sayings—Commentators differ in how they reach the number 10, but 10 is a round number, whose point is in the idea of many sayings as compared to one; and the enumerations here and all through this chapter make two larger points: they function as examples encouraging us to make our own lists, and they are based on the belief or hope that our ordering capacity is a sign that this painful life makes sense, that what seems random can be ordered, that the chaos of history can be understood, made to yield meaning, transformed by an act of understanding. (Neusner, et al) In addition, the divine revelation begins with the Ten [Divine] Utterances, usually called the Ten Commandments.

--- This mishnah is the first of a series of six passages linked by their use of the number 10. They lead from the creation of the world to the creation of Israel as the people of the covenant, down to the Temple where the God of creation was worshipped. The point of this linking device may be the thought that creation is continued, completed, or fulfilled by those who are faithful to their covenant with the Creator. (CS)

--- One who does one good deed thereby maintains, as it were, an entire world created by ten sayings; one who commits one transgression thereby destroys, as it were, a world created by ten sayings. (ARN 31)

--- Great therefore is the merit of those who by their lives help to maintain the moral nature of...Creation; and terrible is the responsibility of those who would destroy it. (Hertz, p. 83)

Avot 5:2

עֲשָׂרָה דוֹרוֹת מֵאָדָם עַד נֹחַ,

לְהוֹדִיעַ כַּמָּה אֶרֶךְ אַפַּיִם לְפָנָיו,

שֶׁכָּל־הַדּוֹרוֹת הָיוּ מַכְעִיסִין לְפָנָיו

עַד שֶׁהֵבִיא עֲלֵיהֶם אֶת־מֵי הַמַּבּוּל.

עֲשָׂרָה דוֹרוֹת מִנֹּחַ עַד אַבְרָהָם,

לְהוֹדִיעַ כַּמָּה אֶרֶךְ אַפַּיִם לְפָנָיו,

שֶׁכָּל־הַדּוֹרוֹת הָיוּ מַכְעִיסִין לְפָנָיו עַד

שֶׁבָּא אַבְרָהָם אָבִינוּ וְקִבֵּל שְׂכַר כֻּלָּם.

THE WERE ten generations from Adam to Noah,[2] to show how patient God was with the provocations of so many generations before bringing the Flood-waters upon them.

There were ten generations from Noah to Abraham,[3] to show how patient God was with the provocations of so many generations before Abraham came along and took the reward that had been meant for them all.

From Noah to Abraham

Perspective

Noah was a righteous man, whole-hearted in his generation (Genesis 6:9). According to Rabbi Yochanan, this means: in *his generation*—but not in other generations. In the view of Resh Lakish, this means: in *his generation*—all the more in other generations. Rabbi Chanina said: How expound Rabbi Yochanan's view? If you put a flask of wine into storage with vinegar, its scent, in that place, will be outstanding, but elsewhere not so.

Rabbi Hoshaya said: How expound the view of Resh Lakish? If you put a flask of perfume among foul odors, and if it is pleasant even there, how much the more would it be pleasant in a place that smells sweet! (Talmud Sanhedrin 108a)

Two Who Walked with God

Noah walked with God (Genesis 6:9). Rabbi Judah said: This is like the case of a king who had two sons, one big, the other little. The little one had to walk with him, while the big one could walk before him.

So with Abraham, whose strength was great, God says (Genesis 17:1), *Walk before Me, and be whole-hearted*. But of Noah, whose strength was minute, it is said (Genesis 6:9), *Noah walked with God*. (Midrash Genesis Rabbah 30)

The Dove

And there, in her beak, was a freshly-picked olive leaf (Genesis 8:11). Where did she get it from? Rabbi Bevi said: The gates of Eden opened for her and she brought it from there. Rabbi Aibu retorted: If she had brought it from Eden, she would have brought something exotic, such as myrhh. No—this was a subtle way of saying:

"Master Noah, I prefer this bitter thing from the hand of the Holy One, than something sweet from your hand." (Midrash Leviticus Rabbah 31; Midrash Songs Rabbah 17)

And there, in her beak, was a freshly-picked olive leaf (Genesis 8:11). The dove was saying to the Holy One: Master of the world, let my sustenance come from Your hand, though it be bitter as this olive, rather than depend on flesh and blood, though then my food be sweet as honey. (Midrash Genesis Rabbah 33; Sanhedrin 108a)

Partners

Now Noah was the first farmer to plant a vineyard (Genesis 9:20). When Noah was about to plant his vineyard, Satan came and said to him: "What are you planting?"
He replied: "A vineyard."
Satan said: "What is its nature?"
Noah replied: "Wet or dry, its fruits are sweet, and with them one makes wine that gladdens the heart."
Satan said: "How about both of us planting together?"
He replied: "Certainly." What did Satan do? He brought a lamb and slaughtered it over the vine; then he took a lion and did likewise; he did similarly with a monkey and a pig; and he took their blood and watered the vineyard. What was his meaning? When you drink one cup, you become like a lamb, meek and mild. When you drink two cups, you become strong as a lion, and begin to talk proudly, saying: "Who is like me?" When you have drunk three or four cups, you become a monkey, dancing about, fooling around, speaking loosely, hardly aware of what you are doing. And when you become drunk, you are like a pig. You foul yourself in mire and lie stretched out in filth.
And all this happened to Noah, the saint... (Midrash Tanchuma, Noach)

Bodies and Bricks

The Tower of Babel had seven steps on its eastern side and seven on its western side. They would haul the bricks up on one side and descend on the other. When a man would fall to his death, they would pay no attention; but if a single brick happened to fall, they would lament it, saying: "What a pity! This will delay the work!" When Abram son of Terach passed by and noticed this, he called a curse down upon them in the name of his God, saying (Psalm 55:9): *Eternal One, confuse and divide their tongues! For I have seen violence and strife in their town.* (Midrash Pirkei de Rabbi Eliezer 24)

A Child is Born

When our father Abraham was born a star rose in the east and swallowed up four stars in the four directions. Nimrod's wise men said: "A boy has been born this hour, whose descendants will inherit this world and the next. Let gold and silver be given to his father, and let us put this boy to death." When this proposal was made to Terach, he replied: "You might as well cut off a horse's head, offering him in compensation a roomful of oats. If you kill my son, who will inherit the wealth you propose to give me?"

In the end, Terach concealed Abraham in a cave for three years, where he was sustained by oil and fine meal provided by the Holy One.

When Abraham reached the age of three years, he left the cave. Upon seeing the world, he reflected: "Who created heaven and earth and me?" All that day he worshipped the sun, but in the evening the sun sank in the west and the moon rose in the east. At his first sight of the moon and her attendant stars, he speculated: "This must be what created all things, and these stars are her retainers and servants." All that night, therefore, he worshipped the moon. But the moon sank towards morning, and the sun shone in the east. He concluded: "Such things have no power; they must all have a Ruler: only that One will I worship!" (Bet Hamidrash 2)

Two Ends of A Rope

Then Abraham approached and said (Genesis 18:23, 25), *Will the Judge of all the earth not do justly?*

Rabbi Levi says: If You want the world to endure, do not weigh it on the scales of justice; if You want sheer justice, there will be no world. Do You want both world and justice? You are holding the rope at both ends! Take hold of only one of them! And if You do not show a little mercy, the world will not endure. (Midrash Genesis Rabbah 39, 49)

The Blessing

Thus may your descendants be (Genesis 15:5). Rabbi Levi said in the name of Rabbi Yochanan: What is the meaning of this blessing? It may be understood through the story of a man who went on a journey in the desert. Many days passed; he found neither city nor inn, neither tree, nor water, nor any living creature. At last he spied a tree far off and went towards it, hoping to find water, and he found a spring. The tree was beautiful, its fruit sweet, its branches pleasant and its shade satisfying. He sat at his ease, cooling himself in its shade, eating of its fruit and drinking the water. Replete and refreshed, he arose to depart, and thus did he address the tree: "O tree, how shall I bless you? What can I say to you? That your wood may be healthy, your shade satisfying, your branches pleasant, your fruit sweet? All these are so already. Shall I wish for you a spring at your roots? You already have one. How then can I bless you? Only with this: let all the plantings that come from you be like you!"

So it was when the Holy One created the world: twenty generations passed without a single righteous human being. Then the Holy One found Abraham in Chaldea and said: "Perhaps he will be the one." When he was cast into the fiery furnace and sanctified God's name, standing fast in his moment of trial, the Holy One summoned him to the land of Israel. There Abraham carried on: he built an inn and sustained all who passed by; he brought people under the wings of the Divine Presence, and spread the knowledge of God far and wide.

And so the Holy One said to him: "Abraham, how shall I bless you? What can I say to you? That you, and Sarah your wife, be whole-hearted and righteous? You are already. That your household be righteous? They too are so. How then can I bless you? Only with this: let all those destined to come from you be like you!" (Midrash Numbers Rabbah 2; Ta'anit 5a)

Banished

And she said to Abraham: Banish this bondwoman and her son! (Genesis 21.10) Rabbi Akiba said: We may conclude that our mother Sarah had observed Ishmael building altars, capturing grasshoppers, and offering them up in pagan worship. Therefore she thought: 'He may teach this to my son, who will do likewise, and the name of Heaven will be profaned.'

Abraham argued: "Does one exalt a person only to degrade him? After we have given her her present status and dignity, shall we expel her from our house? What will people say?" She replied: "Since you claim there is something shameful about this, let God decide between us."

Rabbi Simeon ben Yochai said: This is one of four matters which I expound differently from Rabbi Akiba, and mine is the better interpretation. I say it is inconceivable that the household of that saint should harbor such things! How is it possible that there should be idolatry in the household of him concerning whom it was said by God, *For I have known him...* No—the word *tz'chok*[4] used here of Ishmael refers to the question of inheritance. When Isaac was born people rejoiced and said: "A son is born to Abraham! A son is born who will inherit the world!" And Ishmael would laugh and say: "Don't be fools! I am the first-born, and I will receive a double portion!" (Tosefta Sotah 5:6; Midrash Genesis Rabbah 53)

Judgment

Why are you distraught, Hagar? Have no fear, for God has heard the boy's voice, where he is (Genesis 21:17).

Rabbi Isaac taught: This teaches that we are judged only for what we are at the moment of judgment, as it says of Ishmael: God has heard the boy's voice, **where he is.**

Rabbi Simon added: When God took note of the boy's cry and saved Ishmael and Hagar in the wilderness, the ministering angels were astounded. They complained:

"Holy One, how can You provide water from a well for one whose descendants will cause Your children to die of thirst?"

The Holy One replied: "Here and now—tell Me—is this one righteous or wicked?"

They had to say: "Righteous."

The Holy One continued: "Then understand: I judge My children only for what they are at the moment of judgment. The future must take care of itself." [What follows?]

God then opened her eyes. Looking up, she saw a well. She ran and filled a bottle with water, and gave it to the boy (Genesis 21:18–19). (Talmud Rosh Hashanah 16b)

Avot 5:3

עֲשָׂרָה נִסְיוֹנוֹת נִתְנַסָּה אַבְרָהָם אָבִינוּ,
וְעָמַד בְּכֻלָּם, לְהוֹדִיעַ כַּמָּה חִבָּתוֹ שֶׁל
אַבְרָהָם אָבִינוּ.

OUR FATHER Abraham was subjected to ten trials[5] and withstood them all: to show how great was the love of our father Abraham.

ten trials—The various midrashim do not agree on what exactly the ten trials were, although they are unanimous that there were ten. (Duran)

Abraham, Isaac, Satan—the Last Trial

As Abraham and Isaac set forth for Mount Moriah, Satan appeared before Abraham and said: "Where are you going?"

Abraham replied: "To pray."

"With a firestone and wood on your shoulder?"

"We may be away a day or two, and will have to prepare some food."

"Old man," Satan rejoined, "I was there when the Holy One asked you to take your son. Old man, have you gone mad? Old man, are you going to slaughter the child of your old age?"

"Even so."

"And if yet greater trials await you, will you be able to withstand them?"

"Even more."

"And when tomorrow God calls you a murderer for having shed your own son's blood?"

"Even so."

Satan then turned to Isaac and said: "How many prayers your mother offered up that she might have you! Now this old man has lost his mind and is going to slay you."

Isaac replied: "I will not transgress my Creator's will nor my father's command."

His arguments having failed, Satan now became an impassable stream. Abraham entered it with Isaac and his servants. By midstream the water had reached his neck. Abraham called to God: "Ruler of the universe, You are the Single One who called me, so that I too am unique. You have promised that through me your name will become known in all the world. You have charged me to offer up my son to You. Would You now have us drown? If Isaac drowns with me, who will remain to establish Your word, who will call You One?"

At these words the holy One proclaimed: "As you live, you are the one who will bring Me to the world!"

And the stream dried up.

When Satan saw that he could not prevail, he said: "There will be a ram for you to offer in place of your son."

Such is the fate of the liar—not to be believed even when telling the truth.

Avot 5:4

עֲשָׂרָה נִסִּים נַעֲשׂוּ לַאֲבוֹתֵינוּ בְּמִצְרַיִם, וַעֲשָׂרָה עַל הַיָּם. עֶשֶׂר מַכּוֹת הֵבִיא הַקָּדוֹשׁ בָּרוּךְ הוּא עַל הַמִּצְרִים בְּמִצְרַיִם, וַעֲשָׂרָה עַל הַיָּם. עֲשָׂרָה נִסְיוֹנוֹת נִסּוּ אֲבוֹתֵינוּ אֶת־הַמָּקוֹם בָּרוּךְ הוּא בַּמִּדְבָּר, שֶׁנֶּאֱמַר: וַיְנַסּוּ אֹתִי זֶה עֶשֶׂר פְּעָמִים וְלֹא שָׁמְעוּ בְּקוֹלִי.

TEN WONDERS[6] were done for our ancestors in Egypt, and ten at the Sea. The Holy One, ever to be praised, brought ten plagues on the Egyptians in Egypt and ten at the Sea.[7]

In the wilderness, our ancestors inflicted ten trials[8] on the Omnipresent[9] who is blessed, as it is said (Numbers 14:22), *Yet they have tried Me these ten times and have not hearkened to My voice.*

ten wonders—The ten wonders done for our ancestors in Egypt consisted in the fact that they were spared the ten plagues visited on the Egyptians. (Maimonides)

ten trials—There is...a certain daring simplicity, which perhaps only a Jew can fully appreciate, in...linking together the trials which God and Israel brought on each other. This...is one of the characteristic features of the Hagadah[10] in general, and one which is seldom understood or rightly judged by the Christian reader. (TH)

Avot 5:5

עֲשָׂרָה נִסִּים נַעֲשׂוּ לַאֲבוֹתֵינוּ בְּבֵית
הַמִּקְדָשׁ: לֹא הִפִּילָה אִשָּׁה מֵרֵיחַ בְּשַׂר
הַקֹּדֶשׁ, וְלֹא הִסְרִיחַ בְּשַׂר הַקֹּדֶשׁ
מֵעוֹלָם, וְלֹא נִרְאָה זְבוּב בְּבֵית
הַמִּטְבָּחַיִם, וְלֹא אֵרַע קֶרִי לְכֹהֵן גָּדוֹל
בְּיוֹם הַכִּפּוּרִים, וְלֹא כָבוּ גְּשָׁמִים אֵשׁ
שֶׁל עֲצֵי הַמַּעֲרָכָה, וְלֹא נָצְחָה הָרוּחַ
אֶת-עַמּוּד הֶעָשָׁן, וְלֹא נִמְצָא פְסוּל
הָעֹמֶר וּבִשְׁתֵּי הַלֶּחֶם וּבְלֶחֶם הַפָּנִים,
עוֹמְדִים צְפוּפִים וּמִשְׁתַּחֲוִים רְוָחִים,
וְלֹא הִזִּיק נָחָשׁ וְעַקְרָב בִּירוּשָׁלַיִם
מֵעוֹלָם, וְלֹא אָמַר אָדָם לַחֲבֵרוֹ צַר
לִי הַמָּקוֹם שֶׁאָלִין בִּירוּשָׁלָיִם.

TEN WONDERS were done for our ancestors in the Temple:

No woman ever miscarried because of the smell of the sacrificial meat;

the sacrificial meat never went bad;

no fly was ever seen in the slaughterhouse;

the High Priest never suffered uncleanness[11] on the Day of Atonement.

rain never quenched the fire on the altar;

no wind ever blew away the pillar of smoke;

no defect ever spoiled the Omer, the two loaves, or the show bread.[12]

people standing are crowded together, yet when they lie down in worship they have room enough;

no snake or scorpion ever injured anyone in Jerusalem;

and no one ever had to say, "There isn't room enough for me to stay in Jerusalem."[13]

smoke—The pillar of smoke rose up straight as a rod, until it reached the sky. (ARN 35)

Omer...bread—The sheaf of barley was cut on the second night of Pesach for the wave-offering; the two loaves were baked just before the beginning of Shavuot; the show bread was replaced just before each Sabbath. In all three cases, there would not have been time enough to prepare a substitute, had a defect been found in them. (CS)

room enough—While the Temple stood, economic conditions never compelled a resident of Jerusalem to leave, or to seek charity. (Rashi)

N.B.: The last two wonders refer to Jerusalem the city, not to the Temple.

N.B.: These 'wonders' are all negative and, so to speak, 'preventive'—warding off, over several centuries, various relatively commonplace but undesirable accidents, any of which was likely, in time, to occur. And therein lies the wonder. (Talmud Yoma 21ab)

Avot 5:6

עֲשָׂרָה דְבָרִים נִבְרְאוּ בְּעֶרֶב שַׁבָּת,
וְאֵלּוּ הֵן:
פִּי הָאָרֶץ,
פִּי הַבְּאֵר
פִּי הָאָתוֹן,
הַקֶּשֶׁת,
וְהַמָּן,
וְהַמַּטֶּה,
וְהַשָּׁמִיר,
וְהַכְּתָב,
וְהַמִּכְתָּב,
וְהַלֻּחוֹת.
וְיֵשׁ אוֹמְרִים: אַף הַמַּזִּיקִין, וּקְבוּרָתוֹ
שֶׁל מֹשֶׁה, וְאֵילוֹ שֶׁל אַבְרָהָם אָבִינוּ.
וְיֵשׁ אוֹמְרִים: אַף צְבָת בִּצְבָת עֲשׂוּיָה.

TEN THINGS were created at twilight on [the first] Sabbath Eve. Here they are: The mouth of the earth, (Numbers 16:32) the mouth of the well, (Numbers 21:16–18, 22:17) the mouth of the ass, (Numbers 22:28) the rainbow, (Genesis 9:13) the manna, (Exodus 16:15) the rod, (Of Moses: see Exodus 4:17. Others say: Of Aaron: See Numbers 17:23) the shamir, the writing, the writing implement, and the stone tablets. And some say: the demons, too, and Moses' grave[14], and our father Abraham's ram.[15] And some say: the tongs that made the tongs, too.[16]

the rod—Like the other objects here enumerated, it was not the rod itself that was created at twilight, but the human ability to make use of it. (CS)

the rainbow—The bow, a symbol of war, when 'overturned,' becomes the rainbow, a symbol of peace. (CS)

the shamir—See Exodus 20:22, I Kings 6:7, 16, Mishnah Middot 3:4. No iron tool could be used for the hewing of the stone of the altar; rabbinic legend therefore had it that a remarkable rock–cutting worm hewed the stones. See Talmud Gittin 68a, Sotah 48b.

the writing—That is, on the stone tablets of the Ten Commandments (Maimonides, Duran). Although the letters were cut clear through the stone and were visible on both sides, they held in place.

the writing implement—used for the writing of the Ten Commandments. (Duran).

the demons—The forces of temptation and unrest in us date from the dawn of Creation and are part of the equipment of the human soul from its birth. (Hertz, p. 89)

the tongs—All unexplained beginnings are brought about by divine action. (TH)

--- An example of the general human ability to make tools with which one then makes other tools. Homo faber is a technologist. (CS)

Seven things

Seven things preceded the world's creation: Torah, Repentance,[17] Paradise,[18] Gehenna,[19] the Throne of Glory, the Temple, the Messiah's name. (Talmud Pesachim 54a)

Avot 5:7

שִׁבְעָה דְבָרִים בַּגּּלֶם, וְשִׁבְעָה בְּחָכָם:
חָכָם אֵינוֹ מְדַבֵּר בִּפְנֵי מִי שֶׁהוּא גָדוֹל
בְּחָכְמָה וּבְמִנְיָן,
וְאֵינוֹ נִכְנָס לְתוֹךְ דִּבְרֵי חֲבֵרוֹ,
וְאֵינוֹ נִבְהָל לְהָשִׁיב,
שׁוֹאֵל כָּעִנְיָן וּמֵשִׁיב כַּהֲלָכָה,
וְאוֹמֵר עַל רִאשׁוֹן רִאשׁוֹן וְעַל אַחֲרוֹן
אַחֲרוֹן,
וְעַל מַה שֶּׁלֹּא שָׁמַע אוֹמֵר לֹא שָׁמַעְתִּי,
וּמוֹדֶה עַל הָאֱמֶת. וְחִלּוּפֵיהֶן בַּגּּלֶם.

A CLOD[20] has seven traits and so does a sage:
The wise never speak before one whose wisdom is greater;[21]
they do not interrupt their companions;
they are not hasty to reply;[22]
they ask to the point and reply as they should;[23]
they speak of first things first and of last things last;
concerning something of which they have not heard they say, "I have not heard;"
and they acknowledge the truth.[24]
The reverse is true of fools.

to the point—"The one claimed wheat, and the other granted the claim—about barley!" (Talmud Baba Kamma 35b)

"I have not heard"—The wise are not ashamed to say "I have not heard." Such a person was Moses (see Numbers 9:8). (ARNB) [See, also, 4:1 and 4:5, commentaries.]

--- Teach your tongue to say, 'I don't know,' lest you be caught in error. (Talmud Berachot 4a)

--- When you have not heard something from your teacher, say, "What follows I did not learn from my teacher." If you have your own opinion, give it, but add, "so it seems to me." (Rabbi Jonah ben Abraham)

--- "Rabbi Eliezer said, 'Who teach what they have not learned from their teacher drive the Shechinah out of Israel.'" (Talmud Berachot 27b) (see 2:8–9)

N.B.: The wise are 'complete,' whereas clods are 'incomplete' in the sense of lacking the virtues attributed by our mishnah to the wise. Having an undeveloped mentality, and thus being not yet complete, they are mentioned first. In medieval legend, גלם, 'golem' came to mean a clay figure endowed with life through the instrumentality of the Divine Name. The choice of seven attributes for the sage may be intended to correspond to the seven days of creation. (CS)

Seven hidden things

Seven things are hidden from flesh–and–blood: the day of death, the day anxiety will cease, the depth of Judgment, the heart of others, the course of one's fortunes, when the House of David will be restored, when the House of Edom[25] will fall. (Ibid., 54b)

Careful Speech

1. Weigh your words before you let them out of your mouth. (Midrash Derech Eretz Zuta 3)

2. Teach your tongue to say "I don't know," lest you fall into the habit of lying. (Talmud Berachot 4a)

3. Love the word "perhaps" and hate the word "exactly."

Rabbi Chidka put it a little differently: Love the word "perhaps" and hate going on and on and on. (Midrash Derech Eretz Zuta 1)

4. The less clear a matter is the more proofs people bring. (Jerusalem Talmud Berachot 2:3)

5. People say: "A Medean camel can dance on a handful of beans." Here is the camel, here is Medea, here are the beans—yet it isn't dancing. (Talmud Yebamot 45a)

6. People don't lie about matters that will become public knowledge. (Talmud Rosh Hashanah 22b)

Avot 5:8

שִׁבְעָה מִינֵי פֻּרְעָנִיּוֹת בָּאִין לָעוֹלָם
עַל שִׁבְעָה גוּפֵי עֲבֵרָה:
מִקְצָתָן מְעַשְּׂרִין וּמִקְצָתָן אֵינָן
מְעַשְּׂרִין, רָעָב שֶׁל בַּצֹּרֶת בָּא.
מִקְצָתָן רְעֵבִים וּמִקְצָתָן שְׂבֵעִים.
גָּמְרוּ שֶׁלֹּא לְעַשֵּׂר, רָעָב שֶׁל מְהוּמָה
וְשֶׁל בַּצֹּרֶת בָּא.
שֶׁלֹּא לִטּוֹל אֶת־הַחַלָּה, רָעָב שֶׁל כְּלָיָה
בָּא.
דֶּבֶר בָּא לָעוֹלָם עַל מִיתוֹת הָאֲמוּרוֹת
בַּתּוֹרָה שֶׁלֹּא נִמְסְרוּ לְבֵית דִּין,
וְעַל פֵּרוֹת שְׁבִיעִית.
חֶרֶב בָּא לָעוֹלָם עַל עִנּוּי הַדִּין,
וְעַל עִוּוּת הַדִּין, וְעַל הַמּוֹרִים בַּתּוֹרָה
שֶׁלֹּא כַהֲלָכָה.

SEVEN CALAMITIES enter the world, for seven types of transgression:[26]

When some give tithes and some do not, a famine caused by drought arrives. Some go hungry and some are full.

When everyone chooses not to tithe, a famine caused by disorder[27] and drought arrives.

When people fail to set aside chalah,[28] a complete famine arrives.

Pestilence enters the world because of crimes for which the penalty of death is decreed in the Torah, but over which a [human] court has not been given jurisdiction,[29]

and because of the fruits of the Seventh Year.[30]

The sword enters the world because of justice delayed and justice denied,[31]

and because of those who teach the Torah not in line with Halachah.

penalty of death—for crimes whose punishment is reserved for Heaven (karet), see Exodus 12:15, 19; 31:14; Leviticus 7:20f., 27; 19:8; Numbers 9:13; 15:30f.; 19:13, 20.
the fruits of the Seventh Year—That is, the year during which the land is to lie fallow. *The Earth is God's.* (Psalm 24:1) If, then, this law is flouted by farming the land, it betrays an underlying denial of God's sovereignty, and the appropriate punishment for this is exile from the land [see 5:9]. (Bertinoro, Midrash Shemuel)
justice delayed—Putting off sentence and postponing it for a long time, even though the judge has already decided. (Maimonides)
--- in the meantime, that person, kept waiting and not knowing what the outcome will be, is filled with suffering and worry. (Vitry)
--- "The law's delay" erodes the social contract almost as much as does the denial of justice; it is, in fact, a form of denial. (CS)

Justice in Capital Cases

1. Capital cases are decided by 23 judges.

The Sanhedrin was arranged like the half of a round threshing–floor so that they all might see one another. The Patriarch sat in the middle and the elders sat on either side of him. Before them stood the two scribes of the judges, one to the right and one to the left, and they wrote down the words of them that favored acquittal and the words of them that favored conviction. Rabbi Judah says: One wrote down the words of them that favored acquittal, and one wrote down the words of them that favored conviction, and the third wrote down the words both of them that favored acquittal and of them that favored conviction.

How did they admonish the witnesses in capital cases? They brought them in and admonished them, saying: You may say something that is mere supposition or hearsay or at secondhand, or from someone [you think] trustworthy. Or it could be that you do not know that we will test you rigorously.[32] Now you should be aware that capital cases are not like non–capital cases: in non–capital cases one may pay money and so make atonement, but in capital cases a witness is answerable for the blood [of those wrongfully condemned] and the blood of their posterity [that should have been born to them] to the end of time. For so we find it with Cain, who slew his brother, as it is written (Genesis 4:10), *The bloods of your brother cry out.* It says not 'The blood of your brother,' but *The bloods* (pl.) *of your brother*—his blood and the blood of his posterity. Therefore but a single human being was created, to teach that if you cause a single life to perish Scripture considers it as though you have caused a whole world to perish; and if you save the life of a single person Scripture considers it as though you have saved a whole world. ...Therefore every human being must say: For my sake was the world created. And if you say: "All this being so, why should we be at such pains [to bear witness]?"—it was once written (Leviticus 5:1), *He being a witness, whether he has seen or come to know the matter, if he does not speak up, he shall bear his iniquity.* And if you say: "Why should we be guilty of the blood of this man?"—it was once written (Proverbs 11:10), *When the wicked perish there is rejoicing.*

The more judges test the evidence the more are they deserving of praise.

If [after the examination of witnesses, when the examination of the evidence begins,] one of the disciples says: "I have something to say in favor of conviction," they silence him. If one of the disciples says: "I have something to say in favor of acquittal," they bring him up and set him among them and he does not come down from there the whole day. If there is any substance to his words, they listen to him. Even if the accused says: "I have something to say in favor of my acquittal," they listen to him, provided that there is substance to his words.

If they found him innocent they would set him free; otherwise they would leave his sentence over until the morrow. In the meantime they would go about in pairs, eat a little (but they drank no wine all that day), and discuss the matter all night, and early on the morrow they would come to the court. One who favored acquittal says: "I declared him innocent yesterday and I still declare him innocent;" and one who favored conviction says: "I declared him guilty yesterday and I still declare him guilty." One who favored conviction may now acquit, but one who favored acquittal may not retract and favor conviction. If they all found him innocent [upon declaration], they set him free; otherwise they decide by vote. If 12 favor acquittal and 11 favor conviction, he is declared innocent; if 12 favor conviction and 11 favor acquittal, or even if 11 favor acquittal and 11 favor conviction and one says "I do not know," or even if 22 favor accquittal or conviction and one says "I do not know," they must add to the judges. Up to what number may they add to them? By two at a time up to 71. If then 36 favor acquittal and 35 favor conviction, he is declared innocent; if 36 favor conviction and 35 favor acquittal, they debate with one another until one of them that favored conviction approves the words of them that favor acquittal.

When sentence [of stoning] has been passed they take him forth to stone him. One man stands at the door of the court with a towel in his hand, and another, mounted on a horse, far away from him [but near enough] to see him. If [in the court] one said: "I have something to say in favor of acquittal," that man waves the towel and the horse runs and stops him [that was going forth to be stoned]. Even if he himself said: "I have something to say in favor of my acquittal," they must bring him back, even four or five times, provided that there is substance to his words. If then they found him innocent they set him free; otherwise he goes forth to be stoned. A herald goes out before him [calling]: "So–and–so the son of so–and–so is going forth to be stoned because he committed such or such an offence. This one and that one are witnesses against him. Let anyone who knows anything in favor of his acquittal come and plead it."

When he was about ten cubits from the place of stoning they would say to him: "Make your confession," for it is the way of all who have been condemned to death to make confession, for everyone who makes his confession has a share in the world–to–come. ...If he does not know how to make his confession they say to him: "Say, 'May my death be an atonement for all my sins.'"

They used not to bury him in his ancestral burying–place, but two burying–places were kept in readiness by the court, one for them that were beheaded or strangled, and one for them that were stoned or burnt.

When the flesh had wasted away they gathered together the bones and buried them in their own place. The relatives would come and greet the judges and the witnesses as if to say: "We have nothing against you in our hearts, for you have rendered an honest judgment."[33] (from Mishnah Sanhedrin 4–6)

2. Those who are put to death by the court have a share in the world–to–come, because they confess all their sins. Ten cubits from the stoning–place they say to the condemned: "Confess!"

One man, when they told him to confess, said: "May my death atone for all my other sins, but if I have done this sin, let it not be forgiven me..." When this was reported to the judges, their eyes trickled with tears, but they said: "It is impossible to reprieve him, for then there would be no end to the matter; but the witnesses against him will be judged for his blood." (Tosefta Sanhedrin 9:5)

3. Our sages taught: What is "conjecture?" The judge said to them [the witnesses]: Perhaps you saw someone pursuing his fellow into a ruin and you ran after him and found him holding a sword dripping with blood and the victim breathing his last—if you saw [only] this, you saw nothing.

We have learned: Simeon ben Shetach said: May I [not] see the consolation, if I did not see someone pursuing his fellow into a ruin and I ran after him and found him holding a sword dripping with blood and the victim breathing his last. So I said to him: "Villain, who killed this man, you or I?! Yet what can I do, your fate is not in my hands, since the Torah has said (Deuteronomy 17:6), *On the evidence of two witnesses shall the one who is to die be put to death.* May the One who knows all punish the man who killed his fellow!"

They said: The two hadn't stirred before a snake came and bit the man and killed him. (Talmud Sanhedrin 37b)

4. A Sanhedrin that puts one person to death in a week of years[34] is called 'destructive.' Rabbi Elazar ben Azariah says: "Or one in even seventy years." Rabbi Tarfon and Rabbi Akiva say: "Had we been in the Sanhedrin none would ever have been put to death." Rabban Simeon ben Gamaliel says: "They would even have multiplied the shedders of blood in Israel." (Mishnah Makkot 1:10)

Avot 5:9

חַיָּה רָעָה בָּאָה לָעוֹלָם עַל שְׁבוּעַת
שָׁוְא וְעַל חִלּוּל הַשֵּׁם.

גָּלוּת בָּאָה לָעוֹלָם עַל עֲבוֹדָה זָרָה,
וְעַל גִּלּוּי עֲרָיוֹת, וְעַל שְׁפִיכַת דָּמִים,
וְעַל הַשְׁמָטַת הָאָרֶץ.

בְּאַרְבָּעָה פְרָקִים הַדֶּבֶר מִתְרַבֶּה:
בָּרְבִיעִית, וּבַשְּׁבִיעִית, וּבְמוֹצָאֵי
שְׁבִיעִית, וּבְמוֹצָאֵי הֶחָג שֶׁבְּכָל-וְשָׁנָה
שָׁנָה. בָּרְבִיעִית, מִפְּנֵי מַעְשַׂר עָנִי
שֶׁבַּשְּׁלִישִׁית; בַּשְּׁבִיעִית, מִפְּנֵי מַעְשַׂר
עָנִי שֶׁבַּשִּׁשִּׁית; בְּמוֹצָאֵי שְׁבִיעִית,
מִפְּנֵי פֵּרוֹת שְׁבִיעִית; בְּמוֹצָאֵי הֶחָג
שֶׁבְּכָל-וְשָׁנָה שָׁנָה, מִפְּנֵי גֶּזֶל מַתְּנוֹת
עֲנִיִּים.

WILD BEASTS ravage the world because of false swearing and the desecration of the [divine] Name.

Exile enters the world because of idolatry, immorality, and bloodshed, and neglect of the [law concerning the] release of the land.[35]

There are four periods when plagues increase—in the Fourth Year, the Seventh, after the Seventh[36], and every year at the end of The Festival:[37]

in the Fourth, when people do not give the Third Year tithe to the poor;[38]

in the Seventh, when they do not give the Sixth Year tithe to the poor;

after the Seventh, when people deal in the Seventh Year fruits;

and every year after The Festival, when people steal what is owed to the poor.[39]

Wild beasts—Our abuse of that power of speech which distinguishes us from the beasts brings beasts—or bestiality—upon us. (after Rabbi Jonah ben Abraham)

Exile enters the world—The three commandments against idolatry, immorality, and bloodshed are the gravest of all the commandments. In a time when Jews are being persecuted, if a Jew is told (without an intention of forced conversion), "Commit a transgression and your life will be spared," they may transgress in order to save their life—but not if it involves these three transgressions. In regard to these, they must die rather than transgress. And the punishment for these transgressions is exile—captivity. There is none harsher, for it entails subservience to others and is without a trace of independence. (Aknin)

what is owed to the poor—gleanings (Leviticus 19:9, 23:22); forgotten sheaves (Deuteronomy 24:19); the corners of the field (Leviticus 19:9, 23:22).

Avot 5:10

אַרְבַּע מִדּוֹת בָּאָדָם. הָאוֹמֵר:

שֶׁלִּי שֶׁלִּי וְשֶׁלְּךָ שֶׁלְּךָ: זוֹ מִדָּה

בֵּינוֹנִית. (וְיֵשׁ אוֹמְרִים: זוֹ מִדַּת סְדוֹם.)

שֶׁלִּי שֶׁלְּךָ וְשֶׁלְּךָ שֶׁלִּי: עַם הָאָרֶץ.

שֶׁלִּי שֶׁלְּךָ וְשֶׁלְּךָ שֶׁלְּךָ: חָסִיד.

שֶׁלְּךָ שֶׁלִּי וְשֶׁלִּי שֶׁלִּי: רָשָׁע.

PEOPLE COME in four [basic] types. One says:
What's mine is mine and what's yours is yours: this is the average type. (But some say: This is the way of Sodom.[40])
What's mine is yours and what's yours is mine: simple-minded.[41]
What's mine is yours and what's yours is yours: the best.[42]
What's mine is mine and what's yours is mine: the worst.[43]

the way of Sodom—Those who say that this is the way of Sodom are not in disagreement with the first view, but make an additional point, namely, that such an attitude is very close to the behavior of Sodom. Once you get into the habit of letting no one enjoy what is yours, you will eventually refuse to let people enjoy even that which costs you nothing. (Duran)

mine...yours—See, also, 3:7.

--- *When you take the census of the people of Israel, every one of them shall give half a shekel* (Exodus 30:2). The word ונתנו, *v'natnu*, ('they shall give') is a palindrome, because giving involves movement in both directions: as it has been given you, so shall you give to the Giver.... And the cantellation on that word (v'natnu) is kadma v'azla, meaning, "go forward and back"—another hint of the reciprocity to which we are called. (after Bunim, I, p. 261)

Four

Four are called wicked: one who tries to strike someone—even without actually doing it; one who borrows and does not repay; one who shows arrogance; one who is disputatious. (Midrash Tanchuma, Korach)

Four need whole-hearted commitment: Torah, good deeds, prayer, good manners. (Talmud Berachot 32b)

Avot 5:11

אַרְבַּע מִדּוֹת בַּדֵּעוֹת:

נוֹחַ לִכְעוֹס וְנוֹחַ לִרְצוֹת -

יָצָא שְׂכָרוֹ בְּהֶפְסֵדוֹ.

קָשֶׁה לִכְעוֹס וְקָשֶׁה לִרְצוֹת -

יָצָא הֶפְסֵדוֹ בִּשְׂכָרוֹ.

קָשֶׁה לִכְעוֹס וְנוֹחַ לִרְצוֹת - חָסִיד.

נוֹחַ לִכְעוֹס וְקָשֶׁה לִרְצוֹת - רָשָׁע.

THERE ARE four [basic] temperaments:
Quick to anger and quick to be appeased: its gain is cancelled by its loss.[44]

Slow to anger and slow to be appeased: its loss is cancelled by its gain.[45]

Slow to anger and quick to be appeased: the best.[46]

Quick to anger and slow to be appeased: the worst.[47]

four temperaments—These 'temperaments' are actually within our power to improve or make worse. Otherwise you could not call someone a saint for the one and wicked for the other. (Duran)

anger—The chasid is "slow to anger"—that is, there is no requirement that the chasid should *never* be angry: that is possible only for an angel. (Duran)

--- A Chasidic sage used to say, "I keep my anger in my pocket. I take it out only when I need it." (CS)

--- Their wisdom leaves the wise who give way to anger; and if they are prophets, they lose the spirit of prophecy. And even if Heaven has destined them for greatness, those who let anger control them will be abased. (Talmud Pesachim 66b)

--- Those who give way to rage lose sight even of the Divine Presence. (Talmud Nedarim 22b)

Three

The Holy One loves three: who don't show rage, who don't get drunk, who don't stand on their rights. (Talmud Pesachim 113a)

Every day the Holy One weeps over three: who can learn Torah and don't; who cannot learn Torah and do; and a leader who lords it over the community. (Talmud Chagigah 5b)

The Holy One hates three: who say one thing and think another; who can testify in a case and don't; who see people do wrong and bear uncorroborated witness against them.[48] (Pesachim 113a)

Avot 5:12

אַרְבַּע מִדּוֹת בַּתַּלְמִידִים:
מַהֵר לִשְׁמוֹעַ וּמַהֵר לְאַבֵּד -
יָצָא שְׂכָרוֹ בְּהֶפְסֵדוֹ.
קָשֶׁה לִשְׁמוֹעַ וְקָשֶׁה לְאַבֵּד -
יָצָא הֶפְסֵדוֹ בִּשְׂכָרוֹ.
מַהֵר לִשְׁמוֹעַ וְקָשֶׁה לְאַבֵּד -
חָכָם. קָשֶׁה לִשְׁמוֹעַ וּמַהֵר לְאַבֵּד -
זֶה חֵלֶק רַע.

STUDENTS[49] COME in four [basic] types:

Quick to learn and quick to forget: their gain is cancelled by their loss.

Slow to learn and slow to forget: their loss is cancelled by their gain.

Quick to learn and slow to forget: wise.

Slow to learn and quick to forget: a misfortune.

four types—One who says, "I will go and study Torah, for that is my obligation," is worthy. One who says, "I will go and study Torah, perhaps others will see me at it," is inferior to the first. One who says, "I will go and study Torah, perhaps I will learn something and teach it to everyone else," falls between the first two. And one who says, "I will go and study Torah so that I may be called a 'disciple of the wise' [talmid chacham] is good for nothing. (ARNB)

to learn...to forget—The mishnah does not call an intelligent person with a good memory "a saint," because this is an intellectual quality. Such a person is called "wise." Nor does the mishnah call a person who has difficulty understanding and who suffers from a poor memory "wicked," because this is not within one's power. These are not moral qualities because they cannot be acquired. (Maimonides)

--- "Just as no two faces are identical, so are no two minds identical." (Midrash Numbers Rabbah 21:2)

Avot 5:13[50]

PEOPLE WHO give charity come in four [basic] types:

אַרְבַּע מִדּוֹת בְּנוֹתְנֵי צְדָקָה:

הָרוֹצֶה שֶׁיִּתֵּן וְלֹא יִתְּנוּ אֲחֵרִים

- עֵינוֹ רָעָה בְּשֶׁל אֲחֵרִים.

יִתְּנוּ אֲחֵרִים וְהוּא לֹא יִתֵּן - עֵינוֹ

רָעָה בְּשֶׁלּוֹ.

יִתֵּן וְיִתְּנוּ אֲחֵרִים - חָסִיד.

לֹא יִתֵּן וְלֹא יִתְּנוּ אֲחֵרִים - רָשָׁע.

Who want to give but don't want others to give: they have no consideration[51] for others.

Who want others to give but not themselves: they have no consideration for themselves.

Who want to give and want others to give: the best.[52]

Who won't give and don't want others to give: the worst.[53]

Some make themselves rich, yet have nothing; others make themselves poor, yet they have much. (Proverbs 13:7)

Those with a benevolent eye are blessed, for they give of their bread to the poor. (Proverbs 22:9)

People who give charity—The giver is approved by God. However, there are people who seem to need to be the only ones allowed to help someone: this type our mishnah rebukes quite as much and in the same terms as it rebukes those who do not help others. Perhaps they want thanks more than they want to see the relief of the poor and the afflicted. (CS)

four types—Though two of the types do not actually give, all four types are called 'givers.' (CS)

--- There are three types of people with three ways of helping others. Those who give charity, may blessing descend upon them! Superior to them are they who lend their funds. Superior to all are they who form partnerships with the poor, dividing the profits equally. (ARN 41)

the worst—Who is a deceptive [and] wicked person? Rabbi Abbahu said: "One who gives a denar to a poor person, who then has a full 200 zuz. For we have learned (Mishnah Peah 8:8), 'Whoever has at least 200 zuz is ineligible to take [the following, which are set aide for the poor:] gleanings, the forgotten sheaf, Peah or the tithe owed to the poor (Leviticus 19:9f.; 23:22; Deuteronomy 14:22f.; 24:19–21); but one who has 200 less one denar, may take [a denar] even from thousand householders [simultaneously].'" (Talmud Sotah 21b)

Tzedakah[54]

1. Rabbi Chama, son of Rabbi Chanina, said: Why is it said (Deuteronomy 13:5), *Follow after the Eternal your God*? How can a human being follow after the Shechinah, of whom is has been said (Deuteronomy 4:24), *for your Eternal God is a consuming fire*? This means: follow after the qualities of the Holy One. The Holy One clothes the naked, as it is said (Genesis 3:21), *The Eternal God made for Adam and his wife garments of skins and dressed them.* So should you clothe the naked. The Holy One visits the sick, as it is said (Genesis 18:1), *The Eternal appeared to him [Abraham], at the Oak of Mamre.* So should you visit the sick. The Holy One buries the dead, as it is said (Deuteronomy 34:6), *God buried him [Moses] in the valley.* So should you bury the dead. The Holy One comforts mourners, as it is said (Genesis 21:11), *And it came to pass after the death of Abraham, that God blessed Isaac his son.* So should you comfort mourners. (Talmud Sotah 14a)

2. Rav Assi said: Tzedakah is equal to all the other Mitzvot. (Talmud Baba Batra 9a)

3. Rabbi Elazar would give a coin to a poor man before praying. He would say: Scripture says (Psalm 17:15), *As for me, I will behold Your face in righteousness.*[55] (Talmud Baba Batra 10a)

4. *Let them lay hold of My protection, let them make peace with Me.* (Isaiah 27:5) Rabbi Judah, Rabbi Simon's son, says: This poor man sits and protests: "What am I and what is that one? He lives in his house and I live here! He sleeps on a bed and I sleep on the ground!" You got up and helped him—as you live, I regard you as if you had made peace between him and Me. (Midrash Leviticus Rabbah 34; Yalkut Shimoni, Isaiah 58)

5. *The rich and the poor meet together; the Eternal is the maker of them all* (Proverbs 22:2). A rich man said to a pauper: "Why don't you go get a job? You look healthy, you look fit..." The Holy One said to him: "You weren't satisfied with giving him nothing, so you turn a jaundiced eye on what I have given him!" (Midrash Leviticus Rabbah 34)

6. Be careful about the doors of your house: let them not be shut at the time when you sit down to eat and drink.[56] (Midrash Derech Eretz Zuta 9)

7. Rabbi Aba and Rabbi Simeon ben Lakish (both) said: It is better to lend than to give Tzedakah, and better still to set up a business partnership with the poor. (Talmud Shabbat 63a)

Avot 5:14

אַרְבַּע מִדּוֹת בְּהוֹלְכֵי לְבֵית
הַמִּדְרָשׁ: הוֹלֵךְ וְאֵינוֹ עוֹשֶׂה -
שְׂכַר הֲלִיכָה בְּיָדוֹ. עוֹשֶׂה וְאֵינוֹ
הוֹלֵךְ - שְׂכַר מַעֲשֶׂה בְּיָדוֹ.
הוֹלֵךְ וְעוֹשֶׂה - חָסִיד. לֹא
הוֹלֵךְ וְלֹא עוֹשֶׂה - רָשָׁע.

FOUR KINDS of people attend the House of Study:

Who attend[57] but do not practice [what they have learned]: they have the reward of going.[58]

Who practice but do not attend: they have the reward of doing.

Who both attend and do: the best.[59]

Who neither attend nor do: the worst.[60]

· N.B.: As in 5:13, the mishnah speaks of four types and includes among them two who do not perform the specified action. (CS)

do not attend—See 1:17, commentary, on the 'bad neighbor.' (CS)

Avot 5:15

אַרְבַּע מִדּוֹת בְּיוֹשְׁבִים לִפְנֵי חֲכָמִים:
סְפוֹג, וּמַשְׁפֵּךְ, מְשַׁמֶּרֶת, וְנָפָה.
סְפוֹג, שֶׁהוּא סוֹפֵג אֶת־הַכֹּל.
מַשְׁפֵּךְ, שֶׁמַּכְנִיס בְּזוֹ וּמוֹצִיא בְּזוֹ.
מְשַׁמֶּרֶת, שֶׁמּוֹצִיאָה אֶת־הַיַּיִן וְקוֹלֶטֶת
אֶת־הַשְּׁמָרִים.
וְנָפָה, שֶׁמּוֹצִיאָה אֶת־הַקֶּמַח וְקוֹלֶטֶת
אֶת־הַסֹּלֶת.

FOUR KINDS of people sit before the sages: a sponge, a funnel, a strainer, and a sieve.

A sponge absorbs everything.

A funnel takes in here and pours out there.

A strainer passes the wine and keeps the dregs.

And a sieve passes the chaff and keeps the wheat.[61]

N.B.: Ingenious, but in regard to the fourth comparison the author's ingenuity breaks down, for no sieve was ever devised which would let the coarse meal pass through and keep only the fine flour. (TH)

N.B.: 5:12 speaks of students in terms of how quickly they learn or understand and how well they retain their learning. Here the mishnah speaks only of what they retain. (CS)

N.B.: It has been noted that the mishnah speaks literally not of students but of those who 'sit'—implying that the way to learn is patiently to sit and absorb. Midrash Shemuel observes that the mishnah makes no explicit judgment about the four types, leaving the judgment to us, or leaving us to find some value in each of the four types. (CS)

N.B.: This mishnah might lead us to reflect on children and on what they absorb from their parents. (CS)

Avot 5:16

כָּל־אַהֲבָה שֶׁהִיא תְלוּיָה בְדָבָר,

בָּטֵל דָּבָר, בְּטֵלָה אַהֲבָה.

וְשֶׁאֵינָה תְּלוּיָה בְדָבָר, אֵינָהּ

בְּטֵלָה לְעוֹלָם.

אֵיזוֹ הִיא אַהֲבָה הַתְּלוּיָה בְדָבָר?

זֹאת אַהֲבַת אַמְנוֹן וְתָמָר.

וְשֶׁאֵינָהּ תְּלוּיָה בְדָבָר?

זֹאת אַהֲבַת דָּוִד וִיהוֹנָתָן.

IF LOVE depends on an extraneous cause, it lasts only as long as that cause. If love does not depend on an extraneous cause, it never dies away.

What sort of love depends on an extraneous cause? The love of Amnon and Tamar.[62]

What sort of love does not depend on an extraneous cause? The love of David and Jonathan.[63]

Love that depends...does not depend—Contrasting extremes of love: love which seeks primarily gratification of self, and love which is purely unselfish. (TH)

--- Love does not outlive its cause, and therefore must be based on a permanent ideal, or on more than one cause.

--- The 'particular thing,' in the case of Amnon and Tamar, was physical desire. More generally, however, the point made is about any material benefit one craves from another. The reverse, then, is love that has no ulterior motive. (CS)

--- The Second Temple was destroyed because of causeless hatred (Talmud Yoma 9b). It is time to atone for that hatred by causeless love. (Rav Kook) [See, also, 2:11]

Love and Hate

1. This is what the Holy One said to Israel: "My children, what do I ask of you? Only this: that you love one another and honor one another." (Midrash Tanna De Be Eliyahu Rabbah 26)

2. What is the teaching concerning "hatred of people?" Do not say, "Love the sages and hate the disciples," or, "Love the disciples and hate the unlettered, but "Love them all." (ARN 16 on Avot 2)

3. Our sages taught: *Do not hate another[64] in your heart* (Leviticus 19:17). One might suppose it is [only] forbidden to strike, slap, curse—therefore the Torah teaches *in your heart*—the passage is talking about hatred.[65] (Talmud Arachin 16b)

4. It is said (Leviticus 19:18), *You shall not take vengeance or bear a grudge against any of your people.* I am cutting meat and the knife cuts my hand: should I now hit my knife-hand? (Jerusalem Talmud Nedarim 9:4)

5. We have learned: What is 'vengeance,' and what is 'bearing a grudge?'

One says: "Lend me a knife," and the other refuses. The next day the latter says: "Lend me your shovel," and the first replies: "You didn't lend me what I wanted, now I won't lend you what you want."—that is vengeance.

One says: "Lend me your shovel," and the other refuses. The next day the latter says: "Lend me your hammer," and the first replies: "You refused to lend me what I wanted, but I'm not like you."—that is bearing a grudge. (Talmud Yoma 23a)

6. Love that does not include reproof is not love. (Midrash Genesis Rabbah 54)

7. It's easy to gain a foe, hard to acquire a friend.[66] (Midrash Yalkut Shimoni, Va-etchanan)

8. Who are the strongest of the strong? They who make their foe a friend. (ARN 23)

9. The proverb has it: "You feel for your friend what your friend feels for you." (Midrash Sifre Devarim)

10. My feet lead me to the place my heart loves. (Midrash Mechilta, Yitro)

11. The First Temple was destroyed by [reason of] three things: idolatry, immorality, and bloodshed. But in the time of the Second Temple people were devoted to Torah, Mitzvot, and deeds of loving kindness. What then destroyed it? Causeless hatred.

This teaches that causeless hatred is as grave as these three transgressions: idolatry, immorality, and bloodshed. (Talmud Yoma 9b)

12. Rabbi Yochanan ben Torta said: The first Temple was destroyed because of idolatry, immorality, and bloodshed. But in the days of the second Temple they were devoted to [the study of] Torah and careful about tithes. Why then was it destroyed? Because they loved money and hated each other. Learn then that hatred is a grave sin before the Holy One, that it weighs as heavily as idolatry, immorality, and bloodshed. (Jerusalem Talmud Menachot 13:22)

13. When our love was strong, we could sleep on a bed no wider than a sword's edge; now that our love has grown weak, a bed sixty cubits wide is too small for us. (Talmud Sanhedrin 7a)

Avot 5:17

כָּל־מַחֲלֹקֶת שֶׁהִיא לְשֵׁם שָׁמַיִם

סוֹפָהּ לְהִתְקַיֵּם, וְשֶׁאֵינָהּ לְשֵׁם

שָׁמַיִם אֵין סוֹפָהּ לְהִתְקַיֵּם.

אֵיזוֹ הִיא מַחֲלֹקֶת שֶׁהִיא לְשֵׁם שָׁמַיִם?

זוֹ מַחֲלֹקֶת הִלֵּל וְשַׁמַּאי.

וְשֶׁאֵינָהּ לְשֵׁם שָׁמַיִם?

זוֹ מַחֲלֹקֶת קֹרַח וְכָל־עֲדָתוֹ.

EVERY CONTROVERSY that is for the sake of Heaven[67] will bear fruit. And one that is not for the sake of Heaven will not bear fruit.

What is a controversy for the sake of Heaven? That of Hillel and Shammai.

And one not for the sake of Heaven? That of Korach and his cabal.[68]

controversy—In the first instance, both sides were serving truth as they saw it; in the other example, Korach's was an unjustified rebellion against authority, and nothing more. (TH)

--- Once, when (as usual) they differed, it was said of the disciples of Hillel and Shammai, These and these are the words of the living God—but the Halachah is according to the School of Hillel. (Talmud Berachot 3b) See, also, Acts 5:38–9. [And see above, 'Beit Hillel and Beit Shammai'] (CS)

for the sake of Heaven—That is, to establish truth, or to rebuke people because of their transgression—and not out of a passion to dominate others or to build up a reputation, or to glorify oneself at the expense of others. (Vitry)

Hillel and Shammai—In their debates one of them would render a decision and the other would argue against it, out of a desire to discover the truth, not out of the wish to prevail. That is why, when he was right, the words of the one who disagreed, endured. (Meiri)

Korach and his cabal are named, but not Moses [against whom Korach rebelled], for that would raise Korach to a position of equality with Moses, making it seem as though Moses were a partner in the dispute. But it was in fact one-sided: Korach rebelled in pursuit of personal, unworthy ambition. See Midrash Tanchumah, Korach, 5.

Avot 5:18

כָּל־הַמְזַכֶּה אֶת־הָרַבִּים אֵין חֵטְא בָּא עַל יָדוֹ. וְכָל־הַמַּחֲטִיא אֶת־הָרַבִּים אֵין מַסְפִּיקִין בְּיָדוֹ לַעֲשׂוֹת תְּשׁוּבָה. מֹשֶׁה זָכָה וְזִכָּה אֶת־הָרַבִּים, זְכוּת הָרַבִּים תְּלוּיָה בּוֹ, שֶׁנֶּאֱמַר: צִדְקַת יהוה עָשָׂה וּמִשְׁפָּטָיו עִם־יִשְׂרָאֵל. יָרָבְעָם חָטָא וְהֶחֱטִיא אֶת־הָרַבִּים, חֵטְא הָרַבִּים תְּלוּיָה בּוֹ, שֶׁנֶּאֱמַר: עַל־חַטֹּאות יָרָבְעָם אֲשֶׁר חָטָא וַאֲשֶׁר הֶחֱטִיא אֶת־יִשְׂרָאֵל.

WHO LEADS the people[69] to virtue will never be the cause of wrongdoing. Who leads the people to wrongdoing will never be allowed to repent.[70]

Moses was himself virtuous and led the people to virtue, so the people's virtue was credited to him, as it is said (Deuteronomy 33:21), *He carried out the justice of the Eternal, and his judgments are with Israel.*

Jereboam went wrong and led the people astray, so the people's wrongdoing was blamed on him, as it is said (I Kings 15:30), *For the wrongs that Jereboam committed and that he caused Israel to commit.*

will never be allowed to repent—It would be unjust if he escaped punishment by means of penitence, while those whom he misled suffered. The sins he led others to commit rise in judgment against him, and these sins are beyond the remedial action of his own repentance; see Talmud Yoma 87a. "There is a fine chivalry in this Jewish doctrine. Jewish teachers alone have had the moral insight to discern, and the wisdom to teach, this lesson." (Hertz, pp. 98f., quoting TH)

Avot 5:19[71]

כָּל־מִי שֶׁיֵּשׁ בּוֹ שְׁלֹשָׁה דְבָרִים הַלָּלוּ
מִתַּלְמִידָיו שֶׁל אַבְרָהָם אָבִינוּ; וּשְׁלֹשָׁה
דְבָרִים אֲחֵרִים מִתַּלְמִידָיו שֶׁל בִּלְעָם
הָרָשָׁע.

עַיִן טוֹבָה, וְרוּחַ נְמוּכָה, וְנֶפֶשׁ שְׁפָלָה:
מִתַּלְמִידָיו שֶׁל אַבְרָהָם אָבִינוּ.

עַיִן רָעָה, וְרוּחַ גְּבוֹהָה, וְנֶפֶשׁ רְחָבָה:
מִתַּלְמִידָיו שֶׁל בִּלְעָם הָרָשָׁע.

מַה בֵּין תַּלְמִידָיו שֶׁל אַבְרָהָם אָבִינוּ
לְתַלְמִידָיו שֶׁל בִּלְעָם הָרָשָׁע?

תַּלְמִידָיו שֶׁל אַבְרָהָם אָבִינוּ אוֹכְלִין
בָּעוֹלָם הַזֶּה וְנוֹחֲלִין בָּעוֹלָם הַבָּא,
שֶׁנֶּאֱמַר: לְהַנְחִיל אֹהֲבַי יֵשׁ וְאֹצְרֹתֵיהֶם
אֲמַלֵּא.

אֲבָל תַּלְמִידָיו שֶׁל בִּלְעָם הָרָשָׁע
יוֹרְשִׁין גֵּיהִנָּם וְיוֹרְדִין לִבְאֵר שָׁחַת,
שֶׁנֶּאֱמַר: וְאַתָּה אֱלֹהִים תּוֹרִדֵם לִבְאֵר
שָׁחַת, אַנְשֵׁי דָמִים וּמִרְמָה לֹא־יֶחֱצוּ
יְמֵיהֶם; וַאֲנִי אֶבְטַח־בָּךְ.

WHO POSSESSES these three qualities is a disciple of our father Abraham; who possesses three other qualities is a disciple of Baalam[72] the wicked.

the disciple of our father Abraham:

A generous spirit, an unassuming manner, humility.

the disciple of Balaam the wicked:

An ungenerous spirit, an overbearing manner, arrogance.[73]

How do the disciples of our father Abraham differ [in their fate] from the disciples of Balaam the wicked?

The disciples of our father Abraham delight in this world and inherit the world–to–come, as it is said (Proverbs 8:21), *Those who love Me I endow with substance, and I will fill their treasuries.*

But the disciples of Balaam the wicked inherit Gehenna[74] and go down to the pit of destruction, as it is said (Psalm 55:24), *You, O God, will bring them down to the pit of destruction; people of bloodshed and deception will not live out half their days; but I will trust in You.*

the disciples—Note that the contrast is not between Abraham and Balaam, but between their disciples: a religious system is judged not by its founders, but by the lives that their followers after them lead. The purpose of this mishnah seems to stress the fact that selfishness, pride and haughtiness are un–Jewish vices. The characterization of the followers of Balaam is harsh, but—as a Christian commentator admits—so were the attacks on Jews by contemporaries of the author of this saying. (Hertz, p. 99)

Avot 5:20

יְהוּדָה בֶּן תֵּימָא אוֹמֵר:	JUDAH BEN Tema[75] says:
הֱוֵי עַז כַּנָּמֵר,	Be bold as a leopard,
וְקַל כַּנֶּשֶׁר,	light as an eagle,
וְרָץ כַּצְּבִי,	swift as a gazelle,
וְגִבּוֹר כָּאֲרִי	and strong as a lion
לַעֲשׂוֹת רְצוֹן אָבִיךָ שֶׁבַּשָּׁמָיִם.	to do the will of your Divine Parent.
הוּא הָיָה אוֹמֵר:	HE WOULD say:
עַז פָּנִים לְגֵּיהִינָּם,	The brazen go to Gehenna,[76]
וּבֹשֶׁת פָּנִים לְגַן עֵדֶן.	the modest, to the Garden of Eden.
יְהִי רָצוֹן מִלְּפָנֶיךָ, יְהוָה אֱלֹהֵינוּ,	May it be Your will, Eternal One, our God, to rebuild Your city speedily, in our time, and may Your Torah be our way of life.
שֶׁתִּבְנֶה עִירְךָ בִּמְהֵרָה בְיָמֵינוּ,	
וְתֵן חֶלְקֵנוּ בְּתוֹרָתֶךָ.	

be bold—A student ought to be 'bold as a leopard,' and not ashamed to ask questions. If you have not understood, do not say 'I understand.' And having been taught something once, twice, and three times, and still not understanding, say to your master, 'Teach it to me once again.' And even if your teacher grows angry with you, do not be shamed into silence. If a leopard, a creature without intelligence, uses all his daring to seize his prey and get food, you, a creature of intelligence, all the more must use all your daring to acquire life for your soul in the world–to–come. (Aknin)

swift as a gazelle—Rabbi Tarfon taught in the name of Rabbi Joshua ben Levi: One should always run to do a Mitzvah, even on the Sabbath (when running is discouraged). (Talmud Berachot 6a)

--- Whatever the righteous do, they do swiftly. (Midrash Numbers Rabbah 10:5)

Be bold...light...swift...strong—Strive to serve your Creator with all your powers. (Meiri)

A Sense of Shame

1. This nation is known by three signs: they are compassionate, shamefaced, and kind. (Talmud Yebamot 79a)

2. Ulla said: Jerusalem was destroyed because the people lacked a sense of shame, as it is said (Jeremiah 6:15), *Were they ashamed when they committed abomination?*

No, they were not at all ashamed; they did not know how to blush. Therefore they shall be among those who fall.

3. Be ashamed of your own accord rather than by the judgment of others. (Midrash Derech Eretz Zuta 2a)

Avot 5:21[77]

הוּא הָיָה אוֹמֵר:	HE WOULD say:
בֶּן חָמֵשׁ שָׁנִים לַמִּקְרָא,	Five years old to [study] Scripture,
בֶּן עֶשֶׂר לַמִּשְׁנָה,	Ten for Mishnah,
בֶּן שְׁלֹשׁ עֶשְׂרֵה לַמִּצְוֹת,	Thirteen for the Mitzvot,
בֶּן חֲמֵשׁ עֶשְׂרֵה לַתַּלְמוּד,	Fifteen for Talmud,
בֶּן שְׁמֹנֶה עֶשְׂרֵה לַחֻפָּה,	Eighteen for the Chuppah,[78]
בֶּן עֶשְׂרִים לִרְדּוֹף,	Twenty to pursue,[79]
בֶּן שְׁלֹשִׁים לַכֹּחַ,	Thirty for vigor,
בֶּן אַרְבָּעִים לַבִּינָה,	Forty for understanding,
בֶּן חֲמִשִּׁים לָעֵצָה,	Fifty for counsel,
בֶּן שִׁשִּׁים לַזִּקְנָה,	Sixty for old age,
בֶּן שִׁבְעִים לַשֵּׂיבָה,	Seventy for whitened hair,
בֶּן שְׁמוֹנִים לַגְּבוּרָה,	Eighty for strength,[80]
בֶּן תִּשְׁעִים לָשׁוּחַ,	Ninety for bent back,
בֶּן מֵאָה כְּאִלּוּ מֵת וְעָבַר וּבָטֵל מִן הָעוֹלָם.	One hundred—one is as good as dead and passed away and faded from the world.

N.B.: Life is seen here as having three main periods: preparation, maturity, decline. (TH)

King David lived seventy years, and Scripture says (I Chronicles 29:28), *He died in a good old age.*

aging and death—Rabbi Yosé ben Kisma said: Better are the two than the three; and alas for the one who goes away and does not return. Rabbi Dima came and said: Childhood is a garland of roses; old age is a crown of thorns. (Talmud Shabbat 152a) [Rashi interprets: 'two' are the legs of youth; the third is a cane; Rav Chisda interprets: 'the one who goes away' is youth.]

Avot 5:22

בֶּן בַּג בַּג אוֹמֵר:

הֲפֹךְ בָּהּ, וְהַפֵךְ בָּהּ, דְּכֹלָּא בַהּ,

וּבַהּ תֶּחֱזֵי, וְסִיב וּבְלֵה בַהּ, וּמִנַּהּ לָא

תָזוּעַ, שֶׁאֵין לְךָ מִדָּה טוֹבָה הֵימֶנָּה.

BEN BAG Bag[81] says:
Turn it[82] and turn it again, for everything is in it; reflect on it and grow old and grey in it and do not move away from it, for[83] there is no better way than this.

everything is in it—Ben Bag Bag comes to warn us not to be content with a superficial reading of the Torah; on the contrary, let us go over it again and again. As the sages in the Talmud teach us (Chagiga 9b): "One who studies a text one hundred times cannot be compared with one who studies it one hundred and one times." (Meiri)

--- Each time you study, you will discover new insights. (Duran)

--- Rabbi Yochanan said: *Who tends a fig tree will eat its fruit* (Proverbs 27.18). Why are the words of Torah likened to a fig tree? As long as you search in a fig tree, you will find ripe figs [for they do not ripen at the same time]. So with the Torah: so long as we ponder its words, we will find meaning in them. (Talmud Erubin 54ab)

Avot 5:23

בֶּן הֵא הֵא אוֹמֵר: BEN HEI Hei[84] says:

לְפוּם צַעֲרָא אַגְרָא.   According to the labor is the reward.[85]

Aramaic—The statements of Ben Bag Bag and Ben Hei Hei are given in Aramaic, the vernacular, because they resemble proverbs. (Vitry)

--- We do not understand why the statements of Ben Bag Bag and Ben Hei Hei were given in Aramaic. Perhaps these two sages came from Babylonia, as did Hillel. (Duran)

reward—Rav Assi said: One who intended to do a good deed but was prevented is regarded by Scripture as having done it. (Talmud Berachot 6a)

In Sum

The Mishnah—and Avot—tell us how the sages prevailed against the world. They refused to give up. They held to God, looked to the past (Torah), and created their own Torah (Mishnah). We too are survivors; they can teach us. The sages made choices. Their problems were: how to manage without the cult for atonement; how to explain the disaster; how to build a life in the new age; how to account for the new social structures that had come into being. In their time there were four responses:

The Apocalyptics thought the end of time imminent: the new age was coming, in which God would destroy evil and establish righteousness forever.

The Dead Sea Essenes opened a sectarian monastery and lived apart. They rejected the cult even while the Temple still stood, and awaited the end.

The Christian "church" also rejected the cult and awaited the end. Unlike the Essenes, however, they did not live apart from society. After the Temple's destruction, they argued that it didn't matter, that the Messiah had already come. This was an answer to a question that was different from the one asked by

the Pharisees, who determined to keep the laws of ritual purity *outside* the Temple (as well as inside), because for them holiness inhered in the whole land and people, not only in the cult. If priests can serve God, so can everyone, they held. Thus, after 70, the *people* became the Temple. The sages worked out their ideas in Yavneh, and their message was: survival is (will be) the result of Torah. (Neusner)

•••••••

The following section supplements Pirké Avot, by adding passages from elsewhere in the rabbinic literature that either quote or tell about the sages of Avot.

5:20

Judah ben Temah

Judah ben Temah would say: Always love Heaven, fear Heaven, and rejoice in all the Mitzvot.

If you have done your friend a small injury, let it seem like a great one to you; and if you have done your friend much good, let it seem to you a trifle.

If your friend has done you a small favor, let it seem great to you; and if your friend has done you a great injury, let it seem to you a trifle. (ARN 41)

5:22

Ben Bag Bag

Ben Bag Bag says: Never enter your neighbor's property without permission, even to take something that belongs to you, lest you appear to be a thief. Instead, say clearly: I'm going to take my belongings! (Talmud Baba Kamma 27b)

5:23

Ben Hei Hei

Elijah said to Ben Hei Bei [and some say: to Rabbi Elazar]: *See, I am refining you, but not as silver; I am testing you in the furnace of affliction* (Isaiah 48:10). That teaches that the Holy One, having reviewed every benefit worth conferring upon Israel, found nothing better than affliction. (Talmud Chagigah 9b)

•••••••

Notes

[1]"God said: 'Let there be...'" See Genesis, ch. 1, 2.

[2]See Genesis 5.

[3]See Genesis 11.

[4]'play, smile, or laugh'

[5]See Genesis 12–22.

[6]The Ten Plagues, Exodus 7–11.

[7]There is no Biblical source for this statement.

[8]See Exodus 14–17, Numbers 11.

[9]See Note at 2:9.

[10]That is, rabbinic literature in its speculative, non–legal mode.

[11]From a nocturnal emission which, in addition to preventing him from serving in the Temple on that day, would have shamed him. Disqualifications for other reasons are recorded in Talmud Yoma 12b, 47a.

[12]See Leviticus 23–24, I Samuel 21:7.

[13]on the three Pilgrimage Festivals, when Jerusalem was especially crowded, as people came from all over to celebrate.

[14]See Deuteronomy 34:6, Talmud Sotah 13b–14a.

[15]See Genesis 22:13.

[16]For the way to make tongs is by means of other tongs. Who, then, made the first tongs? You must conclude that they were created by Heaven. (Vitry). Others argue, contra, that the first tongs could have been made with a mold or die, just many other things are. This is perhaps a little more literal than necessary.

[17]Teshuvah, See Glossary

[18]*gan eden*, the Garden of Eden. See Glossary

[19]Hell.

[20]Hebrew גולם, *golem*, an unformed, incomplete being; unfinished matter; a fool.

[21]See, also, 3:13; Proverbs 18:13.

[22]Or, "do not hasten to reply;" or, "are not at a loss for an answer."

[23]That is, 'pertinently;' the Hebrew has the word הלכה, *Halachah*, 'the law.'

[24]That is, they give up their own view when shown to be wrong.

[25]Rome, That is, the current oppressor in any age.

[26]See Leviticus 26:19ff.

[27]That is, (social) unrest.

[28]Dough–offering. See Numbers 15:20.

[29]That is, by the Torah itself, so that pestilence is Heaven's own way of righting or avenging these wrongs.

[30]See Leviticus 25:1–7 for the regulations concerning the Sabbatical Year of the Land.

[31]Or, 'perverted.' See, also, 1:1, 1:18.

³²Literally, by examination and inquiry.

³³Based on the Danby translation with some adaptations.

³⁴That is, 7 years.

³⁵This refers to the release of the land in the Sabbatical Year. See the preceding mishnah and Leviticus 25:1–7.

³⁶That is, in the 1st year of the new seven–year cycle.

³⁷That is, Sukkot, the Festival par excellence.

³⁸See Deuteronomy 14:28f.

³⁹That is, apart from the cyclical tithe. See Leviticus 19:9, Deuteronomy 24:19.

⁴⁰See Ezekiel 16:49. The parenthetical view holds that, far from being the way of the average person, the first type follows the way of intense selfishness, denying all relation between people, leaving each shut away in radical aloneness. (TH)

⁴¹Hebrew עם הארץ, am ha-aretz, 'ignorant,' 'a boor,' etc. See Note at 2:5.

⁴²Hebrew חסיד, chasid, 'loyal [to God],' 'a saint,' 'truly pious.'

⁴³Hebrew רשע, rasha, 'wicked,' an 'evildoer, villain, scoundrel, etc.'

⁴⁴Some versions reverse 'gain' and 'loss.'

⁴⁵See preceding Note.

⁴⁶See Note at 5:10.

⁴⁷See Note at 5:10.

⁴⁸Two witnesses are required; thus nothing is gained but a reputation is blackened and the court's time is wasted.

⁴⁹Or, 'disciples.' The Hebrew of the rest of this passage is in the 3rd person singular.

⁴¹See, also, 3:7, 5:10.

⁵¹Literally, "has a bad eye for others, begrudges others." See, also, 2:9. The Hebrew of the rest of this passage is in the 3rd person singular.

⁵²See Note at 5:10.

⁵³See Note at 5:10.

⁵⁴'Charity,' from Hebrew for 'righteousness.'

⁵⁵ A play on צדקה, Tzedakah, = righteousness and charity.

⁵⁶ See, also, 1:5.

⁵⁷The Hebrew of the rest of this passage is in the 3rd person singular.

⁵⁸See, also, 4:5, commentary.

⁵⁹See Note at 5:10.

⁶⁰See Note at 5:10.

⁶¹Literally, "passes the coarse meal and keep the fine flour."

⁶²See II Samuel 13:15.

⁶³See I Samuel 18:1

⁶⁴Literally, your brother.

⁶⁵Even without overt actions.

⁶⁶Or, It's easy acquire someone who hates you and hard to acquire someone who

loves you.

[67]See 2:2 and, especially, 4:11.

[68]See Numbers 16–17.

[69]Or, 'community.' See. Also, 2:2

[70]Or, '(re)turn [to God]'. Literally, 'to do Teshuvah.' See 2:10. The author may also have had in mind the story of Elisha ben Abuyah (see 4:20).

[71]See, also, 2:9.

[72]See Numbers 22.

[73]See, also, 2:11, 4:21.

[74]See 1:5. Note that the mishnah is silent about how the 'disciples of Balaam' fare in this world, unless we suppose (with Meiri) that their inheritance of Gehenna is in this world, that theirs is a living hell.

[75]Dates unknown.

[76]See 1:5.

[77]"The ages of Man," As You Like It, III:7.

[78]That is, marriage.

[79]That is, a livelihood. Or, righteousness. (Rashi)

[80]See Psalm 90:10.

[81]B–G, the 2nd and 3rd letters of the Hebrew alphabet. The Eng. equivalent would be: X (Anon.) Sometimes this saying is attributed to a proselyte—one of Hillel's disciples, perhaps. If so, the Hebrew B+G=H (2+3=5), and H, is the letter added to Abram's name when he became Abraham, a sign of exaltation; and Abraham is the quintessential convert and the quintessential 'missionary.' This applies also to Ben Hei Hei in 5:23. See first Note to 5:23.

[82]That is, the Torah.

[83]Up to this point the passage has been in Aramaic; it concludes in Hebrew.

[84] H(ei), is the 5th letter of the Hebrew alphabet, and an abbreviation for the word meaning Eternal [One]. To this should be added the comment on Ben Bag Bag, above.

[85]The passage is in Aramaic.

Avot 6

פרק קנין תורה—The Chapter of the Acquisition of Torah

שָׁנוּ חֲכָמִים בִּלְשׁוֹן הַמִּשְׁנָה. בָּרוּךְ שֶׁבָּחַר בָּהֶם וּבְמִשְׁנָתָם.

The sages taught what follows in the style of the Mishnah. Blessed is the One who called them forth to teach.

Chapter 6 is not part of the original Avot. It was attached later in praise of Torah, the grand passion of the Sages.

Avot 6:1

רַבִּי מֵאִיר אוֹמֵר:

כָּל־הָעוֹסֵק בַּתּוֹרָה לִשְׁמָהּ זוֹכֶה לִדְבָרִים הַרְבֵּה.

וְלֹא עוֹד, אֶלָּא שֶׁכָּל־הָעוֹלָם כֻּלּוֹ כְּדַי הוּא לוֹ.

נִקְרָא רֵעַ אָהוּב, אוֹהֵב אֶת־הַמָּקוֹם, אוֹהֵב אֶת־הַבְּרִיּוֹת, מְשַׂמֵּחַ אֶת־הַמָּקוֹם, מְשַׂמֵּחַ אֶת־הַבְּרִיּוֹת.

וּמַלְבַּשְׁתּוֹ עֲנָוָה וְיִרְאָה, וּמַכְשַׁרְתּוֹ לִהְיוֹת צַדִּיק, חָסִיד, יָשָׁר וְנֶאֱמָן, וּמְרַחַקְתּוֹ מִן הַחֵטְא, וּמְקָרַבְתּוֹ לִידֵי זְכוּת.

וְנֶהֱנִין מִמֶּנּוּ עֵצָה וְתוּשִׁיָּה, בִּינָה וּגְבוּרָה, שֶׁנֶּאֱמַר: לִי־עֵצָה וְתוּשִׁיָּה, אֲנִי בִינָה, לִי גְבוּרָה.

וְנוֹתֶנֶת לוֹ מַלְכוּת וּמֶמְשָׁלָה, וְחִקּוּר דִּין. וּמְגַלִּין לוֹ רָזֵי תוֹרָה, וְנַעֲשֶׂה כְּמַעְיָן הַמִּתְגַּבֵּר וּכְנָהָר שֶׁאֵינוֹ פוֹסֵק. וְהֱוֵי צָנוּעַ וְאֶרֶךְ רוּחַ, וּמוֹחֵל עַל עֶלְבּוֹנוֹ.

וּמְגַדַּלְתּוֹ עַל כָּל־הַמַּעֲשִׂים.

RABBI MEIR would say:

Those[1] who engage in the study of Torah for its own sake become worthy of many things; moreover, it would have been worth creating the world for their sake alone.

They are called beloved friends, lovers of God, lovers of humanity, a joy to God, a joy to [God's] creatures.

It [the Torah] clothes them in humility and reverence, and makes them fit to be righteous, loyal, upright and faithful; it keeps them far from sin and draws them near to virtue.

People benefit from their discerning counsel, their strong insight, as it is written (Proverbs 8:14): *Counsel and discernment are Mine; I am insight; strength is Mine.*

It gives them sovereignty, authority, and keen judgment.

The secrets of Torah are revealed to them, and they become ever-flowing fountains, streams that never fail. They become modest and patient, forgiving of insults.

It magnifies and exalts them over all creation.

247

The note of hyperbole struck here is repeated throughout chapter 6. It testifies to the depth of the sages' love for Torah and Torah-study, and to their anxiety that the world's lure not entice people from its study and practice. (CS)

Guardians

Rabbi Judah Nesiah[2] sent Rabbi Chiyah, Rabbi Assi, and Rabbi Ammi on a tour of the land of Israel. They were to go to the cities and appoint teachers of Torah and Mishnah.

They came to a city where there was no teacher, and they called for the guardians of the city.

The local militia was brought to them.

"You call them the guardians of the city?" exclaimed these Sages. "They are the city's destroyers!"

"In that case," the people asked, "whom do you call the city's guardians?"

"The teachers of the Written and Oral Torah, as is is said (Psalm 127:1), *Unless the Eternal watches over the city, they keep vigil in vain who watch over it.* (Jerusalem Talmud Chagigah 1:7)

Avot 6:2

אָמַר רַבִּי יְהוֹשֻׁעַ בֶּן לֵוִי:

בְּכָל־יוֹם וָיוֹם בַּת קוֹל יוֹצֵאת מֵהַר

חוֹרֵב וּמַכְרֶזֶת וְאוֹמֶרֶת:

אוֹי לָהֶם לַבְּרִיּוֹת מֵעֶלְבּוֹנָהּ שֶׁל תּוֹרָה.

שֶׁכָּל־מִי שֶׁאֵינוֹ עוֹסֵק בַּתּוֹרָה נִקְרָא

נָזוּף, שֶׁנֶּאֱמַר: נֶזֶם זָהָב בְּאַף חֲזִיר,

אִשָּׁה יָפָה וְסָרַת טָעַם.

וְאוֹמֵר: וְהַלֻּחֹת מַעֲשֵׂה אֱלֹהִים הֵמָּה,

וְהַמִּכְתָּב מִכְתַּב אֱלֹהִים הוּא,

חָרוּת עַל הַלֻּחֹת. אַל תִּקְרָא חָרוּת

אֶלָּא חֵרוּת, שֶׁאֵין לְךָ בֶּן חוֹרִין אֶלָּא

מִי שֶׁעוֹסֵק בְּתַלְמוּד תּוֹרָה.

וְכָל־מִי שֶׁעוֹסֵק תָּדִיר בַּתּוֹרָה הֲרֵי זֶה

מִתְעַלֶּה, שֶׁנֶּאֱמַר: וּמִמַּתָּנָה נַחֲלִיאֵל,

וּמִנַּחֲלִיאֵל בָּמוֹת.

RABBI JOSHUA ben Levi said: Every day a Divine Voice goes forth from Mount Horeb [Sinai] declaring: 'Woe to those people who despise Torah.' For those who do not engage in the study of Torah are called detestable, as it is written (Proverbs 11:22): *A beautiful woman without sense is like a golden ring in a pig's snout.*

And it says (Exodus 32:16): *And the tablets [given to Moses] were God's own work, and the writing was God's own writing engraved on the tablets.* Do not read it as *harut* (engraved) but as *hérut* (freedom), for no one is free except one engaged in the study of Torah.

And all who regularly engage in the study of Torah are exalted, as it says (Numbers 21:19): *From Mattanah to Nahaliel, from Nahaliel to Bamot.*[3]

The second passage is well-known, a nice example of rabbinic interpretive technique. The interpretation itself is often interpreted to mean that the practice of Torah makes us free, but in fact the passage speaks of study. Yet the broader interpretation is not far-fetched, when we remember the many rabbinic assertions that study must lead to practice. And, also, see 6:5: 'Do more than you have learned.' (CS)

To Whom Torah was Given

And he said: The Eternal came out of Sinai... (Deuteronomy 33.2). At the time of the revelation of the Torah, God appeared not to Israel alone, but to all the nations. Going first to the children of Esau, God said: Will you accept the Torah? They replied: What does it say? God said: *You shall not murder.* Whereupon they replied: But our ancestors were murderers by nature—*The hands are the hands of Esau* (Genesis 27:22)—and they were destined to depend on nothing but the sword—*And by your sword you shall live* (Genesis 27:40). We cannot accept the Torah. God then went to the Ammonites and Moabites, saying: Will you accept the Torah? They replied: What does it say? God said: *You shall not commit adultery.* Whereupon they replied: But we are all descended from adulterers—*And the two daughters of Lot were with child by their father.* (Genesis 19:36). We cannot accept the Torah. God then went to the children of Ishmael and said: Will you accept the Torah? They replied: What does it say? God said: *You shall not steal.* Whereupon they replied: But our whole existence depends on stealing and robbery—*And he shall be a wild ass of a man, his hand shall be against every man and every man's hand against him...* (Genesis 16:22). We cannot accept the Torah. There was not a single nation to whom God did not go and plead, there was no door on which God did not knock, in the hope of finding someone willing to accept the Torah. When, finally, God came to Israel, they said: *We will do and we will hear* (Exodus 24:7).

This is what the verse means (Deuteronomy 33:2): *The Eternal came from Sinai, shining forth upon them from Seir, appearing from Mount Paran and approaching from Riv'vot–Kadesh: at God's right hand was a fiery law for them.* (Midrash Sifre, B'rachah)

Avot 6:3

הַלּוֹמֵד מֵחֲבֵרוֹ פֶּרֶק אֶחָד, אוֹ הֲלָכָה
אַחַת, אוֹ פָסוּק אֶחָד, אוֹ דִבּוּר אֶחָד,
אוֹ אֲפִילוּ אוֹת אַחַת, צָרִיךְ לִנְהָג בּוֹ
כָבוֹד, שֶׁכֵּן מָצִינוּ בְּדָוִד מֶלֶךְ יִשְׂרָאֵל,
שֶׁלֹּא לָמַד מֵאֲחִיתֹפֶל, אֶלָּא שְׁנֵי דְבָרִים
בִּלְבָד, וּקְרָאוֹ רַבּוֹ, אַלּוּפוֹ, וּמְיֻדָּעוֹ,
שֶׁנֶּאֱמַר: וְאַתָּה אֱנוֹשׁ כְּעֶרְכִּי, אַלּוּפִי,
וּמְיֻדָּעִי.

וַהֲלֹא דְבָרִים קַל וְחֹמֶר:
וּמָה דָוִד מֶלֶךְ יִשְׂרָאֵל, שֶׁלֹּא לָמַד
מֵאֲחִיתֹפֶל, אֶלָּא שְׁנֵי דְבָרִים בִּלְבָד,
קְרָאוֹ רַבּוֹ, אַלּוּפוֹ, וּמְיֻדָּעוֹ, הַלּוֹמֵד
מֵחֲבֵרוֹ פֶּרֶק אֶחָד, אוֹ הֲלָכָה אַחַת,
אוֹ פָסוּק אֶחָד, אוֹ דִבּוּר אֶחָד, אוֹ
אֲפִילוּ אוֹת אַחַת, עַל אַחַת כַּמָּה
וְכַמָּה צָרִיךְ לִנְהָג בּוֹ כָבוֹד.
וְאֵין כָבוֹד אֶלָּא תוֹרָה, שֶׁנֶּאֱמַר:
כָּבוֹד חֲכָמִים יִנְחָלוּ, וּתְמִימִים
יִנְחֲלוּ־טוֹב.
וְאֵין טוֹב אֶלָּא תוֹרָה, שֶׁנֶּאֱמַר: כִּי לֶקַח
טוֹב נָתַתִּי לָכֶם, תּוֹרָתִי אַל־תַּעֲזֹבוּ.

IF YOU learn from anyone a single chapter, law, verse, or word—even one letter—you must treat that person with honor. Thus do we find with David king of Israel, who learned nothing from Achitophel, and merely conversed with him, yet [on that account] called him his teacher, mentor, and confidant, as it is said (Psalm 55:14), *You are equal to me, my teacher and confidant.*

Obviously, then, if King David, who learned nothing from Achitophel, and merely conversed with him, called him his teacher, mentor, and confidant, all the more should one who does learn anything from another treat that person with honor.

Honor and Torah go together, as it is written (Proverbs 3:35, 28:10): *The wise inherit honor, and the upright inherit good.*

Good and Torah go together, as it is written (Proverbs 4:2): *Behold, I have given you a good doctrine, My Torah: do not forsake it.*

Obviously, then—Literally, 'Is this not an inference from major to minor?' This is the first of a set of thirteen rules of Torah interpretation laid down by Rabbi Ishmael and incorporated into the daily morning service of the traditional liturgy. (CS)

And merely conversed—We have combined two words so that King David is represented not as having learned two things from Achitophel, as the text would otherwise say, but as having merely conversed with him and had learned nothing—and yet paid him honor. (CS)

Avot 6:4

כָּךְ הִיא דַרְכָּהּ שֶׁל תּוֹרָה:
פַּת בַּמֶּלַח תֹּאכֵל,
וּמַיִם בַּמְשׂוּרָה תִּשְׁתֶּה,
וְעַל הָאָרֶץ תִּישַׁן,
וְחַיֵּי צַעַר תִּחְיֶה,
וּבַתּוֹרָה אַתָּה עָמֵל.
וְאִם אַתָּה עֹשֶׂה כֵן, אַשְׁרֶיךָ וְטוֹב לָךְ.
אַשְׁרֶיךָ: בָּעוֹלָם הַזֶּה;
וְטוֹב לָךְ: לָעוֹלָם הַבָּא.

THIS IS the way of [the life of] Torah:
your food—bread with salt;
your water—measured out; (Ezekiel 4:11)
your bed—the earth;
your life—hardship;
your labor—the Torah.
And if this is what you choose, *Happy are you, fortunate your lot.* (Psalm 128:2)
Happy are you—in this world;
fortunate your lot—in the world–to–come.

This is the way—It is not clear whether this passage is descriptive or prescriptive. Our translation prefers the former; if the latter, it should read: 'This is the way [to acquire] Torah. (CS)

Second Century CE: In the Time of Persecution

The Ten Martyrs, I

When the imperial decree went out to slaughter the saints and sages of Israel,[4] his colleagues asked Rabbi Ishmael the High Priest to ascend to heaven and see whether the decree could be annulled.

Rabbi Ishmael purified himself, wrapped himself in Tallit and Tefillin, and uttered the Ineffable Name.[5]

He encountered the angel Gabriel, who said: "Are you the Rabbi Ishmael whose Creator boasts of having a servant upon earth whose countenance is like that very Creator's?" "I am the one," the rabbi replied. "What are you doing here, then?" "I have come to see whether the decree is final." "You may be sure of it," replied the angel. "I have heard from behind the Veil[6] that ten sages of Israel have been given over to the evil empire for slaughter." "What is our offence?" "You are paying," Gabriel answered, "for the sale of Joseph. Each day Justice stands before the Throne of Glory and says, 'You must not make the Torah void, for it is written (Exodus 21:17), *Who steals and sells a person is subject to death.* The ten tribes sold Joseph, yet neither they nor their descendants have been punished for that crime.'" "Are we, then," Rabbi Ishmael wondered, "the first generation in all that time to merit this punishment?" And the angel said: "Not since that time has the Holy One found a generation with saints and sages like yourselves. You are the equals of the tribes; therefore you pay the penalty [for their crime]."

Samael rejoiced greatly to see that the decree was sealed. That, therefore, was the moment the Holy One decreed the fall of Rome and all its works. This comforted Ishmael as he went about in Heaven. Not far from the Throne of Glory he noticed an altar, and he asked: "What do you offer up here day by day?" Gabriel told him: "We offer up the lives of the righteous." Then Ishmael returned to earth and told his colleagues: "Our fate is sealed."

The Ten Martyrs, II

Simeon ben Gamaliel and Ishmael were seized for execution. Rabbi Simeon began to weep. "You are but two steps from Paradise," Ishmael exclaimed, "and you weep!" He replied: "My heart is breaking because I do not understand what I have done to deserve this." Ishmael responded: "Have you never in your life put off helping someone, even for a moment, because it suited your convenience?" Simeon then said: "You have consoled me, my master.".

Each pleaded with the executioner: "Kill me first; let me not see the death of my friend." "Cast lots," he said.

Simeon ben Gamaliel was first. Immediately, the executioner wielded his sword and beheaded him. Weeping, Rabbi Ishmael held Simeon's head close to him and cried out: "Saintly mouth! Holy lips! Mouth whose utterance was pearl, whose words were gems! Now in dirt you roll, your tongue covered with dust and ashes. Is this Torah, and this its reward?!"

As he wept the emperor's daughter was struck with his beauty, a beauty rare even among the angels. Stirred, she said to her father: "Grant me one boon." "What is it, daughter?" asked the emperor. "Spare this man," she pleaded. "I can refuse you naught but this one thing," he answered. "This man and his colleagues must die."

They began to strip his face of skin. When they reached the place that had held his Tefillin,[7] he uttered a loud and bitter cry. Heaven and earth were shaken. He cried a second time, and the Throne of Glory tottered. The ministering angels wept to see this saint's suffering and pleaded with the Holy One on his behalf: "Is this Torah, and this its reward?!" God then replied: "What can I do for My child? The decree is sealed and I am helpless to undo it." Then a Voice went forth to Ishmael: "Accept this; affirm Me; for if you fail, the world must crumble into chaos!" Ishmael then accepted his fate and said (Job 13:15), *Though You slay me, yet will I trust in You.*

The Ten Martyrs, III

When news of the executions came to Rabbi Akiba, he went into mourning and said to his disciples: "Prepare to suffer. Had this generation been destined for happiness, these men would have been first to enjoy it. Now the One whose word made the world has determined that this great suffering is ordained, and has removed them from our midst, to fulfill Scripture's word (Isaiah 57:1): *The righteous perish...the righteous are removed before the calamity.*

He himself—Akiba ben Joseph—was the man who could draw meaning not only from the words of the Torah, but from the crowns and ornaments that decorated their letters, the man who had revealed meanings of Torah as clearly as Moses himself had done, when standing at Sinai. He was next.

After a delay, during which he was imprisoned, he was taken out and his flesh was flayed with iron combs at the time when the Sh'ma is recited. He said: "Hear, O Israel..." "Even now, Master?" his disciples asked him. He replied: "All my life I was troubled by the verse (Deuteronomy 6:5), *Love your Eternal God with all your being*—love God, though you die on that account! And I prayed always to be allowed to fulfill it; now I can." And with his last breath he uttered: "The Eternal God is One!," prolonging the last word till life was gone.

A Voice proclaimed: "Happy are you, Akiba! You died as you lived, in purity and sanctity."

The Ten Martyrs, IV

Chanina[8] ben Teradion was next. He was a man who pleased all who knew him, and who was pleasing to God, for never did a word of dispraise for another person pass his lips.

When the decree forbidding the teaching of Torah was proclaimed, he assembled a great multitude and expounded Torah.

During this period Chanina visited Rabbi Yosé ben Kisma, who was ill. Yosé remonstrated with him: "Brother, do you not understand that this nation has all the power? It has destroyed God's Temple and slaughtered God's saints and heroes with impunity. And yet you gather crowds and teach them, holding the Scroll itself in your arms!" "Heaven will show mercy," was Chanina's response. Yosé declared: "I reason with you and you tell me about Heaven's mercy! They will burn you and the Scroll together!"

"When I die, Master, what will be my fate?" And Yosé answered: "Is there aught you are ashamed of?" "Well," Chanina rejoined, "I once confused two separate funds and gave the whole to the poor." "Then," concluded Yosé, "let my lot be with yours."

Not long after, Yosé died, and all the Roman worthies went to the funeral and honored him. On their way back they came across Chanina expounding Torah, embracing a Scroll, as usual. "How comes it," said they, "that you defy Rome?" "I obey a higher Power," said he. His death by fire was then and there decreed. His wife, too, was sentenced to die, and his daughter[9] consigned to a brothel.

They wrapped him in a Scroll of the Torah, heaped twigs about him, set fire to him. To prolong his agony they brought water-soaked pads of wool and placed them over his heart. His daughter said to him: "Father, must I see you brought to this pass?" He consoled her: "Had I alone been burnt, I would have found it difficult to bear. But, see, they burn the Scroll along with me. The One whose Torah is burnt is the One whose child is burnt. The One who preserves the Torah will also preserve me."

He gazed into the distance, and his disciples asked: "Master, what do you see?" "The parchment burns, but the letters fly upward." "Do you the same," said they. "The One who gave me spirit will choose the time to take it back."

The executioner said: "Master, if I increase the heat and remove the pads of wool, will you promise me eternal life?" "I will." "Swear it." He swore. The executioner did as he had offered, and death came swiftly. A Voice proclaimed: "Chanina ben Teradion and his executioner have earned eternal life."

Regarding this, Rabbi Judah the Prince said once, with tears in his eyes: "Some earn in a moment what others must labor for over many a year!"

The Ten Martyrs, V

Now it was the turn of Judah ben Baba. Of him they used to say that from the age of eighteen to the age of eighty he slept as lightly as a cat.

The Romans had forbidden the ordination of rabbis, decreeing death to ordainer and those ordained, and destruction for any city in which ordination took place. Rabbi Judah ben Baba ordained five men in the hills between two cities, Shefaram and Usha. When enemy soldiers appeared on the scene, Judah told his disciples to flee. "What will become of you?" they cried. He answered: "I will place myself before them as an immovable rock."

He did—and a hundred Roman lances pierced him. But his disciples escaped.

The Ten Martyrs, VI

It was the eve of the Feast of Weeks, the Festival of Revelation, when Rabbi Judah ben Dama was to be slain. He begged for a little time to sanctify the Festival, to praise God the Source of Torah. The emperor replied: "You still hold fast to the Torah and the God who gave it?" "Yes," said he.

"What reward do you receive for such faithfulness?" "Of this David sang," came Judah's reply: *How great is the good You have stored up for those who revere You.*[10]

The emperor sneered: "No greater fools live than you who believe in another life." To which Judah replied: "No greater fools live than you who deny the living God."

This so enraged the emperor that he had Judah tied by his hair to the tail of a horse and dragged through the streets of Rome. Afterward he was torn limb from limb.

Elijah the prophet then came and gathered his bones, burying them in a cave near the Tiber. From there came lamentations for thirty days.

When the emperor heard of this, he remarked: "I shall not rest until I have had my way with these old men, even if the whole world is reduced to chaos."

The Ten Martyrs, VII

When Chutzpit the Interpreter was slain, he was a man of great age—some say he had lived 130 years. Nevertheless he was a man of graceful appearance with a commanding presence; he might have been an angel, so full of grace was he.

Because of his age, people urged the emperor to spare him. As they talked, Chutzpit asked of him one more day's life. The emperor wondered: "At your age, what difference does another day make?" Chutzpit replied: "It will give me the opportunity to perform two more commandments—I can recite the morning and evening Sh'ma, proclaiming the sovereignty of the Holy and Awesome One."

"Insolent and impudent people!" shouted the emperor. "How long will you keep faith with your god? Do you suppose he would not have saved you already had he been able to?" These words caused Chutzpit to cry out and rend his clothes: "Woe unto you, Emperor!" he declared. "What will become of you and your people when at last you are called to account for what you have done?!"

The emperor then said: "Why should I go on debating with this one? Let him be stoned and then hanged!"

The Ten Martyrs, VIII

Rabbi Chanina ben Chachinai, too, was quite old. They say it had been his practice from the age of twelve to taste no food on weekdays. Now he was ninety–five.

As the Romans led him to be slain, it was a Sabbath eve. His disciples said to him: "Master, would you like a morsel of food to taste before you are put to death?" "All my life," said he, "I have fasted until the Sabbath, and the Sabbath is not yet here. I hardly can tell where my next step will take me, yet you offer me food and drink!"

He then proceeded to begin the recitation of the prayer that proclaims the holiness of the Sabbath,[11] but the Romans killed him before he could conclude.

A Voice proclaimed: "Happy are you, Chanina! In holiness you lived, in holiness you have died."

The Ten Martyrs, IX

As Yesheivav the Scribe was led out to be slain, his disciples said to him: "Our Teacher, what will become of the Torah?"

"My children," said he, "Israel is destined to forget it, for this brazen nation is determined to wipe out this treasure of ours. Would that I could be an atonement for our generation, the means of its salvation. But all I see before me is this: there is no street in all Rome without corpses; this wicked nation spills Israel's innocent blood."

"Teacher, Master," they cried, "what will become of us?"

His answer: "Strengthen one another, love peace and justice, and there may yet be hope for you."

The emperor asked him his age. "Ninety years old am I," he said, "and I see that from the womb I was destined to be handed over to you along with my colleagues. But your fate will overtake you as well—be sure of that!"

The emperor commanded: "Hurry up and kill this one, too, and let us see the power of his god!"

They burnt him at the stake.

The Ten Martyrs, X

Eliezer ben Shamua was the last to die. Of him it is said that he had reached the age of 105, and that from youth onward none had heard him say a foolish word or engage in a quarrel. He was a man modest and unassuming, a man who asked·little for himself and maintained his self–control all his days.

He was to be slain on the Day of Atonement.

His disciples came to him and said: "Master, what do you see?"

"I see," was his reply, "the bier of Rabbi Judah ben Baba being carried in honor; next to him is the bier of Rabbi Akiba ben Joseph. They are debating a point of law."

"And who," said his disciples, "is moderating the debate?"

"Rabbi Ishmael the High Priest."

"And who is winning the debate? Who has the upper hand?"

"Rabbi Akiba, because he poured all his life's strength into the study of Torah."

Eliezer then added: "My children, I see more. I see the soul of every saint purifying itself in the waters of Shiloah, in purity to enter the Academy On High to hear Rabbi Akiba expound the subject of the day, and every saint has an angel bringing him a golden throne on which to sit."

The execution proceeded.

A Voice proclaimed: "Happy are you, Rabbi Eliezer ben Shamua! Pure in your living, pure in your going!" (Midrash Eileh Ezkerah; Talmud Sanhedrin 14a; Talmud Avodah Zarah 8b, 17b, 18b; etc.)

Avot 6:5

אַל תְּבַקֵּשׁ גְּדֻלָּה לְעַצְמְךָ, וְאַל תַּחְמוֹד
כָּבוֹד. יוֹתֵר מִלִּמּוּדְךָ עֲשֵׂה,
וְאַל תִּתְאַוֶּה לְשֻׁלְחָנָם שֶׁל מְלָכִים:
שֶׁשֻּׁלְחָנְךָ גָּדוֹל מִשֻּׁלְחָנָם,
וְכִתְרְךָ גָּדוֹל מִכִּתְרָם,
וְנֶאֱמָן הוּא בַּעַל מְלַאכְתְּךָ שֶׁיְּשַׁלֶּם לְךָ
שְׂכַר פְּעֻלָּתֶךָ.

SEEK NOT greatness for yourself[12] nor covet honor.

Do more than you have learned.[13]

Never yearn for the table of kings:
your table is greater than theirs,
your crown is greater than theirs.
And your employer can be depended upon to pay you your wages.

your table—In Avot 3:3 Rabbi Simeon speaks of three who eat together and speak words of Torah. Then it is as though they had eaten at God's table. (CS)

your crown—Avot 4:13 speaks of three crowns—Torah, priesthood, and royalty—and concludes with a fourth, best of all: 'the crown of a good name.' (CS)

your wages—See 2:16, where Rabbi Tarfon is credited with this thought. (CS)

Avot 6:6a[14]

GREATER IS Torah than Priesthood and Royalty, for Royalty is gained by thirty qualities,[15] Priesthood by twenty–four,[16] and Torah by forty–eight.

גְּדוֹלָה תּוֹרָה יוֹתֵר מִן הַכְּהֻנָה וּמִן הַמַּלְכוּת, שֶׁהַמַּלְכוּת נִקְנֵית בִּשְׁלֹשִׁים מַעֲלוֹת, וְהַכְּהֻנָה בְּעֶשְׂרִים וְאַרְבַּע, וְהַתּוֹרָה נִקְנֵית בְּאַרְבָּעִים וּשְׁמוֹנָה דְבָרִים.

And these are: Study; attentiveness; orderly speech; an understanding heart; a keen mind; awe; reverence; humility; joy; apprenticeship; loyalty to colleagues; debate with students; perserverance; study of Scripture and Mishnah; keeping these to a minimum: [other] work, sleep, talk, pleasure-seeking, play, and ordinary pursuits; and patience, generosity, trust in the sages, and acceptance of suffering;

וְאֵלּוּ הֵן: בְּתַלְמוּד, בִּשְׁמִיעַת הָאֹזֶן, בַּעֲרִיכַת שְׂפָתַיִם, בְּבִינַת הַלֵּב, בְּשִׂכְלוּת הַלֵּב, בְּאֵימָה, בְּיִרְאָה, בַּעֲנָוָה, בְּשִׂמְחָה, בְּשִׁמּוּשׁ חֲכָמִים, בְּדִבּוּק חֲבֵרִים, בְּפִלְפּוּל הַתַּלְמִידִים, בְּיִשּׁוּב, בְּמִקְרָא, בְּמִשְׁנָה, בְּמִעוּט סְחוֹרָה, בְּמִעוּט שֵׁנָה, בְּמִעוּט שִׂיחָה, בְּמִעוּט תַּעֲנוּג, בְּמִעוּט שְׂחוֹק, בְּמִעוּט דֶּרֶךְ אֶרֶץ, בְּאֶרֶךְ אַפַּיִם, בְּלֵב טוֹב, בֶּאֱמוּנַת חֲכָמִים, וּבְקַבָּלַת הַיִּסּוּרִין.

Avot 6:6b

הַמַּכִּיר אֶת־מְקוֹמוֹ, וְהַשָּׂמֵחַ בְּחֶלְקוֹ,
וְהָעוֹשֶׂה סְיָג לִדְבָרָיו, וְאֵינוֹ מַחֲזִיק
טוֹבָה לְעַצְמוֹ, אָהוּב, אוֹהֵב אֶת־הַמָּקוֹם,
אוֹהֵב אֶת־הַבְּרִיּוֹת, אוֹהֵב אֶת־
הַצְּדָקוֹת, אוֹהֵב אֶת־הַמֵּישָׁרִים, אוֹהֵב
אֶת־הַתּוֹכָחוֹת, מִתְרַחֵק מִן הַכָּבוֹד,
וְלֹא מֵגִיס לִבּוֹ בְּתַלְמוּדוֹ, וְאֵינוֹ שָׂמֵחַ
בְּהוֹרָאָה, נוֹשֵׂא בְעֹל עִם חֲבֵרוֹ,
וּמַכְרִיעוֹ לְכַף זְכוּת, וּמַעֲמִידוֹ עַל
הָאֱמֶת, וּמַעֲמִידוֹ עַל הַשָּׁלוֹם, וּמִתְיַשֵּׁב
בְּתַלְמוּדוֹ, שׁוֹאֵל וּמֵשִׁיב, שׁוֹמֵעַ
וּמוֹסִיף, הַלּוֹמֵד עַל מְנָת לְלַמֵּד, הַלּוֹמֵד
עַל מְנָת לַעֲשׂוֹת, הַמַּחְכִּים אֶת־רַבּוֹ,
וְהַמְכַוֵּן אֶת־שְׁמוּעָתוֹ, וְהָאוֹמֵר דָּבָר
בְּשֵׁם אוֹמְרוֹ.
הָא לָמַדְתָּ, שֶׁכָּל־הָאוֹמֵר דָּבָר בְּשֵׁם
אוֹמְרוֹ מֵבִיא גְאֻלָּה לָעוֹלָם, שֶׁנֶּאֱמַר:
וַתֹּאמֶר אֶסְתֵּר לַמֶּלֶךְ בְּשֵׁם מָרְדְּכָי.

knowing your place; rejoicing in your lot; choosing your words with care; not seeking personal credit; being loved; loving God; loving people; loving righteous[17] deeds; loving uprightness; loving reproof; keeping far from honors; not boasting of your learning; not delighting in making legal decisions; sharing the burden with others; being an examplar of virtue; setting people on the path to truth; setting people on the path of peace; concentrating on study; seeking and responding; gaining knowledge and contributing knowledge; learning in order to teach; learning in order to do; challenging your teacher; accurately transmitting what you have learned; and identifying the source of your words.

Thus you learn, that one who quotes a teaching in the name of the one who said it brings redemption to the world, as it is said (Esther 2:22), *And Esther said to the king in the name of Mordechai...*

This continues the list of qualities by which one gains Torah. The passage contains numerous echoes of earlier passages in Avot.

Avot 6:7

גְּדוֹלָה תוֹרָה שֶׁהִיא נוֹתֶנֶת חַיִּים
לְעוֹשֶׂיהָ בָּעוֹלָם הַזֶּה וּבָעוֹלָם הַבָּא,
שֶׁנֶּאֱמַר: כִּי־חַיִּים הֵם לְמֹצְאֵיהֶם
וּלְכָל־בְּשָׂרוֹ מַרְפֵּא. וְאוֹמֵר: רִפְאוּת
תְּהִי לְשָׁרֶּךְ וְשִׁקּוּי לְעַצְמוֹתֶיךָ.
וְאוֹמֵר: עֵץ־חַיִּים הִיא לַמַּחֲזִיקִים
בָּהּ, וְתֹמְכֶיהָ מְאֻשָּׁר. וְאוֹמֵר: כִּי
לִוְיַת חֵן הֵם לְרֹאשֶׁךָ וַעֲנָקִים
לְגַרְגְּרֹתֶיךָ. וְאוֹמֵר: תִּתֵּן לְרֹאשֶׁךָ
לִוְיַת־חֵן; עֲטֶרֶת תִּפְאֶרֶת תְּמַגְּנֶךָּ.
וְאוֹמֵר: אֹרֶךְ יָמִים בִּימִינָהּ, בִּשְׂמֹאולָהּ
עֹשֶׁר וְכָבוֹד. וְאוֹמֵר: כִּי אֹרֶךְ יָמִים
וּשְׁנוֹת חַיִּים וְשָׁלוֹם יוֹסִיפוּ לָךְ.

GREAT IS Torah, for it gives life to those who fulfill it in this world and in the world to come, as it is said[18] (Proverbs 4:22): *For they are life to those who find them, and healing to all their flesh.* And it says (ibid. 3:8): *It will be a healing for your flesh and a refreshment for your body.* And it says (ibid. 3:18): *It is a tree of life to those who hold it fast, and all who cling to it find happiness.* And it says (ibid. 1:9): *For they are a garland of grace for your head and pendants for your neck.* And it says (ibid. 4:9): *It will set a garland of grace upon your head; it will bestow on you a crown of glory.* And it says (ibid. 3:1): *Long life is at her right hand, wealth and honor at her left.* And it says (ibid. 3:2): *For they will give you a long life, years of life and peace.*

Avot 6:8

רַבִּי שִׁמְעוֹן בֶּן יְהוּדָה, מִשּׁוּם רַבִּי
שִׁמְעוֹן בֶּן יוֹחַי אוֹמֵר:
הַנּוֹי, וְהַכֹּחַ, וְהָעֹשֶׁר, וְהַכָּבוֹד,
וְהַחָכְמָה, הַזִּקְנָה וְהַשֵּׂיבָה, וְהַבָּנִים
נָאֶה לַצַּדִּיקִים וְנָאֶה לָעוֹלָם, שֶׁנֶּאֱמַר:
עֲטֶרֶת תִּפְאֶרֶת שֵׂיבָה, בְּדֶרֶךְ צְדָקָה
תִּמָּצֵא. וְאוֹמֵר: תִּפְאֶרֶת בַּחוּרִים
כֹּחָם, וַהֲדַר זְקֵנִים שֵׂיבָה. וְאוֹמֵר:
עֲטֶרֶת חֲכָמִים עָשְׁרָם. וְאוֹמֵר: עֲטֶרֶת
זְקֵנִים בְּנֵי בָנִים, וְתִפְאֶרֶת בָּנִים
אֲבוֹתָם. וְאוֹמֵר: וְחָפְרָה הַלְּבָנָה וּבוֹשָׁה
הַחַמָּה, כִּי־מָלַךְ יהוה צְבָאוֹת בְּהַר
צִיּוֹן וּבִירוּשָׁלַם, וְנֶגֶד זְקֵנָיו כָּבוֹד.
רַבִּי שִׁמְעוֹן בֶּן מְנַסְיָא אוֹמֵר:
אֵלּוּ שֶׁבַע מִדּוֹת שֶׁמָּנוּ חֲכָמִים
לַצַּדִּיקִים, כֻּלָּם נִתְקַיְּמוּ בְּרַבִּי וּבְבָנָיו.

RABBI SIMEON ben Judah, quoting Rabbi Simeon ben Yochai, says:
Beauty, strength, wealth, honor, wisdom, age, gray hair, and children are fitting for the righteous and fitting for the world, as it is said (Proverbs 16:31): *Gray hair is a crown of glory, attained by a righteous life.* And it says (ibid. 20:29): *The glory of the young is their strength, and the beauty of the aged is their gray hair.* And it says (ibid. 14:24): *The wealth of the wise is their wisdom.*[19] And it says (ibid. 17:6): *Children's children are the crown of the aged, and parents are the glory of their children.* And it says (Isaiah 24:23): *The sun will be abashed and the moon ashamed, for the God of heaven's hosts will reign in Zion and Jerusalem, and God's elders shall have honor.*

RABBI SIMEON ben Menasya says:
The seven qualities that the sages ascribed to the righteous were all present in Rabbi [Judah the Prince] and his sons.

The seven qualities—In fact there is some disagreement how to arrive at that number. We follow those traditional texts that include בנים, *banim* 'children,' making eight. Blackman, in his commentary, tells us that Elijah, the Gaon of Vilna, suggests omitting 'wisdom,' as not supported by a biblical quotation, but that the Jerusalem Talmud omits 'old age.' (CS)

Avot 6:9

אָמַר רַבִּי יוֹסֵי בֶּן קִסְמָא:
פַּעַם אַחַת הָיִיתִי מְהַלֵּךְ בַּדֶּרֶךְ וּפָגַע
בִּי אָדָם אֶחָד וְנָתַן לִי שָׁלוֹם,
וְהֶחֱזַרְתִּי לוֹ שָׁלוֹם. אָמַר לִי: רַבִּי,
מֵאֵיזֶה מָקוֹם אַתָּה? אָמַרְתִּי לוֹ: מֵעִיר
גְּדוֹלָה שֶׁל חֲכָמִים וְשֶׁל סוֹפְרִים אָנִי.
אָמַר לִי: רַבִּי, רְצוֹנְךָ שֶׁתָּדוּר עִמָּנוּ
בִּמְקוֹמֵנוּ, וַאֲנִי אֶתֵּן לְךָ אֶלֶף אֲלָפִים
דִּינְרֵי זָהָב וַאֲבָנִים טוֹבוֹת וּמַרְגָּלִיּוֹת.
אָמַרְתִּי לוֹ: אִם אַתָּה נוֹתֵן לִי כָּל־כֶּסֶף
וְזָהָב וַאֲבָנִים טוֹבוֹת וּמַרְגָּלִיּוֹת
שֶׁבָּעוֹלָם, אֵין אֲנִי דָר אֶלָּא בִמְקוֹם
תוֹרָה. וְלֹא עוֹד, אֶלָּא שֶׁבִּשְׁעַת פְּטִירָתוֹ
שֶׁל אָדָם אֵין מְלַוִּין לוֹ לָאָדָם לֹא כֶסֶף,
וְלֹא זָהָב, וְלֹא אֲבָנִים טוֹבוֹת וּמַרְגָּלִיּוֹת
אֶלָּא תוֹרָה וּמַעֲשִׂים טוֹבִים בִּלְבַד,
שֶׁנֶּאֱמַר: בְּהִתְהַלֶּכְךָ תַּנְחֶה אֹתָךְ,
בְּשָׁכְבְּךָ תִּשְׁמֹר עָלֶיךָ, וַהֲקִיצוֹתָ הִיא
תְשִׂיחֶךָ: בְּהִתְהַלֶּכְךָ תַּנְחֶה אֹתָךְ
בָּעוֹלָם הַזֶּה: בְּשָׁכְבְּךָ תִּשְׁמֹר עָלֶיךָ:
בַּקֶּבֶר: וַהֲקִיצוֹתָ הִיא תְשִׂיחֶךָ: לָעוֹלָם
הַבָּא. וְכֵן כָּתוּב בְּסֵפֶר תִּלִּים עַל יְדֵי
דָוִד מֶלֶךְ יִשְׂרָאֵל: טוֹב־לִי תוֹרַת־פִּיךָ
מֵאַלְפֵי זָהָב וָכָסֶף. וְאוֹמֵר: לִי הַכֶּסֶף
וְלִי הַזָּהָב, נְאֻם יהוה צְבָאוֹת.

RABBI YOSÉ ben Kisma said:
On a journey, once, I encountered a man who greeted me and I returned his greeting. He said: "Rabbi, where are you from?" I replied: "I come from a city filled with sages and scribes." He said: "Rabbi, settle among us, and I will give you abundant gold and jewels." I replied: "Were you to offer me all the gold, silver, and jewels in the world I would not live anywhere but in a place where Torah is taught. For when we die, we are accompanied not by gold or silver or jewels, but only by Torah and good deeds, as it is said (Proverbs 6:22): *When you walk it[20] will lead you, when you lie down it will watch over you, and when you awake it will talk with you. When you walk it will lead you*—in this world; *when you lie down it will watch over you*—in the grave; *and when you awake it will talk with you*—in the world-to-come. And thus is it written in the Book of Psalms by David, king of Israel (Psalm 119:72): *I prefer the Torah You proclaim to me to a fortune in silver and gold.* And it says (Haggai 2:8): *Mine is the silver, Mine the gold, says the God of heaven's hosts.*

263

Avot 6:10

חֲמִשָׁה קִנְיָנִים קָנָה הַקָּדוֹשׁ בָּרוּךְ הוּא
בְּעוֹלָמוֹ, וְאֵלּוּ הֵן:

תּוֹרָה קִנְיָן אֶחָד, שָׁמַיִם וָאָרֶץ קִנְיָן
אֶחָד, אַבְרָהָם קִנְיָן אֶחָד, יִשְׂרָאֵל קִנְיָן
אֶחָד, בֵּית הַמִּקְדָּשׁ קִנְיָן אֶחָד.

תּוֹרָה קִנְיָן אֶחָד מִנַּיִן? דִּכְתִיב: יהוה
קָנָנִי רֵאשִׁית דַּרְכּוֹ, קֶדֶם מִפְעָלָיו מֵאָז.
שָׁמַיִם וָאָרֶץ קִנְיָן אֶחָד מִנַּיִן? דִּכְתִיב:
הַשָּׁמַיִם כִּסְאִי וְהָאָרֶץ הֲדֹם רַגְלָי:
אֵי־זֶה בַיִת אֲשֶׁר תִּבְנוּ־לִי, וְאֵי־זֶה
מָקוֹם מְנוּחָתִי? וְאוֹמֵר: מָה־רַבּוּ
מַעֲשֶׂיךָ, יהוה, כֻּלָּם בְּחָכְמָה
עָשִׂיתָ, מָלְאָה הָאָרֶץ קִנְיָנֶךָ!
אַבְרָהָם קִנְיָן אֶחָד מִנַּיִן? דִּכְתִיב:
וַיְבָרְכֵהוּ וַיֹּאמַר: בָּרוּךְ אַבְרָם לְאֵל
עֶלְיוֹן, קֹנֵה שָׁמַיִם וָאָרֶץ.
יִשְׂרָאֵל קִנְיָן אֶחָד מִנַּיִן? דִּכְתִיב:
עַד־יַעֲבֹר עַמְּךָ, יהוה, עַד־יַעֲבֹר עַם־זוּ
קָנִיתָ. וְאוֹמֵר: לִקְדוֹשִׁים אֲשֶׁר־בָּאָרֶץ
הֵמָּה וְאַדִּירֵי כָּל־חֶפְצִי־בָם.
בֵּית הַמִּקְדָּשׁ קִנְיָן אֶחָד מִנַּיִן? דִּכְתִיב:
מָכוֹן לְשִׁבְתְּךָ פָּעַלְתָּ, יהוה, מִקְדָּשׁ
אֲדֹנָי כּוֹנְנוּ יָדֶיךָ. וְאוֹמֵר: וַיְבִיאֵם
אֶל־גְּבוּל קָדְשׁוֹ, הַר־זֶה קָנְתָה יְמִינוֹ.

The Holy One, ever to be praised, has five [particular] possessions in the world, and these are:

Torah is one, heaven and earth another, Abraham a third, Israel a fourth, and the Holy Temple a fifth.

How do we know about Torah? It is written (Proverbs 8:22): *The Eternal possessed[21] me from the beginning of time, the first divine act of long ago.*

How do we know about heaven and earth? It is written (Isaiah 66:1): *Heaven is My throne and earth My footstool: where is the house you can build for Me, and where is My resting-place?* And it says (Psalm 104:24): *How manifold are Your works, Eternal One; in wisdom You have made them all; earth is full of Your possessions!*

How do we know about Abraham? It is written (Genesis 14:19): *He blessed him and said, "Blessed is Abram of the Most High, Possessor of heaven and earth."*

How do we know about the people Israel? It is written (Exodus 15:16): *Until Your people pass over, Eternal One, until this people, Your possession, pass over.* And it says (Psalm 16:3): *As for the holy ones in the land, they are the noble, in whom is all My delight.*

How do we know about the Holy Temple? It is written (Exodus 15:17): *The place of Your abode that You have made, Eternal One; the sanctuary that You, O Eternal One, have established.* And it says (Psalm 78:54): *You[22] brought them to Your holy region, to the mountain that became Your possession.*

Avot 6:11

כָּל־מַה שֶׁבָּרָא הַקָּדוֹשׁ בָּרוּךְ הוּא
בְּעוֹלָמוֹ, לֹא בְרָאוֹ אֶלָּא לִכְבוֹדוֹ,
שֶׁנֶּאֱמַר: כֹּל הַנִּקְרָא בִשְׁמִי וְלִכְבוֹדִי
בְּרָאתִיו, יְצַרְתִּיו, אַף־עֲשִׂיתִיו.
וְאוֹמֵר: יְהוָה יִמְלֹךְ לְעוֹלָם וָעֶד.

EVERYTHING THAT the Holy One, ever to be praised, created in the world, was created solely for the Holy One's glory, as it is said (Isaiah 43:7): *All who are called by My name, whom I created for My glory, whom I formed and made.*
And it says (Exodus 15:18): *The Eternal will reign forever and ever!*

In Sum

רַבִּי חֲנַנְיָא בֶּן עֲקַשְׁיָא אוֹמֵר:
רָצָה הַקָּדוֹשׁ בָּרוּךְ הוּא לְזַכּוֹת
אֶת־יִשְׂרָאֵל, לְפִיכָךְ הִרְבָּה לָהֶם
תּוֹרָה וּמִצְוֹת, שֶׁנֶּאֱמַר:
יְהוָה חָפֵץ, לְמַעַן צִדְקוֹ,
יַגְדִּיל תּוֹרָה וְיַאְדִּיר.

RABBI CHANANIA ben Akashia said: The Holy One, ever to be praised, wanted to bestow merit on Israel, and therefore added on Torah and Mitzvot for them, as it is said (Isaiah 42:21), *The Eternal delights, for righteousness' sake,*[23] *to make the Teaching great and glorious.*

Notes

[1]The Hebrew of this mishnah is in the singular.
[2]Patriarch; grandson of Rabbi Judah the Prince.
[3]A play on place-names. These were stages on the wilderness journey of Israel after the Exodus, and it can be translated as 'From Gift [of Torah] to Inheritance of God ... to High Places.'
[4]At the time of the Roman persecution after the failure of the Bar Kochba rebellion of 132-135 C.E.
[5]The Hidden Name of the Holy One, whose pronunciation is no longer known.
[6]That stands before the Throne of Glory. Thus, the decree comes from the Holy One and is not to be annulled.
[7]That is, his forehead. The Tefillin worn on the forehead symbolizes the mind's union with the Divine.
[8]Known also as Chananiah ben Teradion.
[9]Beruriah, later the renowned wife of Rabbi Meir.
[10]Psalm 31:20
[11]Kiddush, "Sanctification.'
[12]See, also, Avot 1:10.
[13]See, also, Avot 1:17, 3:9, 5:14.
[14]The mishnah has been divided into two sections for the sake of convenience.
[15]See I Samuel 8:11-17 and Mishnah Sanhedrin 2:2ff.
[16]See Numbers 18:8ff. And Talmud Baba Kamma 110b.
[17]Or, charitable deeds.
[18]In all the following quotations from Proverbs, the references are to wisdom or words of wisdom = Torah.
[19]A literal translation would be: 'The crown of the wise is their wealth.'
[20]This refers back to verses 20-21, That is, 'your father's commandment' and 'your mother's teaching.' Thus 'it' might more appropriately be translated by 'them.' Clearly, however, 'it' is to be understood as referring to Torah in general, a singular collective, and is so understood here.
[21]Or, 'created me'.
[22]The Hebrew is in the third person masculine.
[23]See the translation in the UAHC Haftarah Commentary. The sense here would demand a somewhat different translation: 'for the sake of the righteous ones.'

Authorities Cited or Consulted

Passages from the Talmud and Midrash are generally cited by name and number, e.g., Berachot 33b, Genesis Rabbah 11(:3). The Jerusalem Talmud is cited as follows: Jerusalem Talmud Berachot 1:2.

Aknin—Joseph ben Judah ben Jacob ibn Aknin, Spain/North Africa, 1150–1220, *Sefer Ha–Musar* (Commentary).

ARN (*Avot deRabbi Natan*)—the standard version of a Minor Tractate of the Talmud, which in part consists of commentary upon Pirké Avot—the first of many commentaries. See the translation by Judah Goldin, Vol. 10 of the Yale Judaica Series, Yale University Press, New Haven, 1955.

ARNB—Another version of ARN, first published in full in 1887 by Solomon Schechter.

Bertinoro—Ovadiah ben Abraham of Bertinoro, Italy, 1450-1516 His is the standard commentary on the Mishnah.

Buber, *Tales (of the Hasidim)*, 2 vols., Schocken Books, Inc., NY, 1947.

Buber, *Or ha–Ganuz*. A 1976 translation into Hebrew of Martin Buber's Tales of the Hasidim, published in Tel Aviv by Schocken Books, Inc.

Bunim–Irving M. Bunim, *Ethics from Sinai*, a 3-volume anthological commentary (English), second edition, Philipp Feldheim, Inc., NY, 1964

Duran–Simeon ben Zemach ibn Duran, (AKA Rashbatz), Spain/North Africa, 1361-1444, *Magen Avot* (Commentary). A prolific writer, he is a major figure in rabbinic history.

Hertz–*Sayings of the Fathers*, a Commentary (English) by Joseph H. Hertz, Behrman House, Inc., NY, 1945.

Rabbi Jonah ben Abraham (Gerondi)–Spain, 1200–1263, Commentary. An opponent of Maimonides, he was an influential commentator, teacher, and moralist.

Maimonides–1135–1204, *Commentary*. See *The Commentary to Mishnah Aboth*, translated by Arthur David, Bloch Publishing Co., NY, 1968.

Meam Loez–18th century Ladino Commentary by Isaac ben Moses Magriso. See *The Torah Anthology: Avoth*, an English translation by David N. Barocas, ed. by Rabbi Aryeh Kaplan, Moznaim Publishing Corp., NY, 1979.

Meiri–Menachem ben Solomon Me'iri, Provence, 1249–1316, Commentary. A major scholar and commentator, especially on the Talmud.

Midrash Shemuel–Commentary by Samuel ben Isaac of Uçeda, Safed,16th C. Uçeda was a commentator, teacher, and mystic.

Nachmias—Joseph ben Joseph Nachmias, Spain, 14th C., Commentary.

Neusner–*Torah from Our Sages: Pirkei Avot*. A "translation and explanation" by Jacob Neusner, Rossel Books, Chappaqua, NY, 1983.

Schatz–*Ethics of our Fathers in the light of Jewish History*, a Commentary by Rabbi Morris Schatz, Bloch Publishing Co., NY 1970.

TH–*Pirkei Aboth, a Commentary* by R. Travers Herford, Jewish Institute of Religion, NY, 1945.

Vitry–*Machzor Vitry*, 11–12th C. (pupils of Rashi, 11th century).

~~~~~~

In addition, particular mention should be made of:

The Living Talmud: The Wisdom of the Fathers, by Judah Goldin, New American Library, NY, 1957. Prof. Goldin has in this work furnished his translation of Avot, and translated selected passages from the classical commentaries. I am in his debt for drawing my attention to many cogent comments I might otherwise have overlooked.

Sefer Agadah, Selected and arranged by C. N. Bialik and Y. C. Ravnitzky, Devir Publishing Company, Tel Aviv, 1952. Much of the material in the present volume is translated from this, the standard collection of Aggadot from the Talmud and Midrash. It is an invaluable resource for the Hebrew reader. Now well-rendered in English under the title *Book of Legends*, translated by William G. Braude, Schocken Books, New York, 1992.

A Rabbinic Anthology, Selected and Arranged by C. G. Montefiore and H. Loewe, Meridian Books, 1960 (1938). I do not cite this large compendium of Rabbinic teachings, but I consulted it frequently.

The Day God Laughed, Chosen and Translated by Hyam Maccoby, St. Martin's Press, N. Y., 1978. Another useful collection, it adds a number of conversations between Maccoby and Wolf Mankowitz, in which Maccoby describes the Rabbinic world–view as exemplified by the stories and sayings in the collection.

Subject Index